DISCARDED

PARENTING WITHOUT PUNISHMENT

Making Problem Behavior Work for You

John W. Maag, PhD

The Charles Press, Publishers
Philadelphia

To Jack and Lina Maag who taught, through example, the importance of patience and faith in raising children.

Copyright © 1996 by The Charles Press, Publishers, Inc.

The Charles Press, Publishers
Post Office Box 15715
Philadelphia, PA 19103
(215) 545-8933

Library of Congress Cataloging-in-Publication Data

Maag, John, 1956-
    Parenting without punishment: making problem behavior work for you / John Maag.
      p. cm.
    Includes bibliographical references and index.
    ISBN 0-914783-78-5 (alk. paper)
    1. Problem children — Behavior modification. 2. Child rearing.
3. Discipline of children. I. Title.
HQ773.M225 1996
649' .64 — dc20
                                         95-47277
                                           CIP

Printed in the United States of America

ISBN 0-914783-78-5

Contents

Prologue

A quick look through any bookstore will reveal no shortage of books on parenting. In fact, books on parenting and the management of children's behavior problems seem to occupy more shelf space than any other topic except dieting. After reading many of these books and skimming through others, I quickly came to the conclusion that there is no relation between the number and usefulness of these books. Most of the books on parenting are too theoretical, too preachy or heavy on clichés, and most are far too short on practical suggestions. In fact, most of the books are so unspecific that they are of no practical help at all. Without sounding too impressed with my own work, I believe that my book significantly distinquishes itself from the others in several ways.

The methods for parenting presented in this book are based on thoroughly researched theoretical principles of behavior; I am not suggesting a radical departure from these. In fact, it is important for parents to understand these principles and therefore I present this information in easy-to-understand language with specific examples, actual situations and hands-on ways of using these techniques. On the other hand, I do not believe in punishment and I strongly encourage all parents to give thought to the idea that *parenting is not synonymous with punishment*. This suggestion might make you feel completely defenseless — that without punishment you cannot discipline your children. As this book proves, in actuality, nothing could be further from the truth.

Most parents today use some form of punishment when they want to "discipline" their children. When I ask my undergraduate and graduate students which method for managing children's behavior they most want me to address, all of them inevitably answer "punishment." In my private practice as a psychotherapist, parents always ask me how to decease their children's inappropriate behavior. It seems that most parents today are determined to discover the ultimate punishment for decreasing their children's noncompliance, fighting, yelling and any other type of behavior that bothers them.

In diametric opposition to "disciplining" children by punishing them, this book presents an entirely new approach, one that uses the child's own problem behaviors as the basis for introducing positive alternatives. At first, parents may find the idea of making problem behavior work in their favor difficult to understand. However, the premise is simple. Children's problem behaviors can be used to identify and then promote positive behavior. All behavior is purposeful; it is engaged in to accomplish an outcome. Almost every outcome desired by children is appropriate in one situation or another. Problems do not stem from the desired outcome, but rather from the behavior children use to accomplish the outcome. When you realize that inappropriate behavior represents a method children use to accomplish an appropriate outcome or goal, you have taken the first step in understanding how to change problem behavior. By identifying the desired outcome, children can be taught appropriate behaviors that accomplish the same goal. For example, a child may hit another child to impress a peer group with whom he wants to affiliate. The desire to affiliate is entirely appropriate; however, hitting is an inappropriate way of reaching this goal. Consequently, the child who hits can be taught an alternative, more appropriate behavior that accomplishes the same outcome. Talking about a scary movie to a peer group who likes scary movies is a more appropriate way for him to reach the desired outcome of affiliation. In this way, problem behavior "works for us" by providing the clues to the outcome the child desires. The next step is for parents to apply the techniques described in this book to promote the use of appropriate behaviors to accomplish the desired outcome.

Parenting has always been accompanied by difficult challenges — that appear even greater in today's society. Parents now are faced with the seemingly overwhelming task of raising their children and managing their behavior in a society that is ravaged by violence, drugs and sex. Crime is an accepted pattern of behavior for many youngsters. In fact, juveniles account for almost 40 percent of all arrests for homicide, rape, robbery, aggravated assault, burglary, larceny, motor vehicle theft and arson. In addition to crime and delinquency, substance abuse among young children is an overwhelming and frightening problem. Many children have experimented with cigarettes by age 9 and have their first drink by age 12.

These problems continue into adolescence. Almost 92 percent of all seniors in high school have had some experience with alcohol, 66 percent have used it in the last month, 37 percent report at least one occasion of heaving drinking and 5 percent are daily drinkers. Almost one-fifth of these adolescents also are daily cigarette smokers. Nearly 30 percent of adolescents have tried at least one illicit drug, with the primary drug of choice being marijuana. Similarly, teenage sexual activity is common and appears to be increasing. Despite the fact that early sexual experiences are closely associated with a high risk of pregnancy and premature parental responsibility, contracting sexually transmitted diseases, and a variety of psychological and health risks, 63 percent of 12- to 16-year-old boys and 36 percent of same-age girls report having had sexual intercourse at least once. According to the National Center for Health Statistics, over one million adolescents bear over 500,000 babies each year; furthermore, the number of illegitimate births increased from 15 percent of the total teen births in 1960 to 48 percent in 1984.

Behavior problems experienced by youngsters do not end here. Depression represents a major mental health concern for children and adolescents. Recent estimates of depression among children and adolescents range from 2 percent to 10 percent. In addition, there is a frequent association between depression and suicidal behavior in youngsters. According to the Centers for Disease Control, suicide is one of the three leading causes of death among adolescents and young adults and one of the 10 leading causes of death among children ages 5 to 14. The enormity of this problem has prompted the legislatures of several states to mandate suicide prevention programs in their school systems.

And youngsters have still other problems. For example, an estimated 25 percent of all school children demonstrate poor academic performance, and 20 percent of adolescents fail to complete their high school education. These youngsters are likely to have discipline problems, lack motivation and to show high rates of antisocial behavior and unemployment. Other problems include, but are not limited to, a resurgence of hate groups such as the neo-nazi skinheads, the proliferation of gangs both in urban and suburban areas, date rape, and sexual molestation of children by other children. While this list is far from complete, it nevertheless paints a very dismal picture of the state of American youth today.

A variety of factors may contribute to the types of problems experienced by youngsters in the '90s. Many people believe that the deleterious effects of television should be considered near the top of the list. It is estimated that between the ages of 6 and 18, children watch 16,000 hours of television; this compares to 13,000 hours spent in school. These figures translate into an average viewing time of approximately 30 hours of television each week — more time than is spent in any other activity except sleep. According to a study conducted by *U.S. News and World Report*, the average student has seen 1800 murders on television by the time he graduates from high school. This figure is especially troubling considering the positive relation between viewed and committed violence. Ironically, television network executives who express confidence in the behavioral effects of television commercials argue that the effects of television violence on children's social behavior are negligible. Despite the views of network executives, recent hearings by the Senate Subcommittee on Television Violence illustrate the seriousness of this issue, and further evidence is provided by reported increases in teenage suicidal behavior following media coverage of teen suicides.

Another factor that may contribute to the problems of today's youth relates to the increasing influence of peers on youngsters' behavior. The impact of peers is apparent by the time children are 3 or 4 years old at which time they start to band together in groups with a "we" identity that clearly sets them apart from other groups. The influence of peer groups only becomes stronger as children grow older and spend more time with friends and less time with adult family members. Parents often express concern about the degree to which peer groups seem to be at cross-purposes with their values. Results of one study found that conformity to adult pressure decreases steadily between the third and twelfth grade. In today's society, the degree of parent-peer conflict seems to be increasing and taking on even greater significance than in previous generations. For example, peers play a more significant role than anyone else in affecting youngsters' patterns of substance use. By comparison, the overwhelming evidence suggests that parental behavior exerts little more than a "modulating" effect on peer influence. Children are spending more time with their peers and less time with their families during a time when they are developing notions about aggression, sexual behavior and relationships.

Some people attribute the increased influence on children's behavior of television and peers to recent changes in the traditional family structure. The face of the American family has changed dramatically over the past 50 years, and many people view increases in single-parent families, divorce and cohabitation as indicators of a family structure "breakdown" that results from relaxed moral values. Currently, the most common family structure is one in which there are two parents employed outside of the home; approximately 67 percent of all married women between the ages of 18 and 34 are employed outside the home. Frequently, these women are responsible for household and child-rearing duties in addition to the functions that they perform at work.

As a result of the increase in dual-career families, parents have come to rely heavily upon substitute services to carry out many of the functions once performed by family members. For example, the average preschool child today is exposed to a staggering array of substitute service providers, including daycare workers, babysitters, camp counselors, coaches, teachers, tutors, therapists, neighbors and extended family. In dual-career families who do not use or cannot afford substitute care services, the children must learn to be self-sufficient. According to the U.S. Bureau of the Census, an estimated two million children between the ages of 7 and 13 were caring for themselves before and after school during the 1980s. These "latchkey" children typically have less access to adults and tend to rely more on peer groups.

Although family composition in itself may not be a key to understanding why children develop behavior problems, level of conflict among family members, security of parent-child attachment, temperamental characteristics of children and parents and availability of extrafamilial resources are contributing factors. In addition, parental discipline style appears to play a particularly important role in shaping children's behavior. For example, research has consistently shown that parents whose discipline is warm and restrictive are likely to have submissive, dependent, polite, neat children who are friendly, creative, and minimally aggressive. On the other hand, parents who use warm and permissive discipline are likely to have socially outgoing, active, creative, independent children who assume adult roles and show minimal self-aggression. Hostile and restrictive parents tend to have socially withdrawn, neurotic children who are shy or quarrelsome with their peers, show strong self-aggression and have difficulty assuming adult roles. Parents who are hostile and permissive in their discipline tend to have highly aggressive, noncompliant, delinquent children.

The implications and possible combinations of discipline styles can appear confusing to parents. My graduate students, many of whom are parents, often describe how they fall into one or more of the above-mentioned categories, express concern that they are exhibiting less than optimal parental discipline patterns, and increasingly understand why other parents' children have behavior problems. Although there are probably many routes to becoming a good parent, consistency in discipline is probably the most crucial factor for reaching a favorable outcome. Consistency will smooth out difficulties while inconsistency will exacerbate behavior problems.

The terms "consistency" and "discipline" are extremely important. Neither is synonymous with punishment. I use the term "consistency" to describe sameness over time, agreement between parents, predictability of consequences, and congruity between instructions, rewards and models. To the unsuspecting observer, consistent parents can appear either too punitive or too permissive when, in reality, they are neither. For example, consistent parents may have an arrangement in which their child may watch an extra half hour of television at night if he gets ready for bed (brushes teeth, washes hands and face, and puts on pajamas) by 9:00. Consistent parents make no exceptions if the child fails to meet this condition, even if a special show is on television. This consistency can make a parent appear overly punitive. On the other hand, a child who meets this condition receives the extra half hour of television even if he misbehaves in some other way. The consistent parent does not ignore the misbehavior, but also does not withdraw a reward the child has earned for the behavior specified in the original arrangement.

Similarly, "discipline" is not synonymous with punishment, although the terms are often used interchangeably. According to the *American Heritage Dictionary*, discipline refers to "training that is expected to produce a specific character or pattern of behavior, especially training that produces moral or mental improvement." A key word in this definition is *improvement*. Improvement requires one to increase skills or competence in a particular area. On the other hand, punishment, by definition, is designed to decrease certain behaviors. Therefore, punishment is antithetical to promoting discipline.

In this book, I have chosen to focus on positive methods for *increasing* desirable behaviors. This approach is *proactive* in that it requires parents to think ahead and plan how certain skills will be taught and behaviors managed. Punishment techniques, on the other hand, are *reactive* in that they are applied after behavior problems occur. The latter approach literally places parents at the mercy of their children.

I have organized this book around this theme of proactive approaches. Chapter 1 provides an overview of our preoccupation with controlling children's behavior. I also describe why punishment is one of the least effective methods for teaching children and managing their behavior. I end this chapter with a discussion of one of the most frequently used and recommended punishment techniques — time-out — and provide recommendations for its appropriate use.

Chapter 2 focuses on determining the behaviors that are important to change. This point may seem obvious and even trivial; however, the most common way of identifying behaviors for change involves determining what is most bothersome to the parent. The old adage "the squeaky wheel gets the grease" is an appropriate analogy. However, identifying behaviors based on the amount of "grease" they need often results in ineffective use of punishment. Therefore, this chapter presents several "tests" that parents can apply to increase the likelihood that the behaviors they identify are amenable to change.

Chapter 3 provides the reader with specific, positive techniques for teaching children and managing their behavior. I have compiled these techniques from courses I teach and from my experiences working directly with parents and families. I have divided this chapter into three sections: (1) an overview and recommendations for using positive reinforcement; (2) a description of the "star chart" method of tracking and rewarding desired behavior; and (3) how to use contracts to modify children's behavior.

Chapter 4 deals with the important issue of teaching children self-control. Perhaps no other aspect of managing children's behavior is considered as important by adults. This chapter is divided into two basic sections. In the first part I describe specific techniques for teaching children self-control. I present a model based on rational-emotive therapy (RET) for teaching emotional and behavioral control. The second section will help parents gain more personal emotional and behavioral control so that they can better deal with their children's difficult behavior.

In Chapter 5, I discuss the implications of applying a "diagnosis" to children's behavior problems. This chapter serves as a brief introduction to the next two chapters that address two of the most common disorders of childhood: attention deficits and depression. Perhaps no other conditions have received as much attention in the professional literature and popular press. Children with these two conditions are primarily treated by psychiatrists because medication is commonly prescribed. Unfortunately, many parents do not realize that there are also many *nonmedical* techniques they can use to help their children with these problems. One of the biggest obstacles parents must overcome is understanding that a diagnosis has little to do with treatment beyond prescribing medication. Therefore, in this chapter I demystify the nature and treatment of behavioral disorders by examining them from a societal perspective. From this perspective, a diagnosis with a subsequent label is not particularly helpful in guiding the development of intervention strategies. Furthermore, relying too much on diagnosis takes the focus away from the real problem — that the child is engaging in specific behaviors that require intervention.

Chapter 6 presents information on attention deficits. Because there are literally hundreds of books on the subject of attention deficits, I have been careful not to simply repeat information that is available elsewhere. Rather, I take a look at attention deficits from a nonmedical perspective — an angle that has received much less attention. A nonmedical perspective can help parents manage their children's behavior at home. After giving a brief overview of attention deficits, I examine evidence for some commonly believed assessments of attention deficits and suggest an alternative way to view the problem before describing the school's responsibility and techniques parents can use.

Chapter 7, a discussion of depression, focuses on several areas. First, I distinguish depression from normal feelings of unhappiness that we all experience from time to time. I then describe methods of getting children who are depressed to participate in therapeutic activities. Because of a lack of motivation associated with depression, motivating children to become involved in activities can be a daunting task. This chapter concludes with a presentation of several useful models of depression and treatment techniques that parents can use to help their children.

The book ends with a discussion of the management of resistance. No other topic has generated as much interest and resulted in as much parental frustration as has dealing with resistant, oppositional children. This chapter provides an overview of how parents can alter patterns of interaction to reduce their children's levels of opposition and resistance.

After reading this book, readers will have a better understanding of the nature of behavior problems and how the application of consistent, positive techniques can facilitate teaching children and managing their behavior much more effectively than the currently popular punitive approach. This book provides what few other parenting guides can claim — practical, specific, hands-on techniques that will enable parents to alter their interaction patterns with their children. The book demystifies behavior problems and the labels frequently associated with them. Most importantly, by shifting away from punishment and replacing it with positive reinforcement, a whole new world of amazingly effective parenting techniques will be open to you. Not only will you be a happier parent, but you'll have happier kids.

1

The Concept of Control

Henry and Kate Oakley are having dinner out with their good friends, Tim and Nancy Wilder. Both couples are accompanied by their 8-year-old sons, Frank and Steve. When they enter the restaurant, the hostess seats them at a large table located in the middle of the room. A waiter arrives shortly and hands out menus, informs them of the day's specials and gives each boy a "kiddie packet" consisting of a children's menu, two crackers, a crayon, and a placemat with a crossword puzzle, connect-the-dots, and pictures to color. After receiving drinks and ordering dinner, the adults become engrossed in conversation, ignoring their sons who are busy coloring and connecting the dots on the placemat.

After about 10 minutes, Frank turns to his father and whines, "When is dinner gonna be here? I'm hungry!"

"In a little while," replies his father, who then returns to the conversation with the other adults.

Just as Steve's mother is about to pick up her glass, she sees a crayon fly across the table and land directly in a basket of rolls.

"Pick that crayon up this instant," declares Nancy sternly, "unless you're not in the mood for dessert tonight."

"But Mom," replies Steve, "Frank went to grab my crayon before I was finished with it and when I pulled it back, it flew out of my hand."

At this time Frank's father enters the conversation. Glaring at his son disapprovingly, he says, "Frank, you have your own crayon, leave Steve's alone."

Just as Frank starts explaining to his father the relative merits of two-color shading and the importance of sharing, the meals arrive. Order is restored as the boys attack their cheeseburgers and fries and quietly discuss whether Roger Clemons or Dwight Gooden has a livelier fastball.

Throughout the meal, the parents enjoy conversation that ranges from the national budget deficit and the woeful inadequacies of public schools, to the hassles of visiting relatives and where to go for next summer's vacation.

Toward the end of the meal, Frank interrupts their conversation. "Mom, Steve just…" But before Frank can finish, his mother says, "How many times have I told you not to interrupt me when I'm in the middle of a conversation."

"But Mom, Frank flung ketchup on my shirt!"

"That's because Steve put his finger on my cheeseburger after picking his nose," Frank retorts.

"Alright," says Steve's father. "You just lost your dessert, and if you keep it up, when we get home you'll go straight to your room for the rest of the night."

"That goes for you too, Frank," his mother interjects. She wishfully ponders why a meal at a restaurant can't progress without her having to tell her son to stop misbehaving. The boys briefly glare at each other accusingly, and then, like brave Achilles retiring to his tent, they sulk quietly while their parents lament how difficult it is to take their young boys out to dinner without some type of behavior problem occurring.

After about 10 minutes, the boys begin talking to each other in hardy voices. "Mom, can Frank and I go to the bathroom?" asks Steve.

"Alright," replies his mother, "but don't get into trouble and come right back when you're finished." Frank's parents nod approval as they order coffee, keeping a watchful eye on the boys to ensure they do not get into trouble walking to the bathroom. After Steve and Frank engage in the usual bathroom conversations, they return to the table.

"Dad, can Steve and I wait for you guys up front by where you pay the check, *pleeeeease*?" Frank asks pleadingly.

After checking with his wife and Steve's parents, Tim agrees, but only under the condition that the boys don't wander into the lounge area or outside. The boys settle onto the bench by the cashier and begin examining the baseball cards they had both brought.

Back at the table, Tim moans to Nancy about anticipating the day when Steve can remain at home for a couple hours while they enjoy a relaxing meal out with friends.

"That's for sure," chimes in Kate, overhearing what was meant to be a private conversation.

"Boys need firm discipline. When I was their age, my father would have taken me into the bathroom and paddled my fanny if I was messin' around at the dinner table," says Henry as he keeps stirring his coffee long after the sugar has dissolved.

About 10 minutes later, Steve walks back to the table and asks his mother when they can leave. "Mom, Frank and I have been waiting on that bench forever. Can't we leave now?"

Frank eagerly agrees and adds, "Look Mom, I finally got Steve to trade me his Ken Griffey Jr. for my Barry Bonds. See? Now can we go home so I can put it in my collector's book?"

Ignoring the trade her son had just negotiated, Frank's mother replies in an almost pleading voice, "Honey, you know that your father and I almost never get to eat out with our friends. You and Steve need to wait a bit longer and then we'll leave."

"Eating out with grown-ups sucks," Frank murmurs under his breath.

"What did you say, young man?" his father asks as he shoots Frank a disapproving look.

"Nothin'," responds Frank as he gazes at the ground and shifts from one foot to the other.

"That's better," replies his father. "Now go wait by the front door, and we'll be out soon."

With the approval of his parents, Steve follows a dejected Frank toward the front of the restaurant.

The Oakleys and Wilders get up shortly and, while Tim puts on his sincerest face, he offers to pay the check. Henry protests and insists that dinner is on him. Tim contemplates protesting further but thinks better of it, in case Henry agrees.

"Henry," his wife says pensively, "I thought the boys were supposed to wait at the door."

"That's what we told them to do," replies Henry who cannot hide his irritation or his apprehension.

As the Oakleys and Wilders are about to scour the restaurant for their children, Nancy sees Steve and Frank waving at them from the bumper of their car.

"Are you trying to give us a heart attack?" Steve's mother asks as the parents reach the car. "Weren't you told to wait by the door?"

"I suppose so," replies Steve sheepishly. He quickly adds more enthusiastically, "But we knew you guys wanted to be left alone and it was getting crowded by the door with all the people waiting for a table, so we decided to sit on the back of the car until you were finished. We were waving at you guys while you were paying the check."

Both sets of parents stare at their children disapprovingly. Frank's father speaks first. "You have made this one of the worst dinners out we've had in quite some time. You constantly disobey us. When we get home, young man, you go straight to your room for the rest of the night."

"But Dad..." pleads Frank.

"No buts," replies his father, "now get into the car."

Steve gazes at his parents with a look that bespeaks the virtues of mercy and understanding. "We'll discuss your punishment when we get home," says his mother as she turns away and heads for the car, indicating that the conversation is finished.

This scene is commonly experienced by many families across the country and the behavior of the children and their parents in this story is in no way spectacular. Who cannot remember being a child and dining out with family or friends, bored to death as adults droned on endlessly? And how many adults cannot relate to trying to make the best of an evening out with friends without the luxury of a babysitter for their child? There are no "bad guys" in this scene, nor are the parents' or children's expectations unreasonable. Yet the dinner ended in an unpleasant way for both.

The dissatisfactory outcome in this scenario is largely due to a pattern of responding to children that adults take for granted, a pattern that society perpetuates. We expect children to behave well, and we respond with punishment (or the threat of it) when they behave poorly. Adults, whether they are parents or teachers, tend to ignore good behavior and react to bad behavior. Therefore, it is typical when Frank and Steve's parents ignore the boys' good table manners, quiet talking, positive requests to leave the table, and attempts not to bother the adults. However, when the boys misbehave, their parents are quick to administer verbal reprimands and threaten further punishment.

The tendency to ignore good behavior and attend to bad behavior is pervasive throughout our society. This phenomenon is sometimes referred to as the *concept of control.* Exerting control is a method parents use to make their children behave the way they want them to. One major problem with this kind of control orientation is that it causes parents to focus on decreasing (or getting rid of) behaviors. As a result, this approach promotes the use of punitive, and ultimately ineffective, strategies.

By definition, "punishment" refers to any external stimulus that will decrease future occurrences of certain behaviors. I will elaborate on the problems with punishment shortly, but for now, suffice it to say that punishment is only effective as long as outside pressure is present or at least is perceived to be present. Think back to when you were a child and got into fights with a sibling. When you had enough of your brother's teasing, you may have slugged him a good one in the arm or back. This attempt to get your brother to stop teasing you probably resulted in his running tearfully to your parents and tattling on you. The result was predictable: Mom or Dad told you not to hit your brother again or suffer the consequences. This threat of punishment probably was effective only as long as your parent was nearby. The next time you were alone with your brother, he would pay dearly.

We Live in a Controlling Society

In one of my graduate courses I have my students participate in a brainstorming exercise. Most of the students have been working for several years with children who have behavior problems. Toward the beginning of the semester, I ask them to think of one child whom they found particularly difficult to manage—the child of their worst nightmares. Then I pose the following question: "When you think of that child, what behavior do you most want to see change?" For about a minute I watch their facial expressions change from pained looks—presumably from thinking of children that have caused them a lot of grief—to smiles—perhaps indicating vicarious pleasure from thinking of the behavior of those children without having to experience it directly. I then ask them to shout out these behaviors so that I can write them on the chalkboard. Initial responses usually come slowly and often include behaviors such as swearing, crying, tantruming and hitting. However, when I encourage them to be more creative, a chorus of responses ensues with students shouting out behaviors such as nose-picking, running, spitting, yelling, being late, not following directions and the list goes on, usually much faster than I can write it on the board.

After a couple of minutes, I stop writing and tempt the students with an intriguing response to their list. "I have the perfect solution for dealing with every one of these behaviors. It will work every time—regardless of the child—and it's easy and quick to administer. How's that for getting your money's worth out of a class?" As the students ready their pens with looks of anticipation and skepticism, I say "bullet therapy." Invariably, several students, being well-trained to write down anything because it may appear on a test, begin writing down my words; others look at me with a puzzled expression, and others begin to grin sheepishly. I then ask them to re-examine the behaviors written on the chalkboard to determine what they all have in common. After several failed attempts to classify the behaviors according to some diagnostic category, I point out that all are behaviors that they want to *decrease*. I remind the students that my original request was for them to think of behaviors they wanted to *change*, not decrease. "What about increasing cooperation and negotiation skills or talking politely?" I ask. "When you select only those behaviors that you want to decrease, it is analogous to wanting a dead kid. A bullet shot to the head will take care of those behaviors quite nicely." Of course, a less severe way to decrease behavior is with punishment.

The example of "bullet therapy" is not meant to belittle my students, nor are they usually offended by it. I have found the results of the "bullet therapy" exercise to be remarkably consistent from year to year regardless of the students involved. I think this consistency exists because the concept of control and its focus on decreasing behavior is so well ingrained in us. We live in a society that routinely imposes negative consequences as a means of bringing citizens into alignment with various requirements: if you are caught running a red light or speeding, you get a ticket, swearing at a teacher can lead to suspension and not paying taxes brings the auditor to your house at best and a fine or jail sentence at worst. These are just a few examples from an endless list. And, to make matters more complicated, we take for granted this controlling and consequently punitive nature of dealing with unwanted behaviors.

A study conducted by two educational researchers at the University of Oregon illustrates the unintentional and subtle tendency of adults to try to do away with misbehavior. The two researchers asked teachers to rank-order a list of problematic behaviors. Of the behaviors mentioned, teachers responded that "poor attendance" was the least problematic, ranking it lower than all others including profanity, nervous tics and wearing an orthopedic brace. One interpretation of their responses is that many teachers would rather have a child completely gone than have him attend class and be disruptive. Although doing away with behavior is consistent with the concept of control and relies on punishment, it is antithetical to proactive parenting.

In contrast to control which is reactive (punishment is administered *after* misbehavior occurs), positive approaches to behavior management are proactive. They consist of preplanned activities and techniques to increase children's appropriate behavior. Take the example of a parent teaching her child to ride a bicycle. In the riding lesson, who schedules the time and length of instruction, looks for responses, and then provides correction? The parent does, and, therefore, the child is doing the learning. Conversely, when the child exhibits a behavior problem, who schedules it, provides the materials, and decides if the incident need go on? The child does. Who, then, is doing the learning? I believe that reactive approaches to discipline place parents in learning rather than teaching roles with their children—roles they are not used to and often find uncomfortable. Yet parents continue to rely on punitive approaches as a cornerstone of disciplining their children.

The reasons for this phenomenon are apparent in the differing views our society holds toward punishment and its opposite—reinforcement. We can define reinforcement as anything presented after a behavior occurs that tends to increase the future occurrence of that behavior. Although this is the opposite of punishment, it is not synonymous with rewards. A reward is something children usually receive from their parents or others for doing a good job or for behaving well. Although reinforcement can take the form of a reward, it represents much more. It is the preplanned application of specific stimuli after a behavior occurs to increase the frequency or duration of that behavior in the future. I can receive a one-time reward in the form of winning first prize at a piano recital but that doesn't necessarily mean I will now spend 30 minutes more each day practicing the piano.

In our society, punishment is more acceptable than rewards because it does not threaten our autonomy—we believe we are free to choose to behave in responsible ways to avoid punishment. Conversely, rewards are seen as externally applied, thereby intimating that people behave in certain ways not because they are internally motivated but because they are being coerced.

In his book *Beyond Freedom and Dignity*, the psychologist B.F. Skinner wrote about punishment and motivation in the following way:

> The trouble is that when we punish a person for behaving badly, we leave it up to him to discover how to behave well, and he can then get credit for behaving well.... At issue is an attribute of autonomous man. Men are to behave well only because they are good.

What type of child do you think of more highly: the child who, on his own, cleans up his room, or the child who has to be rewarded with a trip to Dairy Queen after his room is cleaned? Without a doubt, we think better of the child who appears to act autonomously than the one who must be coerced with a reward. Although punitive consequences may be more inconspicuous than reinforcement (e.g., a child sits quietly at the dinner table to avoid a stern look from her mother), they are consistent with the concept of control and the premium society places on individual freedom.

The "control mentality" is pervasive throughout society. B.F. Skinner further notes:

> If we no longer resort to torture in what we call the civilized world, we nevertheless still make extensive use of punitive techniques in both domestic and foreign relations. And apparently for good reasons. Nature if not God has created man in such a way that he can be controlled punitively. People quickly become skillful punishers (if not, thereby, skillful controllers), whereas alternative positive measures are not easily learned. The need for punishment seems to have the support of history, and alternative practices threaten the cherished values of freedom and dignity.

Take, for example, our current system for "controlling" speeding. If you are caught speeding, a police officer issues you a ticket. This ticket is a form of punishment, because it costs you something you value (money) and is designed to decrease a certain behavior (speeding). Imagine the unlikelihood of another societal approach toward speeding—instead of punishing motorists for speeding, they get rewarded for going the speed limit!

Imagine a morning DJ providing the following public service message: "We'll be getting back to the music in a few minutes, but first the news. All you drivers on your way to work, the police have set up speed traps on the following streets: 70th Street between Pioneers Boulevard and South Street, Adams just north of 48th Street, and Holdridge between Main and East Campuses. Drivers who are going the speed limit will be randomly stopped and given a check for $100." Even if public funds to reward motorists in this fashion were available, it is highly unlikely that this approach would ever catch on—it appears too coercive and manipulative. We would obey the speed limit not because it was the "right" thing to do but because we were being "paid off."

In the same way, we try to control children with punishment. But the mark of a successful technique is the ability to use it less rather than more often. If punishment is as effective as many seem to think, its use should decrease instead of increase. In reality, though, punishment has enjoyed unparalleled growth in schools. For example, schools have developed elaborate management plans to decrease inappropriate behavior. In-school and out-of-school suspension, expulsion, community work, restitution, phone calls to parents and trips to the principal have increased in recent years. I am not suggesting that children's behaviors that result in punishment—either at school or home—should be tolerated. Rather, I believe there is ample evidence that punishment techniques, when used in isolation, represent exceedingly ineffective approaches to managing children's behavior.

Punishment: Its Addiction and Effectiveness

Punishment is somewhat analogous to drug addiction. Heroin is an addicting drug for several reasons; most notably, it results in a quick and intense high with relatively little effort. Like heroin, punishment can produce very quick results that can be pleasant to the punisher in terms of controlling a child. However, repeated exposure to punishment causes a tolerance to its effects and, as with drugs, requires increasingly more extreme forms of punishment to achieve the same results. The problems with children and parents developing tolerances to punishment are tragic and well-documented in the media—the incidence of child abuse is rising rather than declining.

In addition to the cultural ethos for using punishment and its addictive nature, it is much more difficult to develop and implement appropriate positive methods in a proactive manner than it is to simply respond to a child's misbehavior with a verbal reprimand or a slap on the fanny. Also, the use of punishment is, ironically, reinforced because it does result in rapid reduction in behavior—but only for brief periods of time. Remember the situation I described above of the child who only stops hitting his brother when the punishment exists—that is, Mom or Dad is present. Although most adults believe the solution to this problem is to administer more intense punishment, this approach rarely solves the problem.

Limitations of Punishment

Many authors have elegantly described the many reasons why punishment is ineffective. I will summarize each of these and explain why recommendations for enhancing the effectiveness of punishment are not only impractical but can increase the risk for a child to be physically abused.

Punishment suppresses behavior

One of the major limitations of punishment is, ironically, that it suppresses behavior. That is what punishment is supposed to do; however, it may suppress the undesirable behavior in all situations although suppression is desired only in a specified setting. For example, most of us would like our children to refrain from yelling throughout the house. However, when administered in sufficient intensity and frequency, punishment may suppress yelling in other situations where yelling is desirable. Thus a child playing second base may not yell to the shortstop that he will make the catch on an infield pop-up. It is important to remember that behavior is affected by the context or situation. In this instance, yelling, in and of itself, is not an undesirable behavior. Rather, it is the context in which yelling occurs that dictates how it is viewed.

The idea that context affects whether a behavior is appropriate or inappropriate is an extremely important one. Take, for example, a context in which many people find themselves on Sunday mornings—church. This context gives us cues on how to behave. In many churches and temples in this country, individuals sit quietly, speak only upon cue, dress nicely, and refrain from drinking or eating. Conversation before and after the service is usually polite and friendly. Now imagine a totally different context that dictates different behavior—the baseball park. This context, especially if you are sitting in the bleachers, results in behaviors that include yelling at the opposing players in the outfield, consuming large quantities of hotdogs, beer and peanuts, and wearing shorts or going shirtless if you are a male. Now imagine going into church wearing cutoffs and a sleeveless t-shirt and carrying a bag of hotdogs and cooler of beer under your arm. You take your seat in the pew, pop open a cold one, and begin munching on a hotdog. As the preacher begins his sermon, you stand up and "boo the bum," yelling for him to get off the podium. It probably would not take long for the police to be summoned and for you to be removed. The point is that behaviors we are likely to be punished for in one context may be very desirable in another. By punishing, therefore, we run the risk of appearing contradictory to our children and eliminating very useful behaviors from their repertoire.

A situation in which a friend of mine found himself illustrates how a single behavior can have both negative and positive aspects. Several years ago, Ken served as a school psychologist in Oregon. One day the principal asked Ken to work with Rich, a fifth-grade student. Rich engaged in a particularly annoying behavior—swearing. Specifically, Rich seemed to favor the word "shit." He would say this word to students and teachers in class, to visiting parents passing in the halls, and to motorists waiting at the stop light on the street next to the school yard. Ken, who was always ready for a challenge, began working with this child enthusiastically. He began with 30-minute counseling sessions three times a week to identify the issues that prompted Rich to resort to swearing to draw attention. Although these efforts resulted in a good relationship between Ken and Rich, the counseling had little impact on Rich's swearing. Consequently, Ken called a conference with Rich's parents. Rich's parents agreed the swearing was a problem and promised to support whatever action the school thought necessary to stop the behavior. Ken told them that Rich's teacher would send a note home specifying how many times Rich had sworn in the course of the day. Ken suggested that if Rich swore less than five times, his parents let him stay up an extra half hour to play his favorite Nintendo game. If he swore more than five times, Rich was to go to bed a half hour earlier than usual. Although Rich's parents nodded approval, Ken got the idea that they were less than enthusiastic about having to monitor their child's bedtime after they both had worked a long day. After a few days it was clear that this intervention too was having limited success. Ken was showing the first signs of frustration. Not unlike other adults at this stage, therefore, he resorted to more punitive measures. Specifically, every time Rich swore, Ken had him spend an extra 15 minutes after school completing math worksheets. Alas, this approach also failed.

Finally, sinking to bribery, Ken decided to pay Rich one dollar for every day he could refrain from swearing. Toward the end of the school year, Rich's swearing did, in fact, decrease somewhat. Although Ken was not sure if it was due to Rich's receiving money or staying after school, the important point was that his swearing had decreased. At about this time, Rich's class was heading on a field trip—a hike through the forest and a picnic lunch. Ken accompanied Rich to make sure his swearing did not recur. The hike was proceeding splendidly—the scenery was magnificent, and Rich was not swearing. Then the hikers came to a narrow stream, about 10 feet wide and 18 inches deep, that was dotted with rocks jutting out above the water. The only way to cross the stream without getting wet was to jump from rock to rock. The children readily took to this challenge, but their enthusiasm was replaced with caution when they discovered that the rocks were quite slippery. After watching other children cross the stream, Ken proceeded with Rich at his side. About halfway across, Rich began to slip on a rock covered with a large amount of moss. He instinctively grabbed at an unsuspecting Ken and both of them landed in the water. Ken turned to Rich and, looking him squarely in the eyes, said, "Now you can say 'shit'!"

The story of Ken and Rich illustrates how an undesirable behavior in one context can be a very natural response in another context. Punishment runs the risk of suppressing behavior that may have a very adaptive function. In fact, almost all behaviors are appropriate in some context. Aggression, for example, is very appropriate when one is physically threatened and, in fact, is often used in a court of law to justify murder. The importance of context will be discussed in more detail in the next chapter on identifying behaviors to change.

Punishment elicits avoidance and escape behavior

Besides the unilateral squelching of behaviors across contexts, there are several other adverse side effects of using punishment. For example, punishment can elicit avoidance and escape behavior. A child may learn to avoid or escape from important sources of socialization and education—namely, her parents—if they are also the source of unpleasant stimuli. Probably the most effective teaching tool that a parent has is the ability to reinforce a child socially for engaging in appropriate behavior. Praise, attention and feedback are powerful teaching tools. If parents dispense intense and frequent aversive consequences, a child may not identify adults as positive or potentially positive. Instead of learning appropriate behaviors, therefore, the child becomes skilled at avoiding or getting away from the punisher.

Punishment does not teach appropriate behavior

Another important drawback of punishment is that when used in isolation, it does not teach a child appropriate behaviors. Instead, the use of punishment leaves the development of desirable behavior to chance. For example, imagine a young girl, Tanya, who is sent to her room for hitting her brother. There is nothing wrong with Tanya's parents wanting to limit their daughter's aggressive behavior toward her brother. However, Tanya may have hit her brother to get him to stop teasing her. Teasing and hitting among siblings is a fairly common occurrence, albeit an undesirable one. But what if hitting was the only way Tanya knew to get her brother to stop teasing her? Her parents could go on punishing but still not teach her how to be assertive or to use negotiation skills in place of hitting. Such skills must be taught and promoted.

Punishment does not eliminate negative attention

Not only does punishment fail to teach appropriate behavior, it also fails to eliminate the reinforcement a child may receive from engaging in an inappropriate behavior. Why does the class clown persist in making barnyard animal noises even after his teacher has sent him to the principal's office and moved his desk next to hers? Why does a young girl continue to place the end of a string bean in her nose at the dinner table after being told she will not receive dessert and will go to bed an hour early? Why are these punishments ineffective? The reason is simply that the "payoff" for engaging in the inappropriate behavior is still present—attention from others. The young girl with the bean up her nose may be receiving comments from her siblings like "You are so gross," "What a pig," "I hate eating at the same table as you," "Mom, would you get her to stop." The boy in school making animal noises may hear similar comments from his peers. Ironically, even though the content of these comments is negative, the attention the child receives is a powerful reinforcer for maintaining the inappropriate behavior despite punishment. It is important to remember that *negative attention is better than no attention and much more powerful than punishment.*

Punishment teaches aggression

Another limitation to punishment is that it may elicit emotional and aggressive behavior. If the aversives are strong enough, a child may exhibit anxiety and fear responses that are counter-productive to learning. Or a child may respond to punishment by attacking the punisher or someone else. For example, a punished child may strike back at her parent either verbally or physically. Or, if the child lacks the power to attack the punisher, she may attack someone weaker. Many younger brothers and sisters bear the brunt of their older siblings' anger at having been punished. Similarly, punishment provides an aggressive model for the child. Who is not aware of the irony, usually recounted by comedians, of the father who swats his son's fanny while repeatedly reminding him not to hit his younger brother. In a more serious vein, punishment gives the child a power model—those with strength and power punish and can control others with their power. Children may learn that to affect the behavior of others, punishment is the procedure of choice.

You may be getting the idea that I never advocate punishing a child. That's not the case. However, punishment should be used judiciously and only after other positive methods have been tried; then punishment can be employed, but only in conjunction with positive methods.

Situational Variables

There are four situational variables that can enhance the effectiveness of punishment. Putting these variables into practice is extremely difficult. I will go through each to illustrate the difficulty of administering punishment effectively and the paradoxes inherent in each variable.

It should be impossible to escape the punishment

First, to be effective, the punishment should be unavoidable. Although it is difficult for parents to withstand their child's verbal onslaughts urging leniency, no amount of begging or remorse should change the situation. Punishment frequently is administered as a last-resort strategy by parents reacting to a stressful situation. Hence, it is not uncommon for punishment to be delivered by a parent who is, quite naturally, angry at a child. Often, in the heat of an argument with a child, a parent yells, "You're grounded for a month," only later to renege on this punishment. Or, a mother may say, "Just wait until your father gets home," only to cool off and "forget" to tell her husband. Anger makes us all say things we don't mean and later retract. And that's good because if every parent followed through with the punishments that come out of their mouths in the heat of anger, the incidence of child abuse would be even higher than current estimates of about 170,000 cases yearly. Parents cool down and feel guilty about their behavior during an argument. As natural as this reaction may be, it still results in the child escaping the punishment. This situation diminishes the punishment's effectiveness and illustrates how difficult it is to administer punishment effectively. Hence, there is an inherent paradox in using punishment: The child should not be able to escape or avoid the punishment, yet punishment produces escape and avoidance behavior in the child.

Punishment should be intense

A second influence upon the effectiveness of punishment involves the intensity with which it is administered. In general, researchers have shown that a gradual increase in the intensity of punishment results in a child adapting to it, thereby hampering a punishment's effectiveness to reduce or eliminate behavior. Conversely, a quick increase in the intensity of punishment leads to greater reductions in the child's behavior. Unfortunately, few people would advocate punishing a child at the maximum intensity level for the first offense. Take, for example, the place all parents dread to be with their child—the checkout line at a grocery store. Capitalism exerts no sympathy for parents in this situation. Every grocery store owner knows that putting items attractive to children on shelves by the checkout counter tests parents' mettle and frequently results in unwanted purchases. Most people are familiar with how this scenario plays out.

"Mommy, can I have a pack of that gum?" asks Sally.

"No dear," responds her mother, "we have gum at home."

"But not that type of gum, " Sally retorts. "Please!"

More forcefully, her mother shoots back, "I said no, now stop asking me." Of course, Sally continues and as her whining increases, so do her mother's verbal reprimands. Sally may then begin to pull on her mother's shirt. At this point her mother may respond by saying, "If you don't stop this minute, you'll go straight to your room when we get home."

"But Mom, why can't I have that gum? You bought some for me last time."

As this scene progresses, Sally's mother tells her she will not only go to her room but also lose her dessert. Sally may continue until her mother gets so frustrated that she slaps her rear end. Although Sally begins to cry, she is no longer asking for candy and her mother has saved face. Unfortunately, in this as in most situations, the intensity of the punishment gradually increased. The most effective punishment Sally's mother employed was also the most intense—a slap to the buttocks. However, this gradual increase made it more likely that Sally would adapt to the punishment, thereby limiting its effectiveness. Instead, the most effective approach would have been to use the most intense punishment first. So, when Sally politely asked if she could have a pack of gum, her mother should have immediately hit her. And herein lies another paradox: No one would advocate using that extreme a form of punishment for a child making a request even though the punishment ultimately would be more effective. Parents would run the risk or be accused of child abuse, and rightfully so. So it appears unethical and abusive to increase the effectiveness of punishment by following this recommendation.

Punishment should be applied consistently and early

A third factor, and one related to the previous two, is timing. Punishment should be applied consistently and quite early in the sequence of a child's misbehavior. However, as described above, it is difficult to be consistent with the application of punishment when it is most often used in the heat of argument. Yet punishment that is administered consistently every time is more effective than occasional punishment. In addition, punishment occurring at the beginning of an episode of misbehavior does not have to be as severe as if several minutes, or even hours, pass before the punishment is delivered. Again, this recommendation has an unintended paradoxical effect. Most parents correctly ignore the little misbehaviors that precede a child's temper outburst. Parents ignore their child whining to stay up later in the hopes that she will recognize the folly of the request. Yet ignoring the initial stages of this misbehavior reduces the effectiveness of punishment.

Reinforcement should not be mixed with punishment

A fourth variable impacting upon the effectiveness of punishment involves, again paradoxically, reinforcement. Specifically, when reinforcement is present at the same time as punishment, the effect is as dramatic as accidentally mixing up the positive and negative jumper cables when charging a car battery. Yet it is extremely common for reinforcement to be associated with punishment. In fact, punishment can serve as a cue to a child that reinforcement will be forthcoming. For example, it is not uncommon for parents to comfort and reassure their child immediately after administering punishment. After an argument, both parent and child may apologize to each other and, because of the guilt both may be experiencing for their actions during the episode, consequently go out of their way to treat each other nicely. I can remember many occasions growing up when my mother would punish me for some misbehavior. Afterwards, we would naturally make up and then she may have asked me to help her in the kitchen or to run an errand together. These positive interactions and experiences are reinforcing both to child and parent and represent a natural way to put an argument to rest. However, the child may come to learn that punishment leads to receiving special attention from Mom or Dad.

At this point, it may be helpful to go back to our original encounter at the restaurant with the Oakleys and Wilders. Several things should have become clear from the discussion thus far. For one, Frank and Steve's parents virtually ignored their sons' appropriate behavior. For another, punishment was not applied consistently, nor did it occur immediately. The boys got away with misbehaving with only a warning. Also, by telling the boys they would be punished when they got home, their parents drastically reduced the effectiveness of the punishment. Throughout the restaurant episode, the parents reacted to their sons' behavior rather than engaging in proactive activities to specify which behaviors were acceptable and the positive consequences that the boys would enjoy for engaging in them.

It becomes easy to see how parents can fall into the trap of applying ineffective punishment without even realizing it. Yet punishment procedures continue to be advocated by "experts" and their use is on the rise. For example, one of the most popular punishment techniques is time-out. Although discussions of parenting techniques relying on time-out appear in newspaper columns, on television shows and in scholarly journals, this technique continues to be misunderstood and misused to the point of representing a form of child abuse in extreme cases. Consequently, I have chosen to end this chapter with a discussion of this particularly popular punishment technique.

Why Time-Out Doesn't Always Work

A fairly well-known psychologist writes a syndicated column describing how parents can better teach and manage their children's behavior. His column is kind of like a "Dear Abby" for parents having trouble managing their children: A parent writes a letter describing a problem and the psychologist provides a solution—usually simplistic and punitive. A popular and recurring theme in his column is the use of time-out as punishment for misbehavior. I remember reading a column in which a parent raised a concern about time-out. The parent wrote that she had been using it effectively for about six weeks, but then its effectiveness began to decline. The psychologist's recommendation was to use three "tickets" that the parent would remove contingent upon misbehavior. Once all three tickets were lost, he recommended that the parent place the child in his room for the remainder of the day, regardless of how long that would be.

Although this recommendation entails numerous problems, I will focus on the two most salient. First, the psychologist should have pointed out to the parent that the effectiveness of time-out is minimal when used as an isolated intervention. In fact, to call time-out a punishment is a misnomer. The complete term is "time-out from positive reinforcement." This more accurate term implies that if time-out is to be effective, the time-in setting must be reinforcing. The idea behind time-out is to remove the child from the environment that is maintaining the inappropriate behavior. For example, the girl described above who was sticking the bean up her nose might benefit from time-out because the reinforcement she received in the form of attention from her siblings would be removed. In this case, time-out would not be punishing the child but rather removing her from the attention she received for her misbehavior.

The second problem associated with the psychologist's recommendation is that time-out is ineffective if the time-in environment does not have specific positive consequences for exhibiting appropriate behavior. For example, the child who made animal noises in class received a form of time-out when the teacher sent him to the principal's office. By removing the child from the classroom, the teacher prevented the misbehavior from being reinforced by attention from classmates. However, the behavior might still continue if the time-in setting is not positively reinforcing. If the only attention the child receives in class is negative, no amount of time-out will decrease the inappropriate behavior. Unfortunately, this situation is common because of our tendency to ignore good behavior and react to bad behavior. In fact, for some children, time-out is reinforcing rather than punishing because it allows them to escape chores, household responsibilities, or aversive interactions with parents or siblings.

Appropriate Uses of Time-Out

Although time-out is most associated with excluding or secluding a child, there are a variety of less extreme time-out procedures. In two excellent articles, Robert B. Rutherford, Jr., and C. Michael Nelson described the different types of time-out and recommendations for using these procedures effectively.

A good example of an appropriate use of time-out is a technique called the "time-out ribbon," developed for use with a child with mental retardation. This child was receiving a lot of negative attention from his classmates for engaging in various forms of socially inappropriate behavior such as picking his nose, invading another classmate's personal space and laughing at inappropriate times. His teacher developed a procedure in which a ribbon was tied in a bow around the boy's wrist. While he had the ribbon tied around his wrist, his classmates gave him a lot of positive attention—asking him to join in activities, giving him compliments and helping him with his work. When the boy engaged in inappropriate behavior, the teacher removed the ribbon for two minutes. During that time, his classmates completely ignored him, no matter how obnoxious he was in trying to get their attention. The first appropriate behavior the boy engaged in after two minutes resulted in the ribbon being replaced on his wrist, signifying that his peers and teacher could again give him high doses of positive attention.

The time-out ribbon illustrates two important points. First, time-in must be highly reinforcing so that children will want to remain there. Simply sending a child to her room when she misbehaves is not effective if the child enjoys playing in her room more than she likes being out of her room. Second, time-out should not be considered synonymous with exclusion or seclusion—the two most extreme forms of time-out.

A whole continuum of time-out procedures are less severe but potentially more effective. For example, the time-out ribbon is a form of time-out called "reduction of response maintenance stimuli." This term refers to the practice of eliminating negative attention that maintains inappropriate behavior and increasing positive attention for appropriate behavior. Consider again the girl who was receiving negative attention at the dinner table for sticking a bean up her nose. Her parents could tell the other children that they would get an extra scoop of ice cream for ignoring their sister; anyone warned more than once to ignore her would go without dessert. Furthermore, the girl's parents could provide her with special positive attention when she used good manners.

Another less severe form of time-out is "contingent observation." This technique calls for removing a child or not allowing her to participate in an activity for a fixed period of time when misbehaving. The child remains able to observe her family but she may not participate in their activities or receive any attention from them. For example, if our girl persisted in sticking the bean up her nose, her parents could place her in a chair away from the table where she could observe others eating but not participate in the meal herself. Parents have used this form of time-out for many years, and it is a favorite of many. However, its success depends upon the parent's ability to withhold all attention from the child—not an easy task. If the parents have to tell the child to sit in the chair, not fiddle around and not try to get others' attention, this form of time-out will be ineffective because the child will continue to receive attention. Therefore, the child may learn that the easiest way to get parents' and siblings' attention is to misbehave. This problem serves only to initiate a perpetual cycle of punishment.

Misused Forms of Time-Out

The most common form of time-out is seclusion—being sent to one's room. Despite its commonness, it is also the most abused and misapplied form of time-out. One problem is ensuring that the child receives no reinforcement while in time-out—a difficult feat in a setting like a bedroom where children have access to many diversions. Time-out may even function as a reinforcer for undesired behavior if it allows a child to escape from a minimally reinforcing environment; the opportunity to engage in highly reinforcing behavior during time-out may be a more powerful consequence than positive reinforcement for appropriate behavior outside of time-out. The child may use the opportunity of being sent to her room as a way to talk secretly to friends on the phone or receive special attention from siblings such as being brought food or messages.

There are other ways in which behaviors resulting in time-out may receive more powerful reinforcement than appropriate time-in behaviors. For instance, as mentioned earlier, siblings might directly or subtly provide attention for the child's inappropriate behaviors. Also, a parent's verbal persuasion to get her child to take time-out could function as a reinforcer. If a power struggle develops over taking time-out, the parent's social attention or the child's occasional success in avoiding time-out could reinforce the child's resistance. In addition, the mere presence of positive attention in the time-in environment does not eliminate the possibility that the total environment may be more aversive than positive. For example, although the parents of the child sticking the bean up her nose may provide her positive attention for using good manners, they may still criticize their child for doing poorly at school or for not finishing her chores. Therefore, time-out allows the child to escape from a minimally reinforcing environment.

The remedy for impoverished time-in environments is to analyze the patterns of attention the child receives both for maladaptive and appropriate behavior and subsequently to increase systematically the frequency of positive attention for appropriate behavior. At the same time, the parent should attempt to reduce spurious reinforcement for undesired behavior. The next chapter explains how to analyze factors that maintain inappropriate behavior.

Another problem is ensuring that a child displays appropriate time-out behavior: He goes to the time-out area, remains there, and does not engage in undesired behavior such as yelling, throwing objects, or kicking the walls or door. However, it is difficult to enforce these conditions. Often the child does not respond appropriately when told to take time-out. Such unresponsiveness is not surprising because parents usually apply time-out when they view a child's behavior as out-of-control—both parents and child are usually in an agitated state. A power struggle ensues and may end only when the parent physically escorts the child to the time-out area. It becomes even more difficult to get children to comply with time-out when they are large and more powerful. Again, the attention the child receives in the form of physical contact, even if that contact is negative, can serve to reinforce the inappropriate behaviors that led to the time-out.

The solution to this problem is paradoxical. Most experts believe it is important to "teach" children how to take a time-out appropriately. This may include scheduling training sessions at times other than when time-out is required. This solution is paradoxical because, if the parent can teach the child to take a time-out appropriately in the heat of anger and conflict, then there is no need for the time-out in the first place. The parent can simply tell the child to calm down or redirect her before an argument escalates. However, de-escalation of behavior is not that simple. Therefore, parents have the best chance at getting their child to take a time-out before everyone involved becomes highly agitated. An undesirable effect of this practice is that even mild misbehavior, such as saying "no" to a parental request, may result in time-out. Of course, the opposite also is true. If time-out is applied too late, when the child is out-of-control, two undesirable outcomes may occur. First, the child's behavior may require physical management that might be reinforcing; second, the parent may be unable to ignore aggressive or tantrum behavior in time-out.

Finally, it is easy to abuse specifications regarding the length of time-out. For instance, the child may receive reinforcement for undesired time-out behavior by leaving his bedroom and asking, "Is my time up yet?" In another instance, the parent may simply "forget" that the child is in time-out, leaving him there far too long. If the child's behavior is aversive to the parent, leaving him in time-out for excessive periods of time may be reinforcing to the parent because she gets a break from dealing with an obnoxious child. A common question asked by parents is, "How long should I leave my child in time-out?" There is no evidence that longer periods of time have more positive impact upon a child's behavior than shorter periods. Therefore, the psychologist's recommendation that the child remain in time-out "for the rest of the day" is no more effective than much shorter periods of time, say up to 20 minutes. A much more important consideration is that the child behave appropriately while in time-out, which means sitting quietly doing nothing or writing a contract on how to handle the situation better the next time it occurs. It may take one hour for the child to begin sitting quietly and realizing he will have to do the time-out appropriately. But after they have learned to comply with the time-out requirements, a 2- to 10-minute time-out should suffice for most children between the ages of 4 and 10.

Given the problems with time-out just mentioned, it is easy to see why it is so hard to use time-out effectively. The solution to the time-out dilemmas discussed here is to broaden your repertoire of techniques for managing behavior positively. Then, in situations where time-out is required, you can increase the chance of having the child comply as well as the effectiveness of the procedure. The first step in developing and implementing positive management techniques is to identify exactly what behaviors are important to change.

2

Identifying What
Behaviors to Change

Identifying what to change about children's behavior appears quite simple on the surface. Indeed, there is little to the identification process if one proceeds from a control mentality: Change what is bothering the adult. When I ask graduate students and parents what to change, they often look at me with bewildered and irritated expressions and respond, "Of course I know what to change—that's the easy part. I want Freddy to stop whining when we are at the store, leave his sister alone, not yell from the other room when he wants something, and stop slouching at the dinner table."

Most of my students and parents emphasize that identifying what to change is easy—the hard part is coming up with ways to accomplish this task. Ironically, the opposite is really true—the hard part is identifying an appropriate behavior to change, whereas deciding on a technique for changing the child's behavior is fairly easy in comparison. However, convincing parents of this is difficult because of the well-ingrained belief that bad behavior must be eliminated and good behavior must be expected. It is difficult to convince adults to move away from focusing on negative behaviors (which necessitate the use of reactive approaches) to identifying positive behaviors that lead to proactive approaches. What prevents us from seeing, accepting and understanding this different concept is startlingly simple: paradigms.

"Paradigm" is a word that has become increasingly popular in recent years. The term first received widespread attention in 1962 when Thomas Kuhn published *The Structure of Scientific Revolutions.* Since then, it has been popularized by futurists such as Joel Barker, who lectures to corporations on how to discover new ways of conducting business. The word paradigm means a "pattern" or "model." Barker offers a more functional definition, considering a paradigm as a set of rules and regulations that does two things. First, similar to a pattern, a paradigm establishes boundaries. Second, the rules and regulations of a paradigm explain how to be successful by solving problems within the given boundaries.

Although the focus of Thomas Kuhn's book was to explore how scientists change their paradigms, his conclusions help explain why we so often fail to anticipate and implement new ways of doing things. Kuhn discovered that paradigms act as filters that screen data coming into a scientist's mind. Data that agree with a scientist's paradigm have an easy pathway to recognition. In fact, scientists see that type of data with great clarity and understanding. This phenomenon is similar to the ease with which parents and teachers see children's misbehavior.

Kuhn also discovered that some data cause scientists substantial difficulty, because they do not match the expectations created by their paradigm. In fact, the more unexpected the data, the more trouble scientists have perceiving it. In some cases, they simply ignore unexpected data. Other times they distort the data until they fit their paradigm rather than acknowledging them as an exception to the rules. In extreme cases, Kuhn discovered that scientists were physiologically incapable of perceiving the unexpected data—for all intents and purposes the data were invisible.

To put the concept of paradigms in more general terms: they filter incoming experiences. We view the world through paradigms all the time. We constantly select from the world those data that best fit our rules and regulations, while trying to ignore the rest. As a result, what may be perfectly obvious to a person adhering to one paradigm may be totally imperceptible to a person with a different paradigm. The phenomenon that Kuhn describes for scientists is true for anyone who holds on to strongly held rules and regulations—in other words, everyone. Because of our paradigms, it is our rules and regulations that blind us to creative solutions to difficult problems of managing children's behavior. We look for solutions through old paradigms that keep us from using alternative techniques.

Barker describes the change in watch-making during the past 25 years to illustrate the power of paradigms. In 1968 the Swiss dominated the world of watch-making with a 65 percent world market share and more than 80 percent of the profits. Yet 10 years later, their market share plummeted below 10 percent, and in the ensuing three years they had to release 50,000 of their 65,000 watch workers. Today Japan dominates the world in watch-making, even though they had virtually no market share 25 years ago. How could the Swiss, who commanded the watch-making industry for the greater part of the twentieth century and were known for the excellence of their products, be destroyed so rapidly? The answer is quite simple: They failed to anticipate a change in paradigms. Specifically, they failed to recognize the importance of the quartz movement watch—a watch that is totally electronic and battery-powered and much more accurate than the mechanical watches it replaced.

Ironically, the Swiss invented the quartz watch in their research laboratories. Yet, when the researchers presented this idea to the Swiss watch manufacturers in 1967, it was rejected—the watch didn't have any bearings, gears or a mainspring. Therefore, in the eyes of the Swiss manufacturers, it couldn't possibly be the watch of the future. So confident were the manufacturers in their conclusion that they did not even protect the idea. Later that year, Swiss researchers displayed the watch to the world at the annual watch congress. Texas Instruments of America and Seiko of Japan walked past, took one look, and the rest is history. Why didn't the Swiss appreciate this wonderful invention that their own people had created? Simple: They were blinded by the success of their old paradigm and all their investments in it. When confronted with a profoundly new and different way to continue their success into the future, they rejected it because it did not fit the rules they had already established and mastered.

Paradigms have considerable relevance for identifying behaviors to change. Paradigms help explain why the control mentality is so pervasive and well-ingrained in our collective societal psyche. To shift one's paradigm for managing children's behavior from a negative and reactive approach to one that is positive and proactive is difficult. I will undertake this challenge by presenting a checklist of factors—some of which are framed in terms of whether a child's behavior passes certain "tests." These "tests" are based, to a large extent, on the work of Joe Kaplan at Portland State University and ensure that the identified behavior is appropriate and amenable to our efforts to change it in a positive fashion.

Test 1: If in Doubt, Ask a Stranger

"Beauty is in the eye of the beholder." This age-old saying carries with it an inescapable truth: perceptions of reality are based on our past experiences, and those past experiences necessarily differ from person to person. When we do not have enough information to form a judgment, we make sense of the situation by filling in the gaps with facts that conform to our view of how things "ought to be." This tendency was painfully evident in the trials of the police officers charged and eventually convicted in the Rodney King beating in Los Angeles. The videotape showing the beating Rodney King received was repeated ad nauseam to the general public before the trials and to the jurors during the trials. To some onlookers, the tape showed a clear case of excessive force and police brutality. Yet to others, the police were responding with the amount of force necessary to the situation. Complete strangers can view the same incident and reach different conclusions because of an unconscious process of seeking facts that are congruent with their prior beliefs. Consequently, wrong people may be identified as criminals, because events are construed in ways that are consistent with an observer's emotions and prejudices.

The same forces are at work when we attempt to identify behaviors to change. When I meet with parents for the first time, I usually ask them to describe the problems they are encountering with their child. Parents generally describe their child as being hostile, aggressive, inconsiderate, oppositional, out-of-control, depressed, sad, hyper, impulsive, inattentive, manipulative, lazy, mean, bad, irresponsible, and so forth. One of the problems with these descriptions is that they are very subjective. What constitutes hostility varies from person to person. Some parents may consider a child's frown and terse "No!" when asked to clean his room an indication of hostility. Other parents may view yelling as representing a hostile act. Still others would consider breaking objects or hitting siblings to constitute hostility. We have a tendency to view behavior in very nonbehavioral terms by labeling the child with emotionally laden language that has different meanings to different individuals. Parents often have considerable difficulty describing their child's behavior objectively because it is faster and easier to describe him as hyperactive than to explain that he runs through the kitchen knocking over chairs with his extended arms.

There are many problems with using such subjective terms. First, using these terms changes the focus from the child's behavior to the child. If you use a term like "lazy" to describe a child's behavior, you are not really talking about what the child is doing. Instead, you are implying why the child behaves in certain ways; in essence, you are describing the child. For example, a child may read a book or play with her toys instead of cleaning her room when asked. The parent specifically wants the child to make her bed, place her dirty clothes in the hamper, and put her toys back on the shelf. When the child fails to perform these acts, the parent may label her as "lazy." However, using global and subjective descriptors such as lazy is incompatible with getting the child to change her behavior. Over time, we tend to think of the child's behavior in terms of the descriptor. What does the child do? She fails to make her bed and put her clothes and toys away. Why? Because she is lazy. What is the child? She is a lazy person. But we do not really know if laziness is the cause of a messy room. Instead, perhaps the child does not see any value in a clean room or lacks the necessary skills to clean her room correctly.

A second problem with using subjective terms such as lazy is that a parent may set in motion a self-fulfilling prophecy whereby the child comes to believe she is lazy and acts accordingly; then the individual who hung the label on the child in the first place says ever so smugly, "I told you so." However, if the parent had used more objective terms to describe the specific behaviors desired of the child, the child's *behavior* would have been labeled instead of the child, and she might have been more motivated to improve the cleanliness of her room.

The third and perhaps most important reason for describing children's behavior objectively is that it enables both the parent and the child to more easily detect changes in the child's behavior. If you describe your child's behavior as "lazy" because her room is messy, how will you tell whether the behavior is improving, staying the same, or getting worse? For example, you may call your child "lazy" because she forgets to put her toys away. However, she may have made her bed and put her clothes in the hamper—two improvements over last week. Simply describing the behavior as "lazy" does not help you detect any change.

In a related way, describing the child's behavior subjectively leads to arguments over whether the child's behavior changed. Suppose you tell your child her room is messy. You view it as messy because she failed to put her toys away. Your child, on the other hand, may view her room as clean because she made her bed and put her dirty clothes in the hamper. As the parent, you may either threaten or actually punish your child for having a "messy" room. In response, your child may view you as unfair and may call you a liar. This initiates an escalating chain of events that could have been avoided if objective terms had been used. Over time the use of subjective labels may lead to more arguments and misbehavior and, most importantly, may inhibit a child's growth. Effective use of proactive parenting requires avoiding subjective labels and instead describing a child's behavior objectively. It is to this point that we can apply the "stranger test" to see if a behavior has been specified objectively.

Because people interpret situations differently, it is necessary to describe your child's behavior in terms that would pass what I refer to as the "stranger test." Imagine a complete stranger coming into your house and observing your daily routine and interactions with your children. Although this experience could be disarming, it also could be beneficial in ensuring that you identify specific and observable behaviors for your children to change. Behaviors that pass the stranger test are those that can be understood and observed by someone unfamiliar with your child. For example, if a stranger walked into your house and was asked to note the number of times your child was "hostile," that number could differ significantly from your own count. The stranger might interpret hostility as any hitting, kicking, shoving, and biting, although you might have meant it to mean only unprovoked verbal threats or profanity directed at siblings. Instead, if you had defined "hostility" for the stranger as "each instance of an unprovoked hit," where "unprovoked" means that it was not in retaliation for a physical or verbal attack from a sibling, both the stranger and you would likely obtain the same count because you would both be looking for the same thing. By defining the behavior in these terms, therefore, both the parent and the child are "on the same wavelength," so to speak. This also avoids the parent saying, "Mike, go to your room for hitting your sister." "But Mom," Mike replies, "she hit me first." In this situation, the mother views the hit as hostile while the child views it as self-defense or righteous retaliation. The parent's efforts to change this "behavior" are futile until both understand exactly what is expected of the child.

Describing children's behavior objectively enough to pass the stranger test is fairly easy and straightforward. The key is to use verbs when specifying behaviors. Words such as "hits," "smiles," "cries," and "talks" are less open to interpretation than are adjectives such as "mean," "happy," "sad" or "hyper." Nonspecific terms such as "talks a lot," "hits hard," "smiles inappropriately" and "very hyper" are not used because they are open to misinterpretation—a "hard" hit to one person may be "light," "moderate" or "soft" to another.

Figure 2.1 provides some examples of objective definitions of inappropriate and appropriate behaviors along with their subjective counterparts. Note that the subjective descriptions use global evaluative words that either attribute the problem to the child or may be interpreted quite differently depending on the person and his previous experiences. Yet these subjective descriptors are quite common. How do you feel as a parent when you hear your child's teacher describe him using these terms? Why should we expect our children to feel any different when we refer to their behavior using subjective terms? If you really want to manage your child's behavior effectively, you must avoid using subjective labels and, instead, describe your child's behavior objectively.

Test 2: So What, and If So, Be Judicious: A Lesson Unheeded by Teachers

Once you select a behavior and ensure that it is defined objectively enough for a stranger to observe it in the same way and with the same frequency as you, you need to ask yourself, "So what?" Is it really necessary for the child to change this behavior? I believe that before any parent arbitrarily decides to change a child's behavior, she should apply the "So what" test. This test simply consists of asking yourself if there is any evidence that the child's behavior is presently or potentially harmful to his or another individual's social, physical, emotional or academic well-being. Many behaviors identified by parents or teachers fail to pass the "So what" test because the behavior is merely irritating to the adult. Because standards for acceptable behavior vary from person to person in an idiosyncratic fashion, we run the risk of actually creating misbehavior where none previously existed. Although this statement may sound preposterous, it is, in reality, a quite common occurrence—especially among school teachers.

I had the occasion to supervise a child identified by his school district as having behavior disorders when he moved from a special education classroom to a regular education fourth-grade classroom. The first step in this transition process called for the child to spend mornings in the regular

Inappropriate Behaviors	
Subjective Description	**Objective Description**
• Is lazy	• Leaves clothes and toys on floor of room
• Uses bad language	• Says "shut up" when asked to remove dishes from table
• Is immature	• Cries when doesn't get candy at store
• Looks depressed	• Sits in front of TV and refuses to answer questions
• Is manipulative	• Asks mother after father says "no" to staying out an hour later than usual
• Acts oppositional	• Has to be told three times to put bicycle in garage and threatened with not using it for a day

Appropriate Behaviors	
Subjective Description	**Objective Description**
• Is polite	• Says "thank you" after receiving a compliment
• Acts friendly	• Smiles when talking to others
• Good at sharing	• Lets siblings play with her Barbie dolls
• Has good table manners	• Sits up straight, switches fork from cutting to eating hand, talks only after swallowing food
• Gets along with others	• Plays with children after school
• Exercises self-control	• Cleans room without being asked

Figure 2.1. Subjective and objective descriptors of inappropriate and appropriate behaviors.

education classroom. Prior to the child attending class, I talked to the regular education teacher. She expressed concerns about having a child with a "behavior disorder" mainstreamed into her classroom. Her fears centered, expectedly, around whether the child would be a disruptive influence on the other children. I asked her to specify what she meant by "disruptive." After much discussion, she pinpointed "getting out of the seat" as a behavior she found particularly disruptive. I agreed that this behavior could cause a problem—if children are out of their seats too much, they are not completing school work and could potentially be bothering other students. When asked how many times she would tolerate the mainstreamed child getting out of his seat during the course of any given morning, the teacher replied, "Once." Without challenging her response, I asked if I could observe the classroom off and on for the next week. She readily agreed, assuming that I would be keeping track of the mainstreamed child's behavior—specifically how many times he got out of his seat. Her assumption, however, was incorrect: I was keeping track of the number of times other children got out of their seats during any given morning. A quick count revealed that children got out of their seats an average of eight times each during a given morning. Now, who has the behavior problem? I would contend that the teacher does and that she is creating a behavior problem in this student where none existed because of her biased expectations due to the label "behavior disorder."

I doubt very much that the "more than one time out of the seat" behavior would pass the "So what" test considering the frequency of out-of-seat behavior exhibited by other students in the classroom. However, teachers, like parents, are often threatened by children who do not follow the rules or who question authority by asking, "Why?" whenever they are told to do something. Many teachers are threatened by what they consider to be "excessive" noise and movement in their classroom. Students who question authority or who are noisy or active probably elicit anxiety in a teacher because the behavior suggests that the teacher is not in control of the class—one of the most frightening prospects a teacher can contemplate.

Teachers have been conditioned to believe that noise, movement and questioning of authority are the three warning signs of an impending revolt in the classroom. Conversely, when students comply without question, sit still and stay quiet, teachers perceive themselves as being in control. Perhaps this is why teachers and parents are so quick to punish noncompliance or any questioning of their authority. Unfortunately, punishing noncompliance can create a classroom of passive conformists who are afraid to assert themselves with any adults or authority figures. This is hardly the kind of citizen we hope to prepare to meet the challenges of the real world.

Teachers must recognize that schools are primarily for children, not adults. A situation involving some friends illustrates the problems that can arise from teachers failing to recognize children's roles in schools and not applying the "So what" test to behavior. My friends have four children. The oldest, Audrey, just began second grade. Audrey's father is a physician and her mother was a registered nurse before she decided to stay home with the children. Audrey is a very bright and sensitive girl and, although she is somewhat shy, she is nevertheless very inquisitive and well liked by her peers and most adults. She would never think of misbehaving in school because she cares too much about what her teacher would think. Last year, Audrey loved first grade and very much looked forward to beginning second grade. However, two weeks into the semester, she complained of hating school for the following reason: To maintain control over the class, Audrey's teacher instituted a discipline program that consisted of handing out three sticks to each child at the beginning of each day. Every time a child "misbehaved" one stick was removed. When two sticks were removed, the teacher phoned the parents to notify them of their child's misbehavior. If all three sticks were lost, the child was sent to the principal's office. Audrey lost one stick on several occasions due to two misbehaviors. First, she whistled unconsciously when she was working at her desk. Second, because she is inquisitive, she liked to touch objects rather than just looking at them from a distance. Audrey got very anxious when she lost a stick and was scared of losing two sticks in a day and having her mother called.

Several points may be made about the teacher's "discipline" technique and Audrey's behaviors that resulted in punishment. First, we must ask if either behavior passed the "So what" test. I would emphatically state no. Audrey's whistling did not disturb other children or interfere with her completing work. In fact, many people whistle when engaging in an activity they enjoy. Similarly, the second behavior, touching objects, did not interfere with Audrey's work, nor was it bothersome to her classmates. It just reflected her natural curiosity—something we want to instill in our children, not suppress. Now Audrey no longer likes school and is scared and anxious. In addition to not passing the "So what" test, the teacher's approach focuses on catching students being bad rather than good—a point that I shall elaborate upon shortly.

I have encountered similar problems when working with families of children with attention deficits. One child, Jake, was constantly being punished by his third-grade teacher for fidgeting with objects—getting ink on his hands from pens, tearing up pieces of paper from the corner of math worksheets and tapping his fingers on the desk until other students as well as the teacher demanded that he stop. I had a fairly easy solution to this problem. Upon Jake's first visit to see me I tossed him a plastic egg containing silly putty. He began playing with it in earnest while sitting quietly and answering my questions. Later I called Jake's teacher and asked her if he could be allowed to manipulate silly putty while completing math worksheets. She somewhat reluctantly agreed and was pleasantly surprised to see that Jake could now complete his assignments without tapping his fingers on the desk or ripping up paper. Sadly, the next year Jake's fourth-grade teacher flatly refused to let him have silly putty during class, stating that it would lessen her control of the class and that all students would soon want to play with silly putty if she allowed Jake to. Was manipulating silly putty a behavior, in Jake's case, that passed the "So what" test? No. This behavior did not interfere with Jake or his classmates completing their assignments.

I had a similar experience with a seventh-grade boy with an attention deficit. Being in junior high school, Joe had different teachers for each subject but had a common problem with all of them: He talked incessantly during class. I thought a reasonable and quick solution to this problem would be to have Joe chew a large piece of gum—but not bubble gum—during school. Joe's teachers reacted to this suggestion with mixed feelings; about half agreed and the other half refused. For the teachers who agreed, Joe's talking decreased considerably. Unfortunately, for those teachers who refused, talking continued to be a problem worthy of a variety of punishments.

As has been shown, not all behaviors targeted by teachers fail to pass the "So what" test. I remember a student teacher who applied the "So what" test to a behavior, found it did not pass and consequently ignored the behavior with marvelous results. This student teacher was conducting a reading lesson with 10 remedial students. The lesson was proceeding splendidly, and the children were attentive and involved. The teacher had students take turns reading a paragraph or two of the story aloud. She then would stop and ask the students to provide examples from their own lives that were similar to those experienced by the characters in the story. This technique helped the students to activate prior knowledge and draw meaning from the text. Any difficult words were written on the chalkboard along with their definitions. Then the students used the words in sentences. While this was going on, a boy in the back of the group was beginning to lose interest. It was winter, and he was wearing a heavy coat with a furry hood. While children were reading, he put the hood over his head and pulled the drawstrings so tight that he looked like a walrus. At this point the student teacher could have stopped what was a very smooth-flowing lesson and reprimanded the child. In all likelihood, the reprimand would have prompted the other children to turn in their seats to see what the boy was doing. I imagine they would have started laughing at the walrus-like appearance of his head, thereby providing him with much attention for his behavior. Instead, the student teacher ignored the behavior and carried on with the lesson. Only one child happened to glance to the back of the class and notice the student; she watched for only a minute before raising her hand to answer a question posed to the group. After about two minutes, the boy removed the hood, probably because it was getting hot under there, and proceeded to raise his hand to answer a question.

I was very proud of this student teacher. Yet many teachers fail to apply the "So what" test or heed its results. And the same situation occurs when I work with parents. Applying the "So what" test requires asking yourself in whose interests you are acting—yours or your child's? Most of the time, behaviors fail the "So what" test because adults are acting in their, rather than the child's, interest. For example, how many times do we wish our children would be more outgoing, assertive, or athletic? Are we really concerned about the child, or are we more interested in achieving some type of vicarious pleasure from something that we missed experiencing when growing up? All one has to do is attend any little league baseball, soccer or basketball game to see who gets most upset when a team performs poorly—the parents!

Thus far, I have discussed how behaviors we typically want to see children perform less often fail to pass the "So what" test. Criteria for meeting the "So what" test were defined as whether the behavior interfered with either the child's or peers' physical, emotional or academic well-being. However, children's behaviors often identified for change may not pass the "So what" test. A behavior passes the test if it makes a positive impact on the child's functioning—that is, if it improves the child's relationship with siblings, peers and significant adults. For example, teaching children blind acceptance or compliance with authority figures may make parents' and teachers' lives easier but may fail to prepare children to deal with peer conflict or, even worse, advances by strangers. Children are not likely to continue using behaviors that make adults' lives easier but do little to enhance the quality of a child's interaction with others. The reason is simple: If others do not respond positively when we engage in certain behaviors, then we are less likely to engage in those behaviors in the future. This is the principle of *positive reinforcement.*

An example of a behavior that does not pass the "So what" test and that teachers, therapists and parents routinely identify to teach children is assertiveness. When working as a counselor at a psychiatric hospital for adolescents, I often taught patients how to be assertive. I would begin by defining assertiveness as a way to get what you want while still respecting others' rights. Not a bad definition, and defined as such, assertiveness certainly appears to pass the "So what" test. Next I would create a list of component skills that, if performed correctly, would lead to assertive behavior. These component skills are: (1) telling the person what he is doing that you do not like; (2) telling the person how it makes you feel; (3) requesting a new behavior from the person; and (4) thanking the person for complying. Then the adolescents would role-play these skills in various situations. Many of the teenagers became quite proficient at being assertive. However, I made a startling discovery—even those who became very proficient at being assertive failed to use the skill after being discharged. I was completely dismayed because these adolescents were so polite and good at expressing their needs to staff while hospitalized. In fact, patients who became very good at being assertive made all the therapists and other staff members' days much more enjoyable and less stressful. As I pondered this problem, I started imagining myself in some of the situations which I had the adolescents role-play. One in particular came to mind, illustrating why assertiveness, in actuality, does not pass the "So what" test for adolescents and, in many cases, would not pass for adults either.

To use the four skills listed above, a popular scenario involved waiting in line to get into a movie. The teenager would role-play waiting in line when, all of a sudden, someone cuts in front of him. Now, following the component skills, the interaction should proceed something like this. The patient says, "Excuse me, but you just cut in front of me. I have been waiting patiently for the past 30 minutes and I get frustrated and angry when people don't wait their turn. Would you please go to the end of the line. Thank you." The silliness of this struck me full force: I would never make such a request. Rather than achieving the desired outcome, this behavior would likely result in a dirty look at best and a knuckle sandwich at worst. In fact, I cannot think of too many situations where an adolescent who is assertive with peers will be well received. I believe the same holds true for many adult encounters. So rather than teaching a skill that would likely result in the adolescent receiving positive attention from peers, I taught a skill that would result in a negative response. It was a skill that only had value to the therapists and other staff members working on the hospital unit because it made their job of interacting with the patients more enjoyable. It most certainly did not pass the "So what" test because it would not benefit the child or her peers.

You may be getting the idea that I do not think any behavior passes the "So what" test. But that is not true. There are behaviors that do pass the test. Once such a behavior has been identified, it is important that it be defined objectively—that is, it must also pass the "stranger test." Here is an example of how important it is that a behavior pass both tests. I was working with a couple who were having difficulty keeping their eight-year-old son Randy seated at the dinner table. We went through the "So what" test and determined that the behavior of "sitting at the table" passed the test. Randy's parents reported that when he was out of his seat, he disrupted his siblings and did not get enough to eat himself. I had worked out a program in which Randy was rewarded with 10 minutes of shooting baskets after dinner for every five minutes he remained seated. His parents and I went over this program with him until he understood it. However, I made one oversight. I failed to ask his parents to describe all the behaviors he engaged in while he was out of his seat. Therefore, after the first week of intervention, his parents reported several days when Randy did not earn any extra free time. Upon questioning them, I discovered that Randy twice got out of his seat because his sister forgot to put a fork at his place when she was setting the table. That behavior did not pass the "So what" test and is illustrative of the importance of selecting and defining behaviors judiciously so as not to end up punishing a child inadvertently.

The "So what" test helps minimize the control mentality while still acknowledging that some behaviors need to be decreased because they constitute physical, emotional or academic dangers to a child or others. However, the best way to ensure that a behavior passes the "So what" test is to determine whether the behavior represents a "fair pair." This is the criterion that I will examine next.

Test 3: All's Fair When You Have a Pair

Adults seem to spend an inordinate amount of time focusing on negative aspects of children's behavior. We are very good at catching children being bad and ignoring them when they are being good. This observation is analogous to the old axiom that "the squeaky wheel gets the grease." We take children's behavior for granted when they are doing what they are supposed to do. But when they act out, they receive considerable attention.

In my experiences as a therapist, I have seen this mentality in action. For example, it is not uncommon during family therapy sessions for parents to focus on a child who is causing trouble. In contrast, the "good" child, who rarely misbehaves and is usually as quiet as a mouse, is virtually ignored. However, it doesn't take long for the ignored child to figure out that the best way to get her parents' attention is to misbehave. In fact, it is not uncommon for the "good" child to vie for her parents' attention by trying to engage in more outrageous behavior than her sibling.

The solution to this problem is to focus more attention on children when they are being good. Catching children being good, however, goes against conventional wisdom. I remember observing a school meeting among several teachers, the school psychologist and counselor, and the vice-principal. The meeting was called to discuss how to handle the behavior of a particularly troubling fifth-grade boy. This boy had an amazingly versatile repertoire of behaviors that annoyed both his teachers and peers. The adults at the school meeting characterized his behavior in the following ways: He would draw inappropriate pictures when he should have been working; poke the boy in front of him with his pencil while whistling some inane ditty; take off his glasses and spit on the lenses under the guise of cleaning them; make numerous requests for trips to the pencil sharpener, drinking fountain and bathroom; and pick his nose and place the boogers under his desk when he had the attention of a female classmate. The list went on and on.

After about 10 minutes of the adults lamenting the outrageous nature of this child's behavior, the discussion turned to how to deal with the problem. An immediate litany of past failed attempts was presented: His chair was moved next to the teacher's desk but then quickly moved to the farthest corner of the room with a portable chalkboard placed in front of the student; he was sent into the hall—usually ending up at the principal's office; he was kept in from recess, although his teachers apparently had some private lottery going to see who would have the dubious honor of watching him during what came to be known as the longest 20 minutes of the day; his parents were called and occasionally asked to take him home; he was required to stay after school; and, finally, he was labeled and placed in a special education classroom for students with behavior disorders for several hours a day. This last approach, although disguised as taking the best interests of the child into consideration, was, in essence, a sign of giving up. If all else fails, remove the child from the teachers and classmates whom he has so tormented, and place him with other children who act similarly and with a teacher who is specially trained to deal with "behavior problems." The amazing part of this meeting was that the adults failed to describe any positive behaviors the child exhibited or that they wanted him to exhibit, nor did they offer any positive approaches to managing his behavior. All the lamented efforts were negative, thereby making a case for bullet therapy—an approach I did not suggest at this meeting but that might have been received quite well given the frustration this child's behavior had caused.

Even when positive approaches are instituted, adults tend to revert back to negative management systems when problems arise. A high school in my community provides a notable example of how instituting a positive approach for increasing attendance can be so effective that adults will abandon it in favor of a more negative approach.

In an innovative attempt to increase students' attendance, thereby reducing the number of truancies, this high school instituted the following policy. For every month a student had perfect attendance, he received a free lunch at a local restaurant. Although many students found a free meal reinforcing, students who went an entire semester with perfect attendance received an even more motivating reinforcer: They were exempt from taking final examinations. Unprecedented numbers of students were going entire semesters without being tardy or absent.

There were, however, some problems with this program. One was that no exceptions were made for extenuating circumstances; therefore, students were coming to school even when they were sick. Also, many teachers, especially those teaching college preparatory courses, strongly objected to students being exempted from taking final exams: They viewed final exams as a necessary preparation for college. A final concern was that despite the program's effectiveness in increasing attendance overall, it had minimal impact on the real target population—those students with behavior problems for whom tardiness and truancy were a way of life. Many of those students did not care whether they took final exams or not. And even for those students who did find the idea of no finals reinforcing, it was so delayed (i.e., coming at the end of the semester) that they lost interest and motivation, viewing the reward as unattainable.

Rather than modifying this positive approach to include different reinforcers that could be delivered more immediately, the school decided to go back to a punitive approach for reducing tardiness and truancy. If a student had five truancies for any one class, he was dropped from that class. Students dropped from three classes were expelled from school. After the system had been in effect for four weeks, 200 students were dropped from classes and 15 students were expelled from school. In addition to the punitive nature of this program, it was also time-intensive. Fifth period became a kind of homeroom—teachers had to take attendance and submit it to the office. Students who were truant from class would have to discuss the truancy with their fifth-period teacher, who also had to call the student's parents. Upon a student's subsequent truancies, the fifth-period teacher and the teacher from the class for which the student was tardy had to meet with the student. Each aspect of this process was accompanied with forms to be completed by teachers. Yet this program was viewed by some as effective—apparently because students were removed from class and/or expelled from school. Removing students from school represents the ultimate way of eliminating undesirable behavior.

The problem with getting rid of behaviors, besides being very difficult to accomplish, is that the child is left with nothing with which to replace undesirable behaviors. For example, a child may have 30 specific behaviors in his repertoire. Of those 30, perhaps 20 are positive behaviors such as asking questions, playing with a peer or sibling, coming to the dinner table on time and answering the phone politely. The remaining 10 are negative behaviors such as hitting peers or siblings when provoked, swearing, stealing and lying. If we focus only on the negative and eliminate these 10 behaviors without replacing them with 10 positive behaviors, the child ends up with fewer behaviors in his repertoire than when he started. Instead, our goal should be to ensure that the child has more rather than less behaviors. You might argue that a child with 20 good behaviors and 10 bad behaviors that are subsequently eliminated is actually better off than before we intervened. Theoretically, the child might be better off. Unfortunately, however, what happens in real life is that eliminating a negative behavior without replacing it with a positive one usually results in a return of the same or a similar negative behavior. For example, if you punish a child every time he hits his sibling when he is provoked, you will eventually weaken his hitting behavior. However, assuming that the provocations continue, if you don't teach him how to handle provocations in a positive manner, you will find that he does one of three things: he returns to his hitting behavior because he has nothing else to use in its place; he resorts to less physical forms of retaliation, such as threats, name calling or stealing his siblings' possessions; or he tries to hit without getting caught. If, instead of punishing the child every time he engages in provoked hitting, you teach him a positive response to provocation such as ignoring or being verbally assertive, the chances are that he will not go back to his old behavior or substitute any new negative responses. Not only will the maladaptive behaviors be removed, but the child will have replaced them with adaptive behaviors that were not previously in his repertoire.

This discussion brings us to the concept of the "fair pair." The term "pair" refers to two behaviors, while "fair" refers to the notion that it is only productive to weaken a child's inappropriate behavior if you strengthen an appropriate behavior in its place. Thus, "fair pair" refers to an inappropriate behavior you wish to weaken and an incompatible or competing target behavior you wish to strengthen in its place. The idea behind the fair pair has a profound impact despite its amazing simplicity. It allows you to eliminate a behavior by simply increasing a desirable but incompatible behavior. An incompatible behavior is one that is similar to the misbehavior in form or action, but whose performance physically prevents the child from engaging in the inappropriate behavior.

Let's say that you want to decrease a child's irritating habit of picking his nose. An incompatible behavior that shares the same physical features would be the use of a kleenex. If nose-picking was defined as the "insertion of an uncovered finger into a nostril making a circular motion," then using a kleenex appropriately would prevent the child from engaging in the inappropriate behavior. It is impossible to hold a kleenex over one's fingers and place it at the end of one's nasal passages while also picking one's nose. Similarly, teachers dislike children who continuously tap their desks with a pencil or pen. An appropriate, incompatible behavior would be writing answers on a piece of notebook paper. It is impossible for a child to be writing words and quickly move his pen up and down in a tapping motion at the same time.

The "fair pair" results in two desirable outcomes. First, we eliminate the inappropriate behavior without having to resort to punishment. Second, an appropriate behavior is developed and promoted using reinforcement. Unfortunately, it is not always possible to find an appropriate behavior that is incompatible with the inappropriate behavior. For example, a fair pair for swearing may be talking politely. Yet it is possible for a child to simultaneously talk politely and swear. These behaviors occur together all the time. I would like nothing better than to receive a letter from someone telling me he thought I wrote "one helluva good book." I would take that statement as a polite, genuine compliment. Although not universally applicable, getting into a mindset of selecting a fair pair will go a long way to helping you manage your child's behavior more effectively.

Selecting a fair pair is not always easy and it takes practice. Some examples of fair pairs are presented in Figure 2.2. One way of ensuring a fair pair is to determine whether the behavior passes the stranger test and "So what" test. Another way to make sure you have a fair pair is to subject it to the dead man's test.

Test 4: Dead Men Do Not Misbehave

The dead man's test consists of a single question and ensures that you have a fair pair. The question is: Can a dead man do it? If the answer is yes, it does not pass the dead man's test and it is not a fair pair. If the answer to this question is no, then you have a fair pair. When examining Figure 2.2, the inappropriate behaviors to decrease in and of themselves would not pass the dead man's test. Can a dead man not pick his nose, not hit peers, not lose toys, not shout, not cry and not swear? Yes. Dead men will hardly ever pick their nose, hit peers, lose toys, shout, cry or swear. However, when asking this same question of the incompatible appropriate behaviors, the answer would be no, because a dead man cannot use a kleenex, ask for assistance, put toys away, speak in a soft voice, ask how he can improve his performance or explain problems. These behaviors pass the dead man's test because a dead man does not have the ability to perform them. Therefore, you are assured of having a fair pair. This, in turn, means that positive approaches can be used to increase appropriate behavior as a way of eliminating inappropriate behavior.

Test 5: Determine the Purpose and Outcome But Don't Ask Why

As strange as it may seem, all behavior is purposeful. All of us, including children, engage in behavior to achieve specific outcomes. We may not always be consciously aware of our purpose for engaging in a behavior at any given moment, but the behavior is purposeful nevertheless. In his book *The Divided Self*, R.D. Laing insightfully claimed that even the language of schizophrenics, with its limited or nonexistent logical base, has meaning for the person using it.

Behavior is not only purposeful, it is also intentional—that is, it is directed toward a perceived outcome. It is the achievement of this outcome that shapes the specific form of a behavior. For example, many aggressive children have found that striking an intimidating pose or uttering a few well-chosen words allows them to escape an unpleasant task or interaction. Other children have developed a sophisticated behavioral repertoire that they can use to achieve their desired outcome. Children who manipulate adults are

Inappropriate Behavior to Decrease	Incompatible Appropriate Behavior to Increase
• Picks nose	• Uses kleenex
• Hits peers when provoked	• Asks for assistance from adult
• Loses toys	• Puts toys away when finished playing
• Slouches at dinner table	• Sits up straight
• Shouts at siblings	• Speaks in soft voice
• Cries when criticized	• Asks what to do to improve
• Lies	• Tells truth
• Whines when doesn't get own way	• Politely asks when request can be met
• Swears at parent	• Explains nature of problem to parent
• Tracks mud on carpet	• Takes shoes off at door
• Leaves clothes on floor	• Puts dirty clothes in hamper

Figure 2.2. Examples of fair pairs.

good examples; they have a wide repertoire of techniques they can use to establish control over another person.

Developing and implementing effective interventions involves determining the connection between observed behaviors and the outcomes expected by the child. This is not an easy task, yet it is one that has far-reaching implications for identifying appropriate behaviors to change. It would be wanton and irresponsible of us simply to change children's behavior without taking into account the purpose and outcome. We should assume that behavior patterns children display are the most appropriate responses they have, no matter how bizarre or inappropriate they seem. Yet the purpose and desired outcome of a behavior is not always apparent. I remember working with the parents of a teenage boy who acted out quite a bit. This boy would frequently stay out past his curfew, was caught shoplifting, ran away from home twice, and started fires in his back yard. These behaviors were in addition to the more mundane ones of getting into fights with his sister and refusing to do chores around the house.

After working with this family for several sessions, I began to notice a pattern. One thing that became clear was that the parents were having marital difficulties. Although they tried to conceal these problems from their children, it was clear that no one was fooled. Both of the children expressed concern and fear that their parents were going to get a divorce. Upon questioning them further as to how they knew about their parent's problems, the boy said he heard his parents arguing late into the night and on weekends. On a separate occasion, the parents acknowledged they were having marital problems and argued frequently. After several more sessions, the probable intent of the boy's acting-out behavior became clear: His behavior successfully terminated the parents' arguing because they "pulled together" to deal with their son: knowing his parents had been arguing that day, the son came home after his curfew; his parents quickly worked in a concerted effort to determine their son's whereabouts.

This case raises two important questions. First, whose behavior needs to be modified—the parents' or the child's? Second, is the outcome achieved by the inappropriate behavior in and of itself inappropriate? If a child is acting out in an attempt to bring his parents closer together, then improving the parents' relationship may have a positive impact on the child's behavior. In the process of determining the purpose and outcome of a child's behavior, therefore, you may find that the best way to manage misbehavior is to alter your own first. I once worked with a family in which the mother was constantly nagging her daughter. The mother felt that she knew what was best for her daughter even though the daughter would not listen to her. Consequently, the mother and daughter would get into heated arguments. The purpose of the mother's behavior seemed obvious: She wanted her daughter to listen because, as her mother, she had good information to convey. I asked the daughter how her mother would have to talk to her to get her to really listen and consider what she was saying. The daughter looked at me with a sly grin and responded that her mother would have to treat her like a person. When I asked the daughter to specify what being "treated like a person" means (so that her behavior would pass the stranger test), she replied that her mother would not be yelling, or... I stopped her and asked her to tell me what her mother *would* be doing—what would she look like, what would she sound like? Then the daughter demonstrated a particular tone of voice that she wanted her mother to use. I turned to her mother and told her to pick one of the things that she thought was important for her daughter to know and to try doing it in the way her daughter demonstrated. After a couple of sentences, I interrupted and asked the daughter if her mother was doing it the way she wanted. The daughter responded that her mother's voice was still a little whiny. So I helped the mother adjust her voice, and she started in again. The daughter sat there and listened, and then said she would comply with the request. The mother was shocked. Previously, the daughter had not even heard what her mother was saying because she reacted to the presentation style rather than the content of her mother's messages.

In the last two scenarios, I suggest that the outcome and purpose of the behavior was very appropriate. There is nothing inappropriate about a son wanting his parents to stop fighting with one another. Therefore, the purpose of the behavior similarly was appropriate. In this instance, the acting-out behavior could be viewed as the "best choice" from the boy's perspective, because it was effective for reaching the desired outcome. Unfortunately, there was an unintended negative effect of the boy's acting out. Although the parents' arguing stopped, they focused their attacks on their son. Their son retaliated and that, in turn, led them to seek professional help. The important point is that by determining the purpose and outcome of a problem behavior, we can replace it with a more appropriate one that has the same purpose and achieves the same outcome.

The importance of determining the purpose and outcome of children's inappropriate behaviors is widely recognized. For example, the Colorado Department of Education recently published a monograph providing a description, a rationale and examples for designing responsive instructional programs for youngsters with behavior disorders. A major and recurring theme of this monograph is reflected in an article written by Richard Neel and Kay Cessna discussing the importance of determining the purpose and outcome of inappropriate behavior as a means of designing instructional content. Figure 2.3 presents some possible outcomes for children's behavior described in this monograph. Notice that this list reflects outcomes shared by most people in our society. At the heart of using the information in this figure, which is by no means inclusive, is that children's behaviors work— they serve a purpose. By distinguishing between the purpose or intention of behaviors and the actual acts, it is possible to find new, more acceptable behaviors that satisfy the same intention.

Replacement behaviors not only achieve the same outcomes as the problem behaviors, but they do so in a way that is socially acceptable to the individuals involved. This approach differs from the common practice of reducing problem behaviors through external controls such as punishment. In fact, the behaviors we reduce through punishment may have a very useful function for the child. Therefore, we must view problem behaviors as a means of determining the child's critical purpose and outcome. We must

Outcome	Description
Power/Control	When a child's outcome is the control of events and/or situations. Characterized by a child acting to stay in the situation and keep control.
Protection/Escape Avoidance	When a child's outcome is to avoid a task, activity; escape a consequence; terminate or leave a situation.
Attention	When a child becomes the focus of a situation; draws attention to self; result is that a child puts self in the foreground of a situation; discriminates self from group for a period of time; distinguishing feature is "becoming the focus" as the end product of the behavior.
Acceptance/Affiliation	When a child connects/relates with others; mutuality of benefit is present.
Expression of Self	When a child develops a forum of expression; could be statements of needs or perceptions, or demonstration of skills and talents.
Gratification	When a child is self-rewarded or pleased; distinguishing characteristic is that reward is self-determined; others may play agent role.
Justice/Revenge	When a child settles a difference; provides restitution, or demonstrates contrition; settling the score.

Figure 2.3. Behavior outcomes and their descriptions.

acknowledge the outcome and teach the child a more acceptable way of achieving it.

Determining the purpose and outcome is not an easy or a completely objective task. It most definitely cannot be determined by asking the child "why." In fact, a good rule is to never ask a child why she did something, because it serves no purpose. Determining why will not change the occurrence of the misbehavior; furthermore, children will only make up excuses, lie, or try to transfer the blame from themselves. The end result most often is an argument between parent and child that digresses into speculation with no resolution in sight. But for those of you who still want to know why a child does something, I'll tell you: Because it served a purpose.

You must help determine the purpose and intended outcome of problem behaviors using methods other than asking why. Try focusing on using words such as "what" and "when." Asking a child what she wanted may help identify the purpose or outcome. Therefore, instead of asking Nancy why she hit her sibling, ask her what purpose this behavior served. This may result in an answer such as, "I wanted him to stop playing with my toys," rather than the typical, "I don't know." Asking "when" questions can also be beneficial. For example, asking the child, "When do you most often hit your brother," may lead to the response, "When he plays with my toys without asking me." Such an answer allows you to find new and more acceptable behaviors that satisfy the same intention.

Sometimes you will not be able to elicit good information from a child. For a variety of reasons, the child may not want to divulge what caused her to hit her sibling. She may be afraid of being punished or may just be angry enough to enjoy being oppositional. Regardless of the reason, you may have to do some direct observation to determine the possible purpose and outcome for a specific behavior. Making this determination takes a little work but is a fairly straightforward process. You must determine the events that precede a given behavior (the antecedents), identify the behavior and make sure it passes the stranger test and "So what" test, determine the events that follow the behavior (the consequences), and speculate on the purpose and outcome the behavior served. It is often helpful to put this information down on paper to facilitate a thorough analysis. Figure 2.4 provides a model for this process through several examples.

Although interaction between individuals is never as linear as presented in Figure 2.4, the model nevertheless does illustrate a way of determining the purpose and outcome of children's behavior. Once you have identified the situation, behavior and outcome desired by the child, you can propose a new behavior that satisfies the same intention. Sometimes you may want to try to promote the new behavior without your child knowing; at other times you may want to solicit the child as an active participant. Of course, presenting a new behavior to a child right after a misbehavior is not a good idea—she will not be in a mood to hear it. However, it can be very helpful to enlist the child's participation. I was able to get a positive outcome between a mother who had important information to convey to her daughter and the daughter who never listened because there was no way for them to respond otherwise, assuming I had correctly determined the intent of their behavior. By not listening, the daughter assumed that her mother was right, and the mother was certainly not going to admit that the things she had to say were unim-

Antecedents	Behavior	Consequences	Possible Outcome
Billy calls Tim a sissy	Tim hits Billy	Billy stops calling Tim a sissy	Protection/ avoidance
Dad ignores Mary when she tells him about receiving an "A" on her spelling test	Mary yells at her dad	Her dad tells her to use a softer tone of voice	Expression of self
Parents fight over financial matters	Daughter breaks a glass	Parents stop arguing and punish her	Attention
Mother forgets to take son to store	Son forgets to clean room	Fight over fairness	Justice/revenge
Jimmy goes to drugstore with two new friends	Jimmy steals cigarettes from drugstore	Police arrest Jimmy and have meeting with his parents	Acceptance/ affiliation

Figure 2.4. Model for determining purpose and outcome of behavior.

portant enough to resist changing her tone of voice. Focusing on the intent of wanting to communicate was more important than going after a direct change. Unfortunately, we often go for the direct change and that sets up conflict.

The key point in this section is that the antecedents and consequences of a situation affect the behavior. Changing the context or situation changes the purpose and desired outcome. A very old Chinese Taoist story appearing in the book *Reframing* by Richard Bandler and John Grinder illustrates this idea. The story describes a farmer in a poor country village. He was considered very well to do because he owned a horse which he used for plowing and for transportation. One day the horse ran away. All his neighbors exclaimed how terrible this was, but the farmer simply said, "Maybe." A few days later the horse returned and brought two wild horses with it. The neighbors all rejoiced at his good fortune, but the farmer just said, "Maybe." The next day the farmer's son tried to ride one of the wild horses; the horse threw him and he broke his leg. The neighbors all offered their sympathy for his misfortune, but the farmer again said, "Maybe." The next week conscription officers came to the village to take young men for the army. They rejected the farmer's son because of his broken leg. When the neighbors told him how lucky he was, the farmer replied, "Maybe." Having two wild horses is a good thing until seen in the context of the son's broken leg. The broken leg seems to be bad in the context of peaceful village life but in the context of conscription and war it suddenly becomes good. Therefore, we should not assume that a behavior has no purpose or has an inappropriate purpose until we examine the situation and the context upon which it is expressed. Once this is accomplished, the process of establishing new behaviors can begin using positive management techniques.

3

Positive Management Techniques

I introduced positive reinforcement in Chapter 1 as an effective tool for changing children's behavior. Nevertheless, this concept continues to suffer from a strong but fallible cultural ethos that says it is better to punish than to reward. In Chapter 2, I discussed techniques for targeting a behavior you wish to increase rather than focusing solely on inappropriate behavior to decrease. In this chapter, I will build upon these principles using the concept of positive reinforcement. Without question, positive reinforcement is the most powerful tool at your disposal for effecting change in your child's behavior. Yet it is also one of the most misunderstood concepts as exemplified in the following two comments I hear regularly from both parents and teachers: "I don't want to have to bribe my child to behave" and "Positive reinforcement doesn't work anyway." I have covered the first statement in the previous chapters: We all respond favorably to positive reinforcement. Who among us would work at our job for free? Is not the sporadic recognition of our employer reinforcing? In fact, many people make a good living conducting seminars describing positive methods for motivating employees. The principle at the core of these seminars is the same—reinforcement.

Positive reinforcement may not work for a variety of reasons—many of these are addressed in the next section where I provide guidelines for how to use positive reinforcement effectively. But the biggest reason I have seen for the failure of reinforcement is, ironically, that parents are unwilling to be strict. The irony of this statement lies in the belief of most parents that punishment rather than reinforcement represents a strict approach to discipline. Yet for reinforcement to be effective, parents must be very strict. I will illustrate this point with the following example. In my private practice, it is common for parents to bemoan the lack of cooperation they receive from their child. "Cooperation" usually refers to the completion of chores such as cleaning the bedroom, helping set or clear the dinner table, getting ready for bed without dawdling, or taking out the trash. After ensuring that these behaviors pass the tests described in Chapter 2, I ask the parents and the child to list activities in which the child enjoys engaging. These activities, such as playing Nintendo, will serve as the reinforcer the child can earn after completing the identified chores. Now comes the part where parents must be strict. The child can *only* play Nintendo for a specified period of time *after* completing the specified chores. So, if a child is required, but refuses, to clean her room after school, then no amount of whining, pleading or excuses will result in her being allowed to play Nintendo. No exceptions! And toeing that line is where parents have the most trouble being strict. Some parents feel guilty because they believe they are restricting their child's fun. Yet nothing could be further from the truth. You are still providing the child the opportunity to play Nintendo, but now she must decide which is more important—to avoid cleaning the bedroom or to play Nintendo. The choice is left up to the child.

The key factor to success is to remove the reinforcer prior to starting the program so that the child no longer has free access to it. Strict adherence to this recommendation is crucial if reinforcement is to be effective. In the above example, the child would likely not clean her room after school to receive reinforcement if she could play Nintendo anyway before bedtime, in the morning before school, or at a friend's house after school before coming home. In this instance, therefore, a child's decision not to clean her room would have little impact upon her opportunity to play Nintendo. Consequently, reinforcement would be ineffective. Therefore, an effective reinforcer is not only something the child likes but also something over which the parent has control.

Another factor involves determining for how long the child can have access to the reinforcer once it is earned. If the child has four chores that must be performed daily, how much time can she play Nintendo after completing each chore? This question can be answered by observing the "free access rule." Using the free access rule, the amount of a reinforcer or the duration for which it is available should be less than that which the child would seek if she had unlimited access to it. For example, if a child would spend about one hour a day playing Nintendo, then the total amount of time she could earn Nintendo should not exceed one hour. Therefore, if the child had four chores to be completed at different times of the day, she could earn 15 minutes playing Nintendo after completing each chore. Remember, more is not better. Providing the child with more access to the reinforcer than she would normally seek without any limits could result in satiation. *Satiation* is a condition in which the child has experienced the reinforcer to such an extent that it is no longer reinforcing—and burnout occurs. To prevent satiation, it is important to give only a small amount of the reinforcer each time. In this way, the child will find playing Nintendo reinforcing and, therefore, be motivated to carry out the target behavior.

So, in order for reinforcement to be effective, parents must be strict, but not unfair. I use the word "fairness" to describe a condition in which the child has the opportunity to access the reinforcer but must earn it first. Conversely, children often use the term "unfair" to describe having to work for a reinforcer rather than getting it for free. Being strict also requires being consistent, which is one of the most difficult things for parents to do. Once you give in to the child and let her play Nintendo "just this once" without having earned it, you have opened Pandora's box. Now, the child will test the limits to which you can be pressed. And, almost inevitably, you have created a worse situation than by refusing to acquiesce in the first place. Children are persistent. They will come at you from all angles, and sometimes their arguments make sense or hit our guilty buttons. But just remember, you are not taking away a privilege or an activity, you are only making the child earn it. Once the child figures out you mean business and can't be manipulated, her performance will quickly improve.

A final point about being strict and consistent. It is important never to argue with your child. That recommendation requires considerable self-discipline. But consistent parents rarely need to argue. You have specified the conditions under which the child can earn the reinforcer. Now the ball is in the child's court. You're not telling the child that she must clear her room—that choice is hers. And you're not punishing the child for deciding not to clean her room. The child simply cannot earn access to the reinforcer until she has cleaned her room. You cannot disengage from your child's attempts to circumvent the contingency since the stipulations have been laid out. In fact, simply putting your arms up in a gesture of stop, saying "It's not my decision, you must make the choice" often deflects a potential argument while placing the responsibility back on the child. It lets the child know you will not get into a power struggle, that the agreement is set, and that the decision is hers.

Guidelines for Using Positive Reinforcement

Numerous authors have described recommendations for using positive reinforcement. I will synthesize these recommendations into a series of guidelines for increasing the effectiveness of positive reinforcement.

Reinforce Continually at First

Continuous reinforcement means praising the child after each occurrence of the specified behavior. Most adults have trouble believing this practice actually works. Typical responses from parents when I make this recommendation range from expressions of skepticism to overt hostility. Here is a sample of some of those responses. "Are you kidding? You actually want me to *praise* my child *every* time she is being good?" "Won't I be spoiling my child if I praise her every time she is good?" "Are you telling me that the behavior problems we've been having with our son will magically disappear just by praising him on a regular basis?" "Where in the world do you think I'll get the time to praise my kid every time he's good. Do you think I don't have anything better to do with my time?" "No one in this world gets praised every time they do something good. Why should I treat my child any different than other people?"

These statements represent a powerful reflection of the general belief that children don't need continual recognition for good deeds and that they may otherwise become spoiled and overly dependent upon others for validation. There is some truth to this statement as well as the remarks by the parents. We do not want children to be dependent upon parental praise for performing tasks. Nor do we want children to expect to receive praise every time they behave appropriately. After all, it is often not practical to reinforce each occurrence of a desired behavior right away. Many real-life activities are not reinforced this way. You do not always get good grades after studying. You have to work for an hour before you earn an hourly wage, and you probably get your paycheck on a biweekly or monthly basis. We eventually want children to perform tasks and behave appropriately because of the self-satisfaction they receive from doing so. Unfortunately, promoting self-motivated and self-sufficient children, the topic of the next chapter, requires a gradual shift from parental control to self-control. Reinforcement is always more time-consuming and parent-intensive than punishment. However, the effort and time commitment to use continuous reinforcement will pay long-term dividends far surpassing those short-lived advantages associated with punishment.

There are several reasons why we want to use continuous reinforcement initially. First, it is the most effective method for getting a child to perform a new behavior or a behavior that has previously occurred at a very low rate. The idea is to get the new behavior to occur with some regularity. Once that has been accomplished, it is more desirable to reinforce the behavior only occasionally.

Second, continuous reinforcement at first helps combat the well-ingrained cultural ethos that good behavior is expected and, consequently, ignored. It has been my experience when working with parents that they are 10 times more likely to provide negative feedback to their child than praise. This practice only serves to compound the self-criticism in which most of us have a propensity to engage. Because of early childhood experiences (that is, the way parents treat children, as well as a biological predisposition), we are about 10 times more likely to give ourselves self-criticism instead of positive feedback. This pattern contributes to a habitual way of responding as an adult to various situations and to children's behavior.

Third, by initially engaging in continuous reinforcement, the parent receives feedback that can change his perceptions of his child's behavior. Because of our propensity to ignore good behavior, we are naturally inclined to focus in on bad behavior. In fact, we are very good at catching children being bad. Therefore, we don't perceive that our children behave appropriately. Common statements made by parents such as, "My son *never* says thank you" or "The kids are *always* fighting," reflect well-ingrained perceptions that are probably not true. And when I challenge parents by saying, "So your son has never said thank you in his entire life?" they begin to realize they are overgeneralizing and engaging in dichotomous thinking—commonly referred to as black-and-white or all-or-nothing thinking. Perceiving only children's negative actions prevents us from forming a close relationship with them.

To avoid this pitfall, I ask parents to keep a record of the times they reinforce their children for engaging in specified behaviors. I usually make the stipulation that they must reinforce their child 10 times per hour, each time for a different situation. So, if the behavior is "acting courteously," the parent must reinforce the child for courteous behavior in 10 different situations. The reinforcement can be for simple things such as smiling, picking up a toy or answering the phone. Most parents complain that they run out of things before the end of the hour or make up silly reasons for reinforcing their child. Nevertheless, the exercise is designed to get these behaviors defined as "courteous" performed at a higher rate and to change the parent's perception of how they view their child's behavior. The only way to change parents' perception is to feed back into their system a constant perception of the good things their child does. After a couple days, the process becomes easy, and after about a week parents can shift to more natural and intermittent forms of praise. Here is an example of how continuous reinforcement works.

Mrs. Conrad and her 14-year-old son, Oscar, entered my office. Both sat down stiffly on chairs in opposite sides of the room.

I smiled at each in turn, asking them, "How can I help you?"

Mrs. Conrad glanced at her son menacingly, sighed, returned her gaze to me and said, "Oscar *always* talks rudely to me. He *never* seems to talk or act politely to me. It's gotten so bad that I try to avoid talking to him altogether. Just the other morning I gave him a ride to school because it was cold. As I pulled into the parking lot I saw a lot of kids hanging around the outside of the building. I asked Oscar if the school had a new policy for not letting kids in early. He proceeded to roll his eyes, got out of the car and slammed the door. He didn't even thank me for the ride!"

As Mrs. Conrad was talking, her son slouched lower and lower into his chair while he looked out the window and occasionally made a comment under his breath. I turned to Oscar and asked, "Are you willing to talk to your mother about this problem?"

"All she'll do is lecture me," Oscar replied somewhat curtly.

I motioned subtly to Mrs. Conrad to be quiet, as she appeared ready to tell Oscar not to talk to me so impolitely. I then turned back to Oscar and asked him, "Are you willing to talk to your mother for a few minutes?"

"Do I have a choice?" replied Oscar sarcastically, continuing with a slight hesitation, "Yeah, I guess so."

With a reassuring smile I asked him, "Would you like to get along better with your mother?"

"I don't know," replied Oscar.

"Are you satisfied with how things are going?" I continued.

"No, it sucks," said Oscar dejectedly.

"Would you like to get along better with your mother?" I repeated.

"Yeah, I guess so," came the reply.

"Are you sure?" I asked sincerely.

"Yes, I would like that," replied Oscar.

Feeling reasonably satisfied that Oscar was sincere about wanting a better relationship with his mother, I proceeded to the issue of talking politely and acting courteously. Turning to Mrs. Conrad, I asked "Do you want to talk to your son politely?"

"Yes, but it's so hard when he's rude to me all the time," replied Mrs. Conrad.

"Ignoring the last part of her answer, I again asked, "Mrs. Conrad, do you want to talk to your son politely?"

"Yes," she simply stated.

I pressed the issue further by asking, "Are you sure?"

"Yes, I'm sure," replied Mrs. Conrad.

I now turned to Oscar and asked him the same question, "Do you want to talk politely and act courteously to your mother?"

"Yeah, I guess so, but she is always finding fault with me. Even when I do say something nice, she seems not to notice," replied Oscar.

"Oscar," I said, "do you really want to talk politely and act courteously to your mother?"

"Yes," replied Oscar.

At this point the discussion shifted to identifying exactly what "talking politely" and "acting courteously" entailed. Using the steps described in Chapter 2, we came up with a definition of several specific behaviors for "talking politely" and "acting courteously."

I turned to Oscar and said, "We have agreed that 'talking politely' means saying thank you, answering your mother in a tone of voice you would use with your friends when she asks you a question, and asking her rather than telling her to do something for you. We also agreed that 'acting courteously' means helping with the dishes, putting your dirty laundry in the hamper, and staying out of your brother's room. Can you do these things?"

"Yes," replied Oscar, "but unless everything is just 'perfect,' she'll still yell at me. And besides, even if she doesn't yell at me, I know she'll never let me know how much she appreciates what I do."

I turned to Mrs. Conrad and asked, "Can you refrain from saying anything negative to Oscar when he doesn't engage in one of the behaviors we identified?"

"I guess so," replied Mr. Conrad.

"Looking stoically at Mrs. Conrad I said, "Do you want Oscar to talk more politely and act more courteously?"

"Yes, she said, "and I can refrain from saying anything negative to Oscar."

I smiled and said, "Good. Now, can you praise Oscar *every* time he talks politely and acts courteously?"

"I'm not sure I'd be able to praise him every time. We're both pretty busy."

"Would you like me to give you a technique for ensuring you praise Oscar every time?" I asked.

"Yes," replied Mrs. Conrad enthusiastically.

I smiled at her and said, "Good, because I want you to praise Oscar at least 10 times during the three hours you are together in the evening."

"Oh dear," Mrs. Conrad said in a skeptical voice. "I hope your technique is a good one because that's not going to be easy."

"Here's what I'd like you to do," I began. "I notice that you're wearing one of those 'fanny packs' that have become so popular. Every night during the three hours you and Oscar are together, I want you to wear your fanny pack. You're going to have to empty out the contents, however." Mrs. Conrad gave me a quizzical look. I continued, "I want you to go to a toy store and buy two of the biggest bags of the largest marbles you can find. They're pretty cheap, so it shouldn't be too much of an expense. Then fill your fanny pack with the marbles and put it on when you are with Oscar. Every time you praise Oscar, take a marble out of the fanny pack and place it in a large glass. At the end of each hour, count up the number of marbles you have in the glass and write the number down on a piece of paper with the time and date."

Looking somewhat irritated, Mrs. Conrad commented, "How in the world is lugging around my waist a big pack of heavy marbles going to help Oscar talk more politely and act more courteously?"

"The fanny pack with the marbles serves several purposes, Mrs. Conrad. First, since it will be heavy, it will serve as a reminder for you to praise Oscar. It's easy to go on with our daily routines and forget to praise our children. Second, because you will want to lessen its weight, you will be forced to 'catch' Oscar behaving well. So often, we only praise children when they do something really big or unexpected. The weight of the marbles will remind you to praise Oscar for performing the little behaviors we identified. Third, as you focus on the positive things Oscar does, your perception of his behavior will begin to change. It will be more difficult for you to use words like a*lways* or *never* when describing Oscar's behavior. Such words are sure-fire ways to start an argument because they are most often used inaccurately. Instead, you will begin to see that Oscar does a lot of things you like—things you may not have been aware of before because you've been so busy focusing on the negative."

Mrs. Conrad looked at me with a bit more enthusiasm and said, "I can understand how praising continuously can help Oscar talk politely and act courteously more often and also help me perceive better the positive things he does. But how did our relationship get to this point in the first place?"

"Well, you see, Mrs. Conrad," I began, "you and Oscar have developed a specific way of interacting with each other. Given your busy schedule, it's easy to get into the habit of ignoring your son when things are going well—when he is treating you politely and doing what is expected of him. However, it's so easy to react to him when he is being impolite and discourteous to you. Yet, as strange as it may seem, if the only attention Oscar receives from you is negative, he will strive to get that negative attention even though it is aversive to both of you. As you withdrew even more from your son because the interactions with him were so aversive, he was receiving even less attention from you. Like most of us, Oscar did the only thing he knew: He did more of the same, since talking impolitely and acting discourteously had gotten your attention in the past. We truly are a curious species. When something isn't working, we tend to do more of it, just out of habit."

Oscar nodded furiously, "All I want is some attention from you, Mom. When you're getting ready for work in the morning, taking me to school, or coming home in the afternoon, you look like you don't want to be bothered. So I kinda know how to get a reaction out of you."

"But son...," Mrs. Conrad began to protest before I interrupted her.

"It's easy to get caught up in negative interactions with each other. Looking for positive behaviors and being positive ourselves takes a lot of energy that's often difficult to muster after a hard day at work. However, the payoffs are immeasurable. And besides, all you have to do, Mrs. Conrad, is praise Oscar continuously for one week. If you and Oscar are successful, we switch to having you only praise him occasionally."

Reinforce Intermittently After the Behavior is Established

The recommendations I provided for Mrs. Conrad and Oscar represent only the first step in using positive reinforcement effectively. Once things are proceeding in the right direction, you can ease up a bit on the number of reinforcements. Although continuous reinforcement gets a behavior started, reinforcing on a more *intermittent* or *occasional* basis is a more feasible and natural approach. But most importantly, it is more powerful than continuous reinforcement in the long run. The idea behind intermittent reinforcement is that a child does not know exactly *when* the reinforcer will be given, but does know that reinforcement *will* occur. Therefore, in order to increase the likelihood of obtaining the reinforcer, a child must either engage in the behavior many times over a period of time or engage in the behavior once, but for protracted periods of time. This principle is well established in our society. It is particularly well understood by the owners of gambling casinos. Gambling provides an excellent example of the powerful effects of intermittent reinforcement. Take the operation of slot machines. Gamblers place coins in the slot machine not knowing *when* the machine will pay off, but knowing that eventually it *will* pay off. That's why gambling is so addictive. People engage in high rates of gambling behavior because of the belief that eventually they will win.

Intermittent reinforcement is so effective that behavior will persist even in the face of punishment. Even though people lose thousands of dollars in Las Vegas—certainly a powerful punisher—they nevertheless persist in high rates of gambling behavior, confident in the knowledge that they will eventually hit it big. It is that occasional "big hit" that is so reinforcing and that maintains the behavior, even when previous gambling behavior has been severely punished through the loss of large amounts of money. If nothing else that I have said so far has convinced you of the power of reinforcement over punishment, gambling should begin to do so. And if any doubts remain, count the number of states that run lottery games. The reinforcement inherent in the lottery is even more intermittent than that of casino gambling. Finally, and ironically, although reinforcement is most effective when it occurs occasionally, punishment must be delivered every time the inappropriate behavior occurs. Punishing a child occasionally when he misbehaves only teaches him that it is possible to "get away with stuff."

Let us return to the previous example. When I saw Mrs. Conrad and Oscar the following week, they both reported changes in each other's behavior. I then explained the concept of occasional reinforcement to Mrs. Conrad in private. Needless to say, she was quite pleased to be able to "ease up" on the amount of praise she was required to give. "Not only can you reinforce Oscar less frequently," I noted, "you should be able to maintain the gains you both made this past week." I continued, "Although you will be putting out less effort, you will still have to catch Oscar being good. But you may find yourself catching Oscar doing substantially more appropriate things. Since Oscar knows he *will* be reinforced but not *when*, you may find him taking on added responsibilities in order to receive recognition."

Mrs. Conrad nodded enthusiastically as she said, "Just the other day, Oscar volunteered to vacuum the carpet in the family room. I almost died! That wasn't even one of the behaviors we identified last week."

"Good," I said. "I can see we're making progress. The reason I wanted to talk to you alone was to prevent Oscar from figuring out when you were going to reinforce him intermittently. It's important that you vary the length of time between praises. I notice that you are wearing a digital watch. One way to make sure he can't figure out when you are going to praise him is to set the timer on your watch to beep at random intervals during the hour. After the timer beeps, you then must 'catch' Oscar being good, just as we discussed before. Do you have any questions?"

"Yes," Mrs. Conrad replied. "Oscar is still doing some things that I would classify as 'talking impolitely' and 'acting discourteously.' Also, I'm not sure when to praise him. Sometimes I see him doing something good like removing the dinner dishes from the table, but he's also calling his brother some name or another. How can I deal with those two problems?"

I nodded understandingly and said, "You have raised two of the most commonly asked questions about using reinforcement effectively. The first question has to do with ignoring or attending to inappropriate behavior, the second has to do with the timing of delivering reinforcement."

Ignore Inappropriate Behavior

Perhaps *no one* concept related to reinforcement is so misunderstood and despised by parents as the recommendation to ignore inappropriate behavior. *Ignoring inappropriate behavior* is based on the following premise: negative attention is better than no attention at all. That is, a child will deliberately engage in inappropriate behavior, ranging from making strange noises at the dinner table to throwing a tantrum to making bizarre statements about wanting to eat squashed cat brains. Because parents find these types of behaviors annoying, they usually give their child some form of negative attention—such as a verbal reprimand or a stern look.

From games they play, children learn at a very early age how to get their parents' attention. And parents quite naturally and benignly play into their hands. For example, an infant just beginning to eat cereal in a high chair may throw food or a utensil on the floor. The parent, amused that the child is showing some independence, may turn to the child and, with a smile, say, "You shouldn't do that." As children get older, these games become more sophisticated. My 2-year-old son will run around the dining room and kitchen laughing when I get his coat out to go to the store. My response is to chase him around with the coat, sometimes stopping and going the other way to surprise him as he turns the corner from the dining room into the kitchen. Eventually, I get his coat on and we're off to the store. Nevertheless, I reinforced avoidance-type behavior.

My point here is not to illustrate my inadequacies as a parent, although I have plenty like the rest of us. Neither am I suggesting that we never give our young children attention for any behavior that could possibly be construed as inappropriate. Rather, I want to point out that children learn from an early age to engage in certain behaviors that we as adults eventually come to find "inappropriate," because of the attention they receive from us. Therefore, it should come as no surprise that children will seek our attention even when such attention is negative. It is this cycle that must be broken by beginning to ignore children's inappropriate behavior.

But does ignoring inappropriate behavior really work? Sometimes. I do not recommend ignoring inappropriate behavior when children are being physically assaultive to others, breaking objects, or hurting themselves. But almost any other behavior can be effectively ignored if certain conditions are met. Even when ignoring is used correctly, however, you must be prepared to "ride out the storm." I am very blunt with parents and tell them that when they start ignoring their child's inappropriate behavior, it will get worse before it gets better. The technical term for this phenomenon is an "extinction curve." The everyday term is "riding the bucking bronco." A wild horse that has not been broke will buck furiously. And the more times the horse is able to throw its rider, the longer it will buck when subsequent riders try to break it. The same holds true for children. Children will misbehave more when the attention they previously received for a misbehavior is removed. And if parents give in to their child's attempts to get attention, ignoring subsequent behavior becomes even more difficult. The parent has, in essence, reinforced a higher intensity of misbehavior. Therefore, the child learns that to get his parents' attention, he must misbehave even more. That's why I call ignoring inappropriate behavior "riding the bucking bronco." Once you get on that bronco, you'd better be prepared to ride it to the end or it will be even more difficult to break the next time. Analogously, once you begin ignoring your child's misbehavior, you'd better ignore it completely until it begins to subside, otherwise the misbehavior will worsen.

The classic example of these difficulties occurs when trying to put a resistant child to bed. Many children between the ages of 3 and 5 are hesitant to go to bed at night. They put their parents through a ritual of "one more story," "I need to go to the bathroom again," "I want a drink of water," "I heard a noise," and the list could go on. In most cases, a child engages in these behaviors as a way to avoid going to bed, which is not as reinforcing as staying up and playing with Mom or Dad. So, quite naturally, when the child is put to bed, she will try to prolong the attention she gets from her parents. Usually, parents will meet their child's request for a drink of water, several stories, checking the room for boogie monsters, having the radio on, and maybe even letting her take a toy to bed, depending on how well the parents' tolerance is holding out. Eventually, the parent leaves the room. Some children are satisfied with this level of parental attention; others are not. Those children who want more attention at bedtime from their parents usually escalate their attention-getting behaviors into the whining and crying stage. It is at this point that ignoring can be effective.

Remember what I warned about ignoring: You must be prepared for the behavior to worsen before it gets better and you must ignore *all* instances of the behavior, no matter how bad it seems. It is extremely difficult for parents to ignore their child's crying—especially when it's coming from a toddler. Parents are conditioned to think that when a child cries, he is either in pain or in need of something. We are conditioned in this way when our children are infants. The only way infants have of telling us something is wrong—either they are cold, tired, wet or hungry—is by crying. Parents become experts at discerning what type of cry their infant is using to express certain needs. However, as children get older and begin to talk, they use crying less to express their basic needs but more to get attention since that's what worked in the past. The bonding that takes place between parents and infants makes it extremely difficult for parents not to react emotionally when their child cries. Therefore, parents' natural reaction when children cry is to try to get them to stop. And long after they have outgrown the need to cry to get their basic needs met, children know that crying is a great way to get their parents' attention.

So, the biggest challenge of getting a child to bed who cries and whines to get additional attention is to consistently ignore that child. I was working with a parent who experienced this problem. I explained to her how to use ignoring. The next week she looked at me sheepishly and stated that she ignored her child's crying really well the first couple of days, and after about 20 minutes the child fell asleep. However, on the third day, her child cried for 30 minutes. The mother had had a long day and was tired herself. So, after another five minutes, she went into her child's room and tried to calm her down. Unfortunately, by doing so, the mother reinforced a higher level of crying than was the case previously. Figure 3.1 illustrates this problem. Notice that in the first two nights the crying lasted for an average of 20 minutes before the child fell asleep. When the mother started ignoring the behavior on the third night, the crying increased to 30 minutes. It is at this stage in the process that ignoring becomes extremely important. You must be prepared to weather the storm and not provide attention for the crying. If you are able to ignore the crying when it escalates, then after a couple days it will subside, as pictured in the graph beginning on the fifth day. On the other hand, providing attention when the behavior is escalating only lets the child know that a more intense form of the behavior is necessary to get the parent's attention.

Yet another problem must be addressed in connection with ignoring a

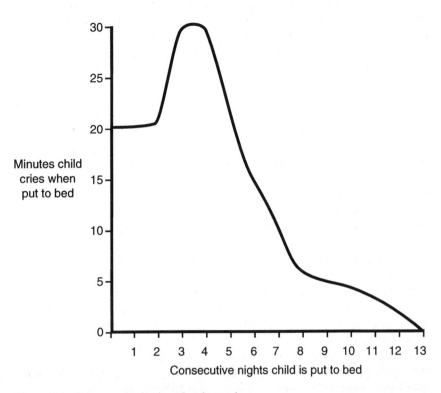

Figure 3.1. Example of behavior when ignored.

child's misbehavior. Even when a parent is able to ignore a behavior sufficiently for it to decrease, it can recur unexpectedly. The technical term is
"spontaneous recovery." I prefer to call it "the hill at the end of the marathon." Just as the marathon runner must face the last test of her endurance
by running uphill before the finish line, so too must parents hold firm when
their child's misbehavior unexpectedly recurs. If parents can hold firm, the
chances that the behavior will subsequently return decline dramatically.

Given these problems, you may begin wondering, as many parents with
whom I work do, why I recommend ignoring inappropriate behavior. There
are two reasons. First, it works better than the method most parents use—
punishment. If parents' attempts at punishing their child's inappropriate
behavior were successful, then they wouldn't be in my office. Unfortunately,
attempts at punishing misbehavior are fraught with the danger that the
parent is unknowingly reinforcing the child through negative attention, in

addition to the other problems described in Chapter 1. And, as the child misbehaves even more, the parents become focused almost exclusively on their child's inappropriate behavior. The level of positive attention parents can provide to their child can be reduced to almost zero.

Second, the only way ignoring inappropriate behavior will work is if parents consciously catch their child being good. "Catching a child being good" is a way to shift away from focusing on the negative to attending to the positive. When parents catch their child being good, they are providing her with a powerful reinforcer—attention. Yet, unlike punishment, the attention is positive rather than negative. Therefore, the child quickly learns that appropriate behavior gets his parents' attention, while negative behavior does not. I believe the single most important reason for the failure of ignoring inappropriate behavior is parents' lack of catching children being good and, consequently, praising them.

A parent once said to me in regard to this idea, "My child doesn't seem to ever do anything good. He's in an especially bad mood when he gets home from school."

I replied somewhat sarcastically, "Well, wait at the door when your child comes home and say 'nice breathing.'" Catching a child being good does not require the child to engage in earth-shaking behaviors. It only requires the parent to pay attention to the little things children do that are so easily ignored when the child is misbehaving. The more parents praise their children for the little things, however, the more effective ignoring becomes. The child will begin to differentiate the types of behaviors that result in parental approval. How many times, upon being questioned, will children say they did something just to see if they could get a reaction out of their parents? And aren't we, more often than not, willing to provide the child with a reaction?

Delivering Reinforcement

As parents become more adept at ignoring inappropriate behavior and catching their child being good, a common question concerns the timing or delivery of reinforcement. Generally, the more quickly a child is praised *after* the appropriate behavior occurs, the more effective will be the reinforcement. The key word in the preceding sentence is *after*. Never reinforce a child before he performs a behavior: Sometimes parents do so in the hopes that the child will subsequently be good, but it doesn't work. Here is a common example that attests to this point.

A parent asked me how to make her son behave when she was shopping at the grocery store. It seemed that this 8-year-old boy would run up and down the aisles often bumping into people, pick up miscellaneous products, and take off to the toy aisle only to return with some object he wanted his mother to purchase for him. When she refused, he would throw a tantrum. In an attempt to stave off his tantrums, his mother told him he could have a toy if he was good the entire time in the store. After arriving at the grocery store, they went directly to the toy aisle and the boy selected a helicopter. He was good for about three-quarters of the time in the store, since he had the helicopter to keep him occupied. However, as they approached the checkout line, the boy began engaging in the usual behavior—running throughout the aisles, knocking products off the shelf, and asking for another toy. The boy's mother could not understand what happened.

In the case above, the reinforcement was not administered contingently. That is, the boy did not have to earn the reward before receiving it. Therefore, there was no reason for him to behave appropriately while in the grocery store. A more effective approach would have been for the mother to define precisely the behaviors she expected from her son in the store. If the child was able to perform them the entire time they were in the grocery store, then, and only then, would he be allowed to pick out a toy. In this way, the reinforcer is administered directly *after* the appropriate behavior. The child will know immediately what he has done that is appropriate, and if you verbally spell out what exactly he did, he will know even more specifically what he has done right. The parent could tell the child, "I like the way you walked down the aisles and kept your hands to yourself. Now you can go and pick out a toy."

There is one potential problem in waiting to reinforce a child until after she has performed the desired behaviors. The child may not be able to maintain the appropriate behavior for the specified length of time. For example, the boy at the grocery store may walk down the aisles with his hands at his side for 10 minutes and then revert back to the inappropriate behaviors. We do not want to reinforce the child with a toy because he failed to perform the desired behaviors the entire time at the store. Yet we want to give the child credit for any improvement. So the question becomes one of how to provide reinforcement for the appropriate behavior when it occurs without reinforcing inappropriate behavior. Often children get frustrated when they see that the amount of behavior and the length of time during which it must be performed are too great. A child can start out strong at the store, but then go downhill as time passes. The way to deal with this situation is to reinforce approximations of the identified behaviors.

Reinforce Approximations

One of the most difficult things for adults to understand when using principles of reinforcement is that behavior is not always performed in one swoop. Often we set goals for children that are too high. That leads to both frustrated children and parents. Most new behaviors will not be performed at first like you hoped—they need to be shaped in the right direction. We learn through a step-by-step process when acquiring a new skill. Therefore, we want to reinforce children for performing behaviors that approximate the desired ones. Unfortunately, most adults want to see an immediate turnaround and will settle for no less. I have seen this thinking in both teachers and parents.

I was working with a third-grade teacher who had a student who was extremely resistant to completing multiplication worksheets. The teacher had tried sending the student to the principal, getting her additional help in math, and calling her parents. None of these techniques had worked. When I met with the teacher, the student had about 12 uncompleted worksheets, each containing 20 problems. At this point, the student had little motivation to complete any of the worksheets—she couldn't see any light at the end of the tunnel. So she simply refused to do any of them. Nevertheless, the teacher gave her a new worksheet every day, just like everyone else in the class. The teacher was at a loss as to what to try next. With an exasperated look she said, "Dr. Maag, do you have any suggestions?"

"Yes," I replied. "But before I tell you what to do, I would like to ask you a question. What is your goal for this student?"

The teacher gave me a puzzled look and responded, "To have her do better in school, of course."

"Could you be a little more specific?" I asked. "The problem area seems to be in completing her math worksheets. What would you like to see change?"

"Well, I'd like to see her complete more worksheets," said the teacher.

"How successful have you been in helping your student reach that goal so far?" I asked.

"Not very," the teacher replied. "But that's why I asked for your help."

"Okay, but I think our goal needs to be a little more modest than completing the worksheets," I replied. "Would you consider it progress if the student completed a portion of the worksheet?"

"Yes, I think that would be a good start," replied the teacher.

"Good. Then here's what I want you to do. First, I want you to throw out all the old worksheets that have accumulated in the student's folder. Chances are that she is feeling overwhelmed and believes it is impossible to catch up, and, consequently, has given up trying. Second, I want you to write one multiplication problem in the middle of a piece of white paper. Put nothing more on the paper except a place for her to write her name." The teacher's initial expression of hope when I started telling her what to do was vanishing. In its place, she was developing a frown. "Third, I want you to tell the student that if she completes the problem on her 'new' worksheet, she can spend the rest of the 15-minute session drawing at the free-time table in the back of the room."

The teacher looked at me with an expression that could only be described as disdain for those ivory tower professors who know nothing about the real world. "You expect me to let her get away with only having one problem on her worksheet when all the other students in class have 20 problems on their worksheets?"

Before I could answer, she continued, "I'm not going to reward bad performance by letting this student get away with a worthless assignment. What type of teacher do you think I am?"

"A very concerned one," I replied quickly. "But let's look at the situation realistically. Currently this student is completing no math problems, yet she is receiving a new worksheet every day. Now, if you get her to complete one problem—which is certainly well within her ability—she will have completed 100% more problems than she has in the last two weeks combined! Wouldn't you consider a 100% improvement in math-problem completion a pretty good initial progress?"

I then went on to explain how this approach represented only the first step. What we were trying to accomplish, in essence, was to "set the student up for success." Once we got her to complete one problem, we doubled the number the following day, and so on, until she was able to complete the entire worksheet, which took about two weeks. The important point is that I did not expect an immediate turnaround of behavior in the student. By starting small with approximations of the desired outcome, the student was more likely to experience success, and as the saying goes, "nothing succeeds like success." Also, the teacher was less likely to be disappointed in the student's performance. Instead, she ended up helping the student toward the final goal by encouraging each step in the right direction. Once behaviors are learned, they become habitual—it doesn't matter whether they are considered appropriate or inappropriate. It is difficult to break a child of a bad behavior in one day. Therefore, it is important to give a child the necessary time, attention and praise to encourage her to keep on trying.

Returning to the example of the mother who wanted her child to behave while in the grocery store, I recommended that she reinforce approximations of the desired behavior. Specifically, I told the mother to have the expectation in place only for the last 2 minutes of shopping. Therefore, if her son could walk down the aisles with his hands to his side for 2 minutes right before they left, then she could buy him a toy. If 2 minutes were too long, then the time would have to be set at 60 seconds, or even 30 seconds if necessary. The idea is to shape the desired behavior by setting up the child for success. That is much more desirable than having the child behave appropriately the entire time in the grocery store except for the last 5 minutes and then lose the reward.

Similarly, many parents I work with complain that their children do not clean their rooms. They lament how their children don't pick up their clothes, or stuff them under the bed, leave toys and garbage in the room, throw stuff in the closet, and fail to make the bed. Instead of starting out with an elaborate "star chart," which is the focus of the next section, I ask the parent to pick one aspect of the dirty room for the child to improve. Therefore, if the child puts all the dirty clothes in the hamper, for example, he is reinforced. After that little part of "cleaning the room" becomes habitual, we incorporate additional behaviors. The biggest challenge I have is convincing parents that they are not letting their child "get away with something." However, when I point out that any small change would be an improvement, they usually are ready to give it a try. Change, as I pointed out previously, is like a kaleidoscope. If you turn the tube just a little bit, the whole pattern changes—so too does changing behavior. Once we get a change in the right direction, albeit a small one, three-quarters of the battle is won. Then, assuming we have identified things that a child truly finds reinforcing, changing behavior becomes a fairly straightforward and easy process.

Reinforcement is Individual

The last recommendation for using reinforcement that I alluded to at the beginning of this chapter is that reinforcement is individual. Therefore, what one person finds reinforcing may not be so to somebody else. In fact, what one person finds reinforcing may actually be punishing to another person. For example, some children respond extremely well to verbal praise or encouragement. Other children, often those whose self-esteem is impaired, fear that verbal praise only means that a more difficult task will be forthcoming—one at which they will ultimately fail. Consequently, such children find verbal praise punishing because of the message believed to be implicit behind the praise. Therefore, it is crucial to find something that the child truly finds reinforcing.

There are several ways to determine reinforcers for your child. The first approach is simply trying and seeing what happens. If the reinforcer selected results in an increase in the desired behavior, then what you selected was, in fact, reinforcing. On the other hand, if the appropriate behavior does not increase, then what you selected was not reinforcing. When you are selecting reinforcers for your child, remember that what you may find reinforcing your child may not. Nevertheless, parents know their child's likes and dislikes better than any other adult. I suggest making a list of everything your child may find reinforcing. Have your child add to your list. Then ask the child to rank her preference for each item, with "1" being "most liked" and so on until each item is rated.

It is helpful to solicit children's input as to what they find reinforcing. In this way, a child feels some sense of ownership and involvement in the process. However, children don't always know offhand what they would like for a reinforcer. Children have difficulty grasping the concept of reinforcement, although they usually have no problem understanding rewards. Even when asking them what rewards they would like, children often are at a loss for coming up with things. Recently I was working with a mother and her 8-year-old son. He was unable to come up with any "rewards" other than playing outside longer after school and staying up later. However, when encouraged to describe his daily routine, the boy was able to come up with a variety of things, such as being able to make a snack himself before bedtime. Specifically, this boy really liked to cook scrambled eggs, although his mother rarely let him do so. When he mentioned being able to cook scrambled eggs himself before bed, his mother looked at me and shrugged her shoulders as if to say—whatever. Often, the reinforcers children think of would hardly appear to be reinforcing to adults. And therein lies the benefit of soliciting reinforcers from children.

Another way to determine what would make good reinforcers for children is to simply watch them when they are given a chance to do what they like. In any situation children are more likely to perform some behaviors than others. A friend of mine was teaching first graders. Six-year-olds' behavior is typically motor-oriented and quite verbal. When my friend stepped out of the room to talk to another teacher in the hall for a few seconds or when her students were moving from one activity to another, she noticed the following behaviors. Some students would be screaming or talking very loudly, others would be making animal noises, two students were running around the classroom, one was pushing a noisy chair across the floor, and another was playing with a puzzle. She wanted to control their behavior without using punishment or tangible reinforcers such as candy or trinkets. When thinking about the behaviors her students were engaging in, she realized they all seemed to be having fun. It appeared that when children were given free rein, there was a great likelihood of these behaviors, or GLOBs for short, being engaged in by her students. She also observed that the students had great difficulty sitting quietly, paying attention, and working on assignments. Therefore, there was a small likelihood of these behaviors, or SLOBs, being performed by her students without much prodding. Consequently, the teacher simply made engaging in the GLOBs contingent on the students doing a small amount of work—the SLOBs. The first request was for them to sit quietly at their desks and work on math problems for 30 seconds. This was followed by the command, "Everybody run and scream for 30 seconds."

The approach used by this teacher illustrates how some of the most unusual things can be reinforcers if we just observe what children do and say. I remember working with a boy who was in the seventh grade. He was having great difficulty getting homework assignments completed in his history class. In addition, he was regularly reprimanded by his teacher for talking during class and mumbling under his breath when the teacher brought these behaviors to his attention. The teacher had met with the parents and had implored them to get their son to finish his assignments and improve his "attitude" in class. Having little success, the parents brought their son to see me. Among other things, the boy related a fairly strong distaste for his history teacher. He had no trouble discussing at great length the personal and professional shortcomings of his teacher. This strong distaste gave me an idea. The junior high schools in town were sponsoring a carnival on Saturday, two weeks from my meeting with the boy. One of the carnival games was "dunk the teacher." A staple at carnivals, this game involves having a person sit on a chair while patrons take turns throwing balls at a bull's-eye. When a ball hits the bull's-eye, the person falls into a tank of water. It is great fun for everybody.

After the family left my office, I called the school and asked to talk to the boy's history teacher. After he explained the problems to me, I told him I thought I had a way to increase the boy's assignment completion and appropriate behavior in class. In turn, I would require a "small" favor of him. I asked him if he would be willing to sit in the dunking chair for one of the half-hour time slots. There was a pause and then he asked why. I replied that I wanted to use him as a reinforcer to increase the boy's assignment completion and behavior in class. I explained that the boy seemed to have some negative feelings toward him and that I thought the boy would work well for the opportunity to dunk him in water. He somewhat skeptically agreed.

At my next session, I presented the boy with the opportunity to dunk his history teacher. His eyes immediately lighted up, but then he asked, "What's the catch?"

"The catch is," I replied, "that you must complete your assignments and improve your behavior in his class." I went on to explain exactly what "improved behavior" meant. I also told the boy that every time he completed an assignment, he would receive one ticket for the carnival. After further conferring with the teacher, I told the boy he would also receive one ticket for every 10 minutes in class he was being polite and attentive. I reminded him that three throws at this carnival game equaled three tickets. Therefore, he could potentially earn about 30 chances to dunk his teacher. Needless to say, the boy was very excited about the prospect of being able to dunk his teacher. As a result, his assignment completion and classroom behavior improved dramatically.

In essence, dunking his teacher was a GLOB, while assignment completion and appropriate classroom behavior were SLOBs. The process of using a GLOB to increase the performance of a SLOB is technically known as the Premack Principle. According to the Premack Principle, a high-probability behavior (dunking the teacher) can be used to strengthen a low-probability behavior (assignment completion and appropriate classroom behavior).

There is another name for the Premack Principle—*Mom's Rule*. Mothers are adept at using the Premack Principle. How many of us cannot remember from our childhood being told that if we wanted dessert, we'd better finish our vegetables, or if we wanted to go out and play, we must first clean our room. Eating dessert or going out to play are GLOBs since if children are given free rein to do what they want, they are more likely to eat dessert and play than to clean their rooms and eat vegetables—the later two representing SLOBs.

Besides selecting things that children will find reinforcing, it is also important to have a large supply of reinforcers from which children can choose. After an initial meeting, it is very common for parents to enthusiastically report to me the following week on how well the program I set up has been working for their child. However, a few weeks later, they may comment that "the program" no longer works. A common response from parents is, "I guess reinforcement only works for a short period of time." After hearing this comment repeatedly, I have learned to anticipate it. Therefore, I point out to parents that reinforcement will work forever. However, the specific things that serve as reinforcers may lose their effectiveness after a period of time. Earlier in the chapter I noted that the technical term for this phenomenon is "satiation." Satiation refers to a condition in which a child has experienced the reinforcer to such an extent that it is no longer reinforcing. The everyday name for this condition is "burnout." I described how satiation can be prevented by limiting a child's access to the reinforcer and by only giving a small amount of the reinforcer. A third way to prevent satiation is to have a large number of potential reinforcers available from which the child can choose. This reduces the chances that the child will "burn out" on any one thing.

Satiation can result not only in the loss of a reinforcer's effectiveness, but in some cases, what was once reinforcing to a child can actually become punishing. There are several examples of this phenomenon happening to us as adults. How many adults have a dislike for bologna sandwiches because of the tremendous number they consumed as children? Quite a few of you probably had the experience in younger days of drinking too much hard liquor that led to a session bowing into the toilet. What did you feel like the next time you saw or smelled that particular type of liquor? In the late 1970s and early 1980s there was a famous institute that had considerable success in getting people to quit smoking. Although its success at having people maintain a smoke-free lifestyle was arguable, the approach was fairly straightforward. A client would go into the clinic, be instructed to sit at a table with an ashtray and smoke as many cigarettes as quickly as he could within a certain period of time. Satiation readily occurred. Although the passage of time can lessen the effects of satiation, the best defense against its occurrence is to have a large supply of things children potentially will find reinforcing.

Figure 3.2 lists some things I have found to be reinforcing to children with whom I have worked. The list is not meant to be exhaustive, and the items may not be appropriate for every child and household. Nevertheless, this list is intended to provide parents with an idea of the variety of things children may find reinforcing. In this way, I hope to stimulate parents' creativity and knowledge of their children to better determine potential reinforcers. Notice that I have included in the list activities that children can easily engage in around the house. Obviously, children will work for expensive toys. However, the idea is not to break the household budget. Notice also that many of the reinforcers involve parental participation. Although this requires additional work, it is another way to encourage parents to give their

---

Ideas for Reinforcers

- Staying up an extra 30 minutes
- Selecting special item at grocery store
- Fixing a special snack before bed
- Having a sibling do a favor
- Playing catch with Dad
- Going to the dump to scrounge around
- Hitting cans with a sling shot
- Shooting baskets with Mom or Dad
- Looking for money in cushion

- Playing a board game with Mom and Dad
- Helping Mom bake cookies
- Having Mom fix a special meal
- Selecting a TV show for the family to watch
- Making popcorn during a movie
- Having a friend spend the night
- Sitting on the roof with Dad
- Checking out books from the library
- Sitting on parent's lap and steering the car

Figure 3.2. Ideas for reinforcers available around the house.

children positive attention which, in turn, will make ignoring inappropriate behavior more effective. Finally, we want children to move away from tangible and even activity rewards so they eventually become able to reinforce themselves—one of the topics of the next chapter.

I want to make a final comment about the boy in the dunking example above, which leads into the next technique. The reinforcement of getting to dunk his teacher was two weeks away, yet the boy was expected to complete all his assignments and behave appropriately in class on a daily basis up until the carnival. The carnival would be too delayed a reinforcer to improve the boy's assignment completion and classroom behavior on a daily basis. Therefore, the tickets he received gave him immediate feedback in the form of tangible evidence indicating the amount of reinforcement he was eventually to receive. In this way, something generally considered too delayed to be effective can acquire reinforcing properties.

The Star Chart: Making Use of the Token Economy

We know from the recommendations described above that for something to be reinforcing: (1) it must be delivered immediately after the behavior occurs, (2) it must be valued by the person receiving it, and (3) it must be resistant to satiation—that is, the child should not burn out on the reinforcer. In the perfect and controlled world of writing this book, I can confidently make these recommendations. However, the real world is not perfect, nor do we have supreme control over what happens. Therefore, it is not always possible to reinforce a child every time a behavior occurs or directly after the behavior occurs. Furthermore, although they may be highly reinforcing, some of the things children find reinforcing may be impractical to deliver on a daily basis, for example, renting a video cassette. If you drove to the store and rented a video every time your child talked politely or followed a direction on the first request, chances are you would not have a life, you would be broke in a short period of time, and your child would burn out on videos. A video would be too much reinforcement for one instance of talking politely or following a direction upon the first request. Nevertheless, a child may find a video very reinforcing.

What is a Token Economy?

One way to deal with these dilemmas is to develop a behavior chart. Sometimes called a "star chart" because stars are placed on a piece of paper when children complete certain behaviors, the chart is based on the principles of a *token economy*. A token economy is simply a system whereby symbols or objects, called tokens, are awarded to the child immediately after she performs specified behaviors. The tokens are later exchanged for a reinforcer of value to the child.

A token economy is analogous to the use of money. Money is nothing more than a token. Although it is not reinforcing in and of itself, money takes on reinforcing properties based on the endless number of things for which it can be exchanged. If, on the other hand, money could only be used to buy socks, it would quickly lose its reinforcing properties since we would satiate on buying socks in little time. One of the advantages of using a program based on a token economy is that satiation is unlikely to occur. It is possible to have a wide variety of activities and objects that are reinforcing to a child and that she can purchase with the tokens she has earned for performing the appropriate behaviors.

Although I did not know it at the time, my first encounter with a token economy system was when I was about 6 or 7 years old. My mother was an avid collector of S&H green stamps. Whenever we went to the grocery store, she would receive a number of S&H green stamps proportional to the amount of money she spent. I can vividly remember her taking the S&H booklet out of her purse and sticking the stamps on the pages before leaving the check-out line. I used to enjoy browsing through the catalog of things that could be purchased by exchanging booklets full of stamps. There seemed to be literally hundreds of items. The behavior that was being reinforced here, of course, was shopping at a grocery store that gave S&H green stamps. But how long would my mother shop at this particular grocery store if the stamps could only be exchanged for two items—a lamp or a clock. She would have reached the satiation point very quickly. To be effective, a program based on a token economy must include a large and varied number of reinforcers a child can potentially purchase with his tokens. Therefore, the program must consist of two components: the token itself and a variety of back-up reinforcers.

Components of a Token Economy

The tokens

The token is delivered immediately after the desired behavior occurs. The token serves to meet the recommendation of delivering reinforcement immediately after the behavior occurs and, initially, upon every instance of the behavior. The token acts like a reinforcer as long as the child can later exchange it for items that are reinforcing. Consequently, it bridges the gap in time between the behavior occurring and access to the reinforcer. Often the term "back-up" reinforcer is used to describe the object or activity for which the child exchanges the tokens. In essence, the reinforcer "backs up" or supports the effectiveness of the token.

Remember, tokens won't work unless they can be exchanged for something. They are rarely reinforcing in and of themselves, but only attain their reinforcing value by being exchangeable for items that are reinforcing. I have often seen parents develop a chart on which stars are placed when their child performs an appropriate behavior, but without the opportunity for the child to exchange the tokens for something else. These parents think that stars are a sufficient reinforcer. That view is analogous to the likelihood of money continuing to be reinforcing to us if we couldn't use it to purchase anything. Although the child's motivation and interest are whetted, they quickly wane when it becomes apparent that there is nothing she can purchase with the accumulated stars.

Common objects used as tokens include things such as a poker chip, a button or play money. Tokens can also be a symbol, such as a check mark, a hole punched in a card, points or stickers.

If objects are used as tokens, there must be a designated place for storing them. Some parents use marbles as tokens that are accumulated in a jar placed on the kitchen counter. With this system, a child can actually see the amount of tokens earned. Other parents stick an envelope on the refrigerator in which they place play money earned as tokens. Still others have laminated cards worn around their child's neck on a string. Holes are punched on the card every time the child performs the appropriate behavior. If symbols are used as tokens, such as stars or stickers, these may be placed on a piece of cardboard divided into sections. Other quite ingenious methods have been used as well. For example, with young children, a dot-to-dot representation of the back-up reinforcer is drawn. Each time a child performs the desired behavior, two dots are connected. When all the dots are connected, the picture is complete and the child receives the reinforcer portrayed in the picture. Another technique is to take a Polaroid snapshot of the back-up reinforcer and then cut the picture into pieces. A child receives one piece of the picture each time he performs the desired behavior. The piece is pasted on a sheet of paper containing an outline of the position of the pieces as in jigsaw puzzles. When selecting tokens, make sure they are portable, durable and easy to handle.

The reinforcers

With grade school children, most parents prefer using a symbol, such as a star placed on a chart to specify the behaviors and potential rewards—hence the term "star chart." A star chart can be developed to encompass behaviors expected to be performed in the morning, afternoon and evening, or for one specific time. The selection of the back-up reinforcers is probably the most difficult aspect of the star chart. The parent must have a wide enough assortment of back-up reinforcers to provide a motivating item for a child.

Possible reinforcers include edibles (a special snack), activities (shooting baskets with Mom or Dad), objects (earning a game, small toy or crayons), and privileges (staying up a half hour later at night, playing a video game). Sometimes these reinforcers are referred to as a menu since the child can select whatever he wants just as one would select a particular meal from a menu at a restaurant.

I provided some examples of reinforcers in Figure 3.2. Besides these items, some of the best reinforcers involve using things children already enjoy doing—and then making them earn them. For example, many children enjoy playing Nintendo; some children will play for hours, if given the opportunity. Other children have favorite television shows and, similarly, would watch for hours if given the opportunity. Both activities can be highly reinforcing. However, you must be prepared to tell your child she can no longer play Nintendo or watch television unless she earns it. It is important to understand that this suggestion is not to be considered as punishment. Punishment is something that is administered directly after a child misbehaves. Instead, you are simply telling your child that she must earn these things. In fact, she could potentially earn more time doing these things than she previously did. The key consideration is that parents must be willing to cut off all access to Nintendo and television viewing unless it is earned.

What a Star Chart Looks Like

Several things should appear on the star chart. Figure 3.3 depicts a completed chart for a 9-year-old boy. First, there should be a place to write down the exact behaviors that are expected of the child. I usually get a poster board and divide it into squares. Along the top I list the days of the week. Along the left side, I list the behaviors. All the recommendations presented in Chapter 2 apply here. However, even when behaviors are specified, problems can still arise. Take the seemingly specific behavior to "put away clean clothes." The parent thinks this behavior means putting the clothes in the dresser drawers, while the child thinks this means stuffing them under the bed or in the closet. We need to be more specific, so we tell the child that "put away clean clothes" means placing them in the dresser drawer. Alas, the child then stuffs the clothes in the drawer. So we go back and say, "neatly fold the clothes and place them in the dresser drawer." By this time the behavior is not only sufficiently specified, but the standard for doing it and receiving a star (or other type of sticker) has been set.

Another important consideration is placing a time limit on performing the behavior. In Figure 3.3, the child has 2 minutes to get dressed, 2 minutes to wash hands and face, and 1 minute to brush teeth. He can earn one token for each behavior completed correctly during each time interval. The easiest

Star Chart					
	Monday	**Tuesday**	**Wednesday**	**Thursday**	**Friday**
Morning Behaviors					
• Get dressed	*		*	*	*
• Wash hands and face		*	*	*	*
• Brush teeth	*	*	*	*	*
Afternoon Behaviors					
• Make bed	*		*	*	*
• Fold clothes and put in dresser		*		*	*
• Put toys on shelf	*		*		*
• Throw away trash	*	*	*	*	*
Evening Behaviors					
• Turn down bed	*		*	*	*
• Put on pajamas	*	*		*	*
• Wash hands and face		*	*	*	*
• Brush teeth	*	*	*	*	*
Daily Total	8	7	9	10	11

	Weekly Total	45

	Reward	**Bonus**
Morning	10 minutes of TV or Nintendo per star	Special breakfast if 3 stars are earned
Afternoon	10 minutes of TV or Nintendo per star	Playing game with parent if 4 stars are earned
Evening	10 minutes of TV or Nintendo per star	Fixing special snack before bed if 4 stars are earned
Daily		Staying up extra 1/2 hour, taking special toy to school, or calling Grandma
Weekly		Renting video, dinner at favorite restaurant, roller skating, movie, or friend spending night

Figure 3.3. Sample star chart for doing chores.

way to monitor the time is to set a kitchen timer. That way differences of opinion between child and parent are reduced.

Along with listing the behaviors, it is important to list how many stars can be earned for each behavior. If "cleaning the room" entails (1) making the bed, (2) folding and putting clothes in dresser drawer, (3) putting toys on shelf, and (4) throwing trash (soda cans, candy wrappers) in garbage can, then each could be worth one star apiece. In addition, the number of tokens required to purchase various back-up reinforcers should be specified at the bottom of the chart. Listing the number of stars that can be earned and the price of the back-up reinforcers allows the child to decide whether the reinforcer is worth the required behavior change. To get the process going quickly, price the reinforcers at a level that allows your child to quickly acquire tokens. This recommendation follows the logic of "catching your child being good" described previously. The number of tokens needed to purchase back-up reinforcers can be modified as needed—either decreased if the child is not earning enough to buy back-up reinforcers or increased if the child earns so many that he buys everything available at one time.

I like to use a "layering" process when specifying the amount of tokens required to earn various back-up reinforcers. Layering is analogous to offering bonus rewards. For example, in Figure 3.3, behaviors are grouped according to when they must be performed: morning, afternoon or evening. For morning behaviors, children can exchange one token for 10 minutes of television or video game time (up to 30 minutes total). However, if all three tokens are earned before the timer goes off, a parent will make a special breakfast. The special breakfast represents a "bonus" reward. The same procedure can be used for afternoon and evening behaviors.

At the end of the day I layer by counting up the total number of tokens earned for that day. If the child has earned at least 9 out of the 11 possible tokens for the day, he may get a bonus reward at the end of the day, in addition to the reinforcers available for performing the evening behaviors, such as staying up a half hour later. Alternatively, the bonus for the day may be given the next morning, such as being able to take a special toy to school to play with at recess (it is important to check with your child's teacher about the feasibility of bringing a toy and the teacher's willingness to hold the toy before and after recess).

The final layering of reinforcers can occur at the end of the week. During this time, special reinforcers can be given, such as eating at a restaurant of the child's choice, renting a video, or going to a movie or baseball game. These rewards do cost money and we would not want them available every day. Also, if they were, the child would quickly tire of them and you would have to find even more elaborate things to use as reinforcers. Therefore, out of a possible total of 55 tokens a week (assuming the program is used Monday through Friday with weekends off), if a child earns at least 49 tokens (about 90 percent), he is entitled to select an end-of-the-week bonus reward.

In the sample chart appearing in Figure 3.3, the child earned 20 minutes of TV or Nintendo time for morning behaviors on Monday and Tuesday. He did not receive the morning bonus reward on these two days. However, he did earn all three stars from Wednesday through Friday, so on these days his mother made him a special breakfast. In the case of afternoon behaviors, the child only earned a bonus of playing a game with his mother or father on Friday. For evening behaviors, the child received a bonus reward on Thursday and Friday because he earned four stars on each of these days. The child earned a daily bonus of either staying up an extra half hour, taking a special toy to school the next day, or calling his grandmother on Wednesday, Thursday and Friday. However, the child did not receive a weekly bonus because his weekly total of 45 points was below the established criterion. Remember, you may need to modify the point totals and criteria for rewards.

Other types of behaviors can be added to the star chart in Figure 3.3 or substitutions may be made. For example, you may want to include a half hour of doing homework as one of the afternoon behaviors. Homework is generally completed most successfully when done in the afternoon or early evening, but many children want to put off doing homework until late in the evening. The usual reason is that otherwise they won't have time to play or watch their favorite television shows. As a parent, you need to decide what takes precedence—homework or play. Most parents place homework above playing; yet they also feel sorry for their children if they do not have time to play or watch television after the homework is completed. Just like any other behavior that appears on a star chart, it is important that homework begin at the specified time. Complicated negotiations about alternative times should be avoided, although exceptions can be made in certain situations, such as having to pick up a relative at the airport. If children have activities after school on certain days, the specified time for afternoon and evening behaviors should be modified accordingly. I will provide more information on dealing with homework completion in Chapter 5.

As children get used to the star chart, you can make modifications to simplify its management. For example, instead of setting the timer for every behavior involved in the morning, afternoon or evening, it can be set for just one time during which all behaviors must be performed. However, although it is more work to set the time for individual behaviors, children respond much better when they are trying to "beat the clock" on successive trials. Therefore, it is important not to modify the structure too soon.

There are two drawbacks to using a star chart. First, it is very time-consuming. Although the payoff is great considering the energy previously expended on trying to get your child to perform these behaviors, you still must be prepared to put in a great deal of effort. The second drawback is that older children, those of junior or senior high school age, often find token economies "gimmicky" or childish. For these children, a contract can accomplish the same goals while having more "face validity" to the youngster. In addition, even with younger children, once they have performed the desired behaviors using a token system for a period of time, they too can move to a contract. While it requires some work to set up, a contract can be managed more easily than a token economy.

Contracting with Children

According to the *American Heritage Dictionary*, a contract refers to "an agreement between two or more parties, especially one that is written and enforceable by law." Contracts based on this definition have been used by therapists, teachers and parents to encourage children to perform a variety of behaviors. In fact, I have worked with parents for whom contracting has become the primary method of structuring expectations and interactions between family members. Although a plethora of research studies have documented the effectiveness of contracting, I find parents like this system basically because it is straightforward, logical and relatively easy to implement. However, I must caution you against oversimplification.

Contracting is not as simple as it is often presented, whether used with a delinquent teenager to increase his compliance with curfew and school attendance or to get an otherwise well-behaved 8-year-old to clean her room. Central to the effectiveness of contracts is the ability of both parties to negotiate and compromise. I have found that some parents cannot talk productively with their children because their interactions have become so strained. In these cases, it may be necessary to use a third party to negotiate various aspects of the contract, as I sometimes do with clients. But in most cases, with some simple ground rules, parents and their children can develop a contract without seeing a psychotherapist. In fact, the process of developing a contract can function as a catalyst to more positive parent-child interactions. With this background information, I will now describe a contract and show why contracts work.

What is a Contract?

The definition of a contract cited from the *American Heritage Dictionary* provides a good foundation for our discussion. However, the definition is somewhat simplistic. Therefore, I would like to expand upon it. A *contingency* or *behavioral contract*, is a written document that specifies a contingent relation between the performance of specified behaviors and access to a specified reward. The word contingent, in this context, simply refers to an if-then relation—*if* you clean your room, *then* you can go out and play. The key point is that in order for the child to go out and play, she must first clean her room.

A defining feature of a contract is that it specifies how two or more people will behave toward each other. This feature is often ignored when parents or teachers use contracts with children. Typically, we want to focus only on the child's behavior. Contracts are doomed to fail unless the parent's behavior is also specified. A *quid pro quo* agreement makes the parents' and child's behavior dependent on each other. Although parents initially want the contract to stipulate only what their child will do, their own behavior must also be part of the contract. Therefore, the contract includes both the mother's and father's behavior as well as their child's. Specifically, if Mom washes the dishes, the child dries them, and Dad puts them away. Contracts must be based on this behavior-exchange principle.

In addition to the if-then rule implicit in behavior exchange, contracts must be written down. Verbal agreements can be considered contracts in the legal sense, but in making a verbal contract with children, there are two drawbacks. First, the act of signing the contract and the physical document itself are integral to the effectiveness of contracting. Second, in the absence of a written document, it is easy for parents and children to get into arguments regarding the specifics of the contract. That is, without a written record, it is difficult to remember the specific components of the contract and, consequently, these become open to reinterpretation.

Components of a Contract

In their book, *Sign Here: A Contracting Book for Children and Their Parents,* Jill Dardig and William Heward described three components that must appear in a contract: a description of the task, a description of the reward and a task record. In Figure 3.4, I have provided a sample contract containing these three components to help a 16-year-old girl be home by 10:00 p.m. on weeknights. Notice how the contract is divided into three parts: task, reward and task record.

The task

The task side of the contract consists of four parts. *Who* is the person who will be performing the task and earning the reward—in this case, Nancy. *What* refers to the task the person must perform. Nancy must be home by 10:00 p.m. four out of five weeknights. Notice that the *what* in this contract only applied to four nights. This lets Nancy know that she can be late one night and still earn the weekly reward. Otherwise, if she was late one night toward the beginning of the week, she would lose the reward at the end of the week and, therefore, would have little reason to be on time for the rest

CONTRACT	
Task	**Task**
Who: Nancy	**Who:** Mom and Dad
What: Be home by 10:00 p.m. four out of five weeknights	**What:** Use the family car or have a friend spend the night
When: Sunday through Thursday	**When:** Saturday night
How Well: Nancy will be in the door at 10:00 p.m. She has a 10-minute grace period. She must call by 9:30 to ask for an extension. If the extension is not granted, she must still be home by 10:00 p.m.	**How Much:** Nancy can use the car Saturday night from 6:00 p.m. to midnight. Mom or Dad will see that car has sufficient amount of gas. Nancy can have a friend spend the night. Mom and Dad will buy a pizza and rent two videos.

Bonus Reward: If Nancy is home by 10:00 p.m. all five nights, then she can stay out an extra half hour later on Friday and Saturday night.

_____   **Date:** ___May 6, 1994___

_____   **Date:** ___May 6, 1994___

_____   **Date:** ___May 6, 1994___

Task Record

S	M	T	W	TH	S	M	T	W	TH
*		*	*	*	*	*	*	*	*
*	*	*	*	*	*		*	*	*

Figure 3.4. Sample contract for a 16-year-old girl.

of the week. Notice from the task record that, in fact, Nancy was late the first Monday the contract was in effect. Yet she was on time the remaining days, so along with being on time the previous Sunday, she still earned the weekly reward. *When* identifies the time during which the task must be completed—

Sunday through Thursday. *How well* specifies the acceptable criteria for completing the task. In this instance, Nancy must be in the door at 10:00 p.m. She has a 10-minute grace period, which means that she can be up to 10 minutes late without penalty. The grace period is one way to eliminate squabbling over whether being 30 seconds late, 1 minute late, or 2 minutes late constitutes failure to perform the task. In addition, Nancy has the option to call by 9:30 to request an extension (for example, if band practice is running late or if the person taking her home has car trouble). This stipulation is another way to avoid arguments over excuses. The information contained in *how well* is the most important part of the contract. Without this specific information, contracts are doomed to fail.

The reward

The reward side of the contract requires as much specification as the task side. Reward statements such as "can stay up later" or "can rent a video when I get a chance" are too general and thus not fair to the child. The *who* on the reward side refers to the parents who judge whether the task was completed correctly and who deliver the rewards. *What* is the reward—using the family car or having a friend spend the night. *When* specifies the time the reward can be obtained by the child. As with any use of reinforcement, the reward must be administered *after* the child completes the task—no exceptions. *How much* refers to the amount of reward that can be earned by completing the task. Note that when specifying how much, parental expectations also are described. Remember, a contract will only work if both the child's and the parents' behaviors are specified. Therefore, in this contract the *quid pro quo* agreement makes Nancy's behavior of coming home on time dependent upon her parents' behavior. In this case, her parents must let her use the car, ensure it has gas, buy a pizza and rent a video.

The contract in Figure 3.4 also includes a bonus reward—Nancy can stay out an extra half hour on Friday and Saturday nights if she is home by 10:00 p.m. the other five days. A bonus reward is a way to "layer" reinforcement—a concept I introduced when describing how to use a star chart. By layering, we include various ways in which children can earn a variety of rewards, thereby increasing the likelihood that the child will perform the specified task. If needed, another layer of rewards could be built into Nancy's contract. Note that she only has access to a reward at the end of the week. This time frame may work well for Nancy, but not for other children who may need more immediate reinforcers, even in a contract. Therefore, we could build into the contract appearing in Figure 3.4 a condition whereby Nancy would earn an extra half hour talking on the phone or listening to her stereo every night that she was home by 10:00 p.m. Under this condition, Nancy could earn a reward every night, at the end of the week, and a bonus reward as well. In other words, she is being presented with both short-term and long-term rewards contingent upon her daily performance of being home on time.

The task record

The last component of the contract in Figure 3.4 is a task record—a place to mark the child's progress. In their book *Applied Behavior Analysis*, John Cooper, Timothy Heron and William Heward said that having a place to mark progress on a contract serves two purposes. First, recording the child's successful completion of the task provides her with immediate feedback about her progress toward obtaining the reward. Parents also receive feedback, which helps them focus on positive aspects of their child's behavior. In this way, the task record helps remind both parents and children of the contract on a daily basis.

Second, making a mark on the contract every time the task is completed correctly represents a kind of token economy system. These marks, such as the stars on the contract in Figure 3.4, bridge the gap between each completion of a task and presentation of the reward at the end of the day or week. Marking the contract in this way increases a child's motivation to perform the task until she has earned the reward. It is also helpful if parents place little sticky notes at the bottom of the contract, by the task record, with short messages of congratulations and encouragement for the child. Although not formally a part of the contract, such notes of praise serve as a further way to layer rewards.

Why Do Contracts Work?

The principle behind a contract appears deceptively simple—application of reinforcement. However, in most contracts the reward is too delayed to reinforce the specific behavior directly. Remember, for a reinforcer to be maximally effective, it should be delivered *directly* after the behavior occurs. Because it is not always possible to reinforce a child's behavior directly after it occurs, I introduced the "star chart," which is fashioned after the token economy. In a token economy, the tokens are presented directly after the behavior occurs, thus bridging the gap between the behavior and the subsequent reinforcer. A task record in a contract functions as a kind of token. Nevertheless, the reward is often too delayed to function as an effective reinforcer.

In addition, I have seen things function as reinforcers in a contract that were totally ineffective when presented without a contract. For example, I worked with a teenage boy who refused to bring home his homework. Even on the rare occasions when he did bring his homework home, he would refuse to complete the assignments, or tell his parents he had completed them when, in fact, he had not. An interview with the boy indicated that he enjoyed listening to music and talking on the phone to his friends—two typically motivating activities for teenagers. Therefore, I suggested that the parents make listening to music and talking on the phone contingent upon their son's bringing home and completing his homework assignments. This program had no effect on the boy's rate of homework completion. When I next saw the boy he told me that he could live without music and talking on the phone, that "it was no big deal," and that "sitting in my room reading magazines was better than doing homework any day."

My next move was to use a contract with this boy. I spent about an hour with the boy and his parents. When it came time to specify the *what* on the reward side of the contract, the boy came up with the suggestion of being able to listen to music and talk on the phone. I thought to myself, "This is crazy. Here's another bright, manipulative teenager trying to get the best of his parents and me. "Nevertheless, both his parents and I agreed to this reward since it was the boy's suggestion. To our surprise the boy worked diligently to complete his homework in order to earn the use of his stereo and phone every evening. I have subsequently observed how something that did not function as a reinforcer when presented immediately after a behavior or task was performed, worked when incorporated into a contract. So how do contracts work? Obviously reinforcement is involved, but in a more subtle manner than one would expect. There seem to be at least two prominent factors that cause a contract to be effective when a reinforcer without a contract is ineffective.

First, B.F. Skinner, the noted behavioral psychologist, suggested that a contract works because it is based on the principle of rule-governed behavior. That is, a contract constitutes a statement of a strong rule: performance of a certain behavior or task will produce a specified positive outcome or reward. The contract itself serves as a cue for this rule. Therefore, presentation of a reinforcer that typically is too delayed to be effective, such as using the family car on Saturday night, can, nevertheless, exert control over behavior, such as coming home on weeknights by 10:00 p.m., by acting as a reminder to the child that every day she performs the behavior correctly, she is another day closer to receiving the reward. The child, in essence, is providing her own encouragement. Such verbal encouragement takes the form of covert self-statements—that is, statements said to oneself. The use of self-statements that cue performance of a behavior or task is a central focus of the next chapter on teaching children self-control.

Second, it may be that the reward has some, although very little, control over the performance of the specific task or behavior. However, the major reason why a task or behavior is performed is that the contract makes the agreement public. Therefore, I suggest to parents that once a contract is successfully negotiated and signed, it should be placed on the refrigerator door where all concerned parties can see the agreement and their signatures. Consequently, it may be that the behavior or task is performed to escape "feeling guilty." Performing at a level below what was stipulated in the contract produces covert guilt statements that can be escaped only by better performance. Under contractual arrangements, the child is involved in coming up with behaviors specified in the contract, agrees to perform them, helps think of appropriate rewards, and finally signs the contract. In other words, the child has assumed a degree of "ownership" for the contract and failing to complete the task can be traced back to the child—there is little opportunity to come up with excuses for not performing the behavior or task. Therefore, being aware of this, the child tells herself that in order to avoid feeling guilty, she must perform the specified behavior or task. Again, the type of statements a child tells herself plays a prominent role in performing the behavior or task specified in the contract.

Negotiating a Contract

One of the key elements in developing a contract is the willingness of both parents and children to negotiate. Without negotiation, no contract can be successful. Any contract that imposes the parents' desires on the child without acknowledging his desires is doomed to fail. In fact, such agreements are not contracts since the child does not have the freedom to help determine the terms and conditions, and may even be forced to sign or accept it. I have seen this happen numerous times both with parents developing "contracts" with their children and with teachers doing the same with their students.

A friend of mine once told me he had developed a contract with his 12-year-old son to cut the lawn on Saturday morning so he could play soccer with his friends Saturday afternoon. My friend wrote the contract and had his son sign it. It didn't work and he couldn't understand why. I talked to his son and found out that his friends played soccer on Saturday morning, not in the afternoon. In the afternoon, most of his friends had chores to complete or errands to run with their parents. His father stated that he didn't want the lawn cut Saturday afternoon or any time Sunday because that's when he liked to work in the yard planting flowers, trimming and pruning. My friend wanted the lawn cut before he worked in the yard. His son obviously wanted to cut the lawn Saturday afternoon or Sunday morning so he could be with his friends Saturday morning. My friend knew this, so he wrote the contract himself to save the hassle of arguing with his son. The contract failed for this very reason. Of course, a compromise could have been reached. For example, his son could mow the lawn Friday after school. Yet this obvious solution was not thought of because the son was not involved in the process of negotiating the contract.

I have seen the same type of problem occur in our schools. A teacher once photocopied a contract she had developed and required her fifth-grade students to sign it the first week of class. The contract stipulated that each student would complete and turn in 10 extra-credit math problems by the end of the week in order to have a popcorn party the last 15 minutes of school on Friday. She couldn't understand why most students were not turning in more extra-credit work on Friday. What this teacher did not realize was that the students were left out of the "loop" for helping to decide the task and reward.

I later helped a teacher develop an effective classwide contract using the following negotiation procedure. She divided the class into groups of four students and asked each group to generate a list of five tasks related to the mathematics lesson for the week and five possible rewards. Each group presented its tasks and rewards to the other groups. The teacher served as facilitator and wrote each group's tasks and rewards on the chalkboard for everyone to see. The students then ranked the tasks and rewards in order of their preferences. Finally, the teacher selected the five most popular tasks and rewards and randomly assigned one task and one reward to each day. Any reward that was selected by all the students was provided at the end of the week.

The previous example illustrates an important aspect of negotiation—facilitating back-and-forth communication designed to reach an agreement when you and your child have some interests that are shared and others that are opposed. In their book, *Getting to Yes*, Roger Fisher and William Ury stressed the importance of not bargaining over positions as the key to successful negotiation. It is unlikely that parents and children will make converts of each other. In fact, the more you defend your position, the more committed you become to it. Parents and children each try to "save face" by refusing to change their respective positions. Although the purpose of a contract is to bring parents and children together and, indirectly, enhance the relationship with each other, arguing over positions damages relationships. Positional bargaining becomes a contest of will. And parents always want to win—otherwise, they believe their authority and control over their children will erode. How many times have you had a discussion with your spouse that focused on "not giving in" or "not sending the wrong message" to your child?

On the other hand, being nice is not the answer either. Parents often realize that arguing over positions with their child takes a toll on the relationship. Therefore, they hope to avoid an argument by trying to be nice. This "parents as friends" approach results in parents making concessions and "trusting" the child to follow through in order to avoid confrontation.

Although this approach may produce a quick contract, the agreement is not likely to be kept. The child is reinforced for being manipulative and will come to view the process of contracting as a means of attaining a victory over the parents. Parents, in turn, will come to distrust their child and view the goal of contracting in terms of the concessions they can get from their children as a condition of the relationship.

Contracts do not have to end in one-sided agreements in which one party feels used or manipulated. Successful negotiation leads to successful contracts. Four basic principles of negotiation described by Fisher and Ury help in the process of developing fair contracts.

Separate the child from the problem

First, it is important for parents to separate their children from the problem. We have strong emotional reactions to our children, especially when they have been misbehaving. And, let's face it, if you are developing a contract with your child, you are trying to improve his behavior. Therefore, there's a good chance that you're angry at the way he has been behaving. Unfortunately, emotions frequently become embroiled with the specific goals each party is trying to achieve. Therefore, both parents and children should view themselves as working together to tackle the problem, not each other. The old adage parents are fond of telling their children, "I don't dislike you, just your behavior," applies here.

Focus on interests rather than positions

The second point is to focus on interests, not positions. When parents and children fall into the trap of trying to negotiate a position, it obscures the interests that both parents and children may have in common. For example, a child and parent may share the common interest of arguing about the condition of the child's room. The parent's position may be that the room needs to be cleaned. The child's position may be that since it is her room, she should be able to keep it in whatever shape she likes. No contract is likely to produce lasting effects when these two positions are the focus of the negotiation. Instead, the underlying interest both parties have in common—arguing less with each other—should be the focus of the negotiation. When this happens, parent and child can work together to reach this common interest.

Generate a variety of tasks and rewards

The third principle is to generate a variety of possible tasks and rewards before deciding on any one specific task or reward. Both parents and children will feel some pressure when they are developing a contract—each side wants to make a good showing. However, having a lot at stake can stifle creativity. Also, searching for the one right task or reward can interfere with creativity. It is possible to offset this problem by setting a designated time within which to think up a wide variety of tasks and rewards—such as the brainstorming procedure I helped the teacher use with her class. The goal of this procedure was to help the students invent options for mutual gain before trying to reach an agreement.

Base results on an objective standard

The fourth point is to insist that the results of the negotiation be based on some objective standard. Throughout this chapter, I have emphasized the importance of clarifying performance or task standards. By discussing standards with a child, rather than focusing on what a child is willing or unwilling to do, neither parent nor child need give in to the other—both can defer to a fair solution. For example, many children balk at having to "clean their room" because they believe that their parents have an unrealistic definition of "clean." However, the standard for clean can be negotiated and agreed upon, making arguments about compliance with the contract less likely to occur. Furthermore, when such arguments do occur, the parent can refer the child back to the contract, rather than defending the importance of a "clean" room.

These four principles will help ensure that a contract is properly negotiated and freely agreed on by both child and parent. Negotiation must be systematic and precise. As the adult, the parent has an obligation to ensure that the negotiation session is productive. Below is a step-by-step negotiation procedure parents can use with their children. These steps are based on the negotiation process developed by James Walker and Thomas Shea in their book *Behavior Management*.

1. Parent explains purpose of the meeting
2. Parent gives simple definition of a "contract"
3. Parent and child discuss tasks
4. Parent and child discuss rewards
5. Parent and child agree on ratio of task to reward
6. Parent and child agree on time to be allotted to perform task
7. Parent and child identify criteria for performance of task
8. Parent and child agree on delivery of reward
9. Parent and child agree on data for renegotiating contract
10. Parent and child write contract
11. Parent and child read contract aloud
12. Parent elicits child's verbal affirmation of contract terms

13. Parent and child sign contract
14. Parent congratulates child for making contract

Successful negotiation goes a long way toward improving the relationship between parents and children. In this respect, a contract not only serves as a method for changing children's behavior, but also as a way to enhance communication between parents and children by focusing on problem solving rather than blaming.

Putting a Contract Together: Specific Guidelines

Once the behaviors or tasks, the rewards and the task record have been negotiated, the contract is written and all parties involved sign it. A variety of guidelines and rules for using contracting have been published. Most authors make similar recommendations. However, Cooper, Heron and Heward stress that three are especially important.

The contract must be fair

There must be a fair relationship between the amount of the task to be performed and the amount of the reward. Giving too much of a reward results in a child satiating. Giving too little, on the other hand, frustrates a child. Remember, contracts should result in a win-win situation, unlike contracts between industry and organized labor in which each party seeks maximum advantage over the other.

The contract must be clear

One of the desirable side effects of contracts is that they specify each person's expectations exactly. When a parent's expectations are clearly stated, the performance of many children automatically improves. Ironically, many children are more willing to be specific than adults, who often claim the privilege of changing their minds.

The contract must be honest

When the task is successfully completed, the reward must be delivered at the time and in the amount specified. In my experience, parents break with honesty more often than with fairness or clarity. Parents are not trying to swindle or cheat their child. On the contrary, such breaks with honesty most often happen because parents promise too much.

Disappointments are a part of life, and children must learn to handle them. However, a child's first contract designed to change an important behavior is not the place for such learning to occur. Therefore, parents must guard against making unrealistic promises. Similarly, parents do a child a disservice by delivering a reward even though the task was not completed as specified in the contract. When this occurs, a child is being rewarded for performing poorly, which increases the likelihood that the child later will make excuses for his performance or try to manipulate obtaining the reward without actually earning it.

Summary

The techniques presented in this chapter focused on the use of positive reinforcement. They have the direct effect of helping a child increase the frequency or duration of appropriate behavior. Further, they have the indirect effect of focusing parents' attention away from children's negative behavior and on to their positive behavior. And in some instances, as in contracting, the quality of the parent-child relationship is enhanced simply because the two parties engage in the process of negotiation. These techniques represent positive and effective ways to get children to perform more appropriate behaviors; however, they rely on the parent for implementation and monitoring. As children grow older, we want them to move away from depending on a parent to specify what to do and which reward they will receive, and begin taking on this responsibility themselves. Independence, pride in accomplishment and self-motivation, to name but a few, are traits parents want to see their children develop. For some children, this process occurs quite naturally. Other children, however, require direct help in order to become self-reliant. The next chapter focuses on teaching children self-control.

4

Teaching Children
Self-Control

In response to the information and recommendations presented in the previous chapters, some readers might express the concern that parents are made to assume the responsibility for changing their children's behavior. Several authors have indirectly chided recommendations such as these as being simplistic and as overindulging children. The popular author John Rosemund recently wrote a column emphasizing that parents should not give children "too much" attention and that too much attention is as destructive as giving children too much food. Instead, Rosemund recommends that the focus should be on teaching children self-control. Numerous parenting books describe ways to teach children self-reliance, self-discipline, self-concept, and the big "R" word—*responsibility*. Ironically, teaching self-discipline and self-reliance is not at odds with the information presented in the first three chapters. In fact, the recommendations offered in Chapter 3 are prerequisites for teaching children self-control.

Briefly, the suggestions I have presented are designed to help children make choices and assume responsibility for their own behavior and its consequences rather than to blame parents. Earlier I described how to make reinforcers available to children *contingent upon* performing some task or behavior. The child is free to either perform the behavior or not perform the behavior—no punishment is involved. However, available reinforcers provide incentives for the child to make "wise" or "responsible" choices. This approach makes it more difficult for parents to become scapegoats for a child's refusal to complete an agreed-upon behavior or task while complaining about the unfairness of not receiving the reward. Through the techniques described in the previous chapter, children learn that their behavior has a direct effect on the consequences they receive—both positive and negative.

Understandably, once children learn that a particular behavior consistently brings a reward or, conversely, that a certain behavior results in a reward being withheld, they are motivated to regulate their behavior so that it brings the desired outcome. For example, children who know that they will be rewarded by their parents for receiving a good grade on the weekly spelling test may arrange study sessions for themselves, and perhaps even deprive themselves of desirable activities, until they master their spelling words. Once children begin the process of self-control and find that it starts to bring them personal and social rewards, they are motivated to continue practicing self-control in the future. They set goals of desirable conduct for themselves, monitor their behavior more closely, chastise themselves when they fall short of their standards, and praise themselves when they match or exceed their standards for appropriate behavior. The methods presented in Chapter 3 are important because (1) they help children identify what behaviors are essential to self-regulate and (2) they provide the necessary support system to sustain children's efforts at self-regulation. In essence, children adopt self-regulatory systems because they recognize that, in the long run, self-control can produce positive effects.

It is when children are insulated from the consequences of their behavior that they become overly reliant on their parents and lack sufficient self-control. However, it is rare that children appreciate relying on their parents. More often, they react to over-reliance by blaming the parent. Unfortunately, however, parents easily fall into the trap of taking on too much responsibility for their children for an obvious reason: we want to insulate our children from experiencing too much of the pain and hurt that the world dishes out.

I worked with a family where this problem was quite evident. At the time, the daughter, a 17-year-old high school senior, had a strained relationship with her mother. The big complaint from the mother was that her daughter never treated her with respect but felt entitled to everything while giving nothing in return. The mother described a typical situation where her daughter was angry with her for not buying a couple of frozen pizzas at the grocery store. According to the mother, the daughter started yelling as she stepped over three bags of groceries on the floor rather than picking them up and placing them on the kitchen counter. The mother also related how her daughter would be furious if she failed to get her up for school if she overslept, yet would yell at her if she came into her bedroom on other occasions to wake her up. It seemed that the mother couldn't win—her daughter had her in a catch-22 situation.

Parents get caught in such situations by taking on too much responsibility for their children. While talking to the mother, I found out that she would do such things as going to her daughter's school to pick up her homework if she forgot it, paying for any library fines she acquired, filling out job applications for her, and calling to make appointments to get her hair cut

These were but a few of the ways in which she insulated her daughter from assuming responsibility for her actions. Consequently, the daughter would blame her mother for any bad thing that happened to her. Although this did not make for a good relationship between mother and daughter, it resulted in two more serious consequences.

First, the daughter's ability to move toward independence was impaired. Because she was insulated from failure, she also was insulated from success. And when she did experience success, she attributed it to factors external to her own ability. For example, when the daughter got a good grade on a test, she thought it was because the teacher was in a good mood when he graded the papers rather than because she studied hard. Second, and more important, such reliance on others severely impaired the daughter's self-esteem. One way to view self-esteem is to see it as a measurement of how many demonstrations of love and affection we receive from others. Some people ignore their own accomplishments just as they blame others for their failures. Often these people suffer from depression. They simultaneously feel helpless to act on their own, are angry at themselves for having to rely on others, and yet are scared at the prospect of significant others not being there to assume responsibility for them.

Parents can help break this vicious circle by initially using star charts and later contracts with their children. I describe children in this situation as lacking self-control. Although they can behave impulsively, I am using the word "self-control" in a more global sense. Self-control means being able to monitor and evaluate one's own behavior and its effect on others. It has to do with developing intrinsic motivation—the ability to reinforce oneself, interpreting situations logically so as to get only reasonably upset when things happen rather than getting overly upset and behaving inappropriately. It also has to do with viewing one's self-worth as a byproduct of one's total experiences rather than an isolated incident.

The techniques presented in Chapter 3 began to address each of these factors in the following ways. First, any type of star chart or contract helps children monitor and evaluate their own behavior since they provide a written record of the child's behaviors and performance on the tasks. Every time a child performs a behavior, a star is placed on a chart, thereby increasing her awareness of the behavior. And by looking at the number of stars from day to day, she is able to evaluate her performance on an ongoing basis. When they earn a reward, children are more likely to feel a sense of pride. "Feeling a sense of pride" can be defined as children telling themselves they did well.

lications of reinforcement, particularly through star charts and con-
in the process of moving a child from relying on the parent
liant. Children begin this process by learning that their
others' choices—directly impact their ability to get what

they want. Getting what one wants in an appropriate fashion is a way of conceptualizing the attainment of goals. Yet star charts and contracts are only a first step. The process of teaching children self-control requires that children learn to interpret situations sensibly and engage in activities that increase or decrease the occurrence of certain behaviors or performance of certain tasks. Much of the process involves children becoming aware of how they interpret events in their life which, in turn, lead to an emotional and behavioral reaction.

What is Self-Control?

Joey and his sister, Susie, are sitting at the kitchen table. "Go on, take another cookie, Sis," urges Joey with a mischievous smile.

"But Mom said we could only have two cookies after dinner," replies Susie.

"Well, Mom isn't in the kitchen now, she's on the phone in the bedroom. And besides, by the time she gets off the phone, you will have eaten them," exclaims Joey confidently.

"I guess so," says Susie. "They sure are good."

Susie grabs two cookies from the cookie jar. Joey smiles at her and grabs a handful himself. They both race downstairs and proceed to polish off about six cookies apiece.

Later Susie complains to her mother of having a stomach ache. After some questioning, Susie admits having eaten close to a half dozen cookies. "Susie," her mother begins sympathetically, "didn't you suspect that eating that many cookies would give you a stomach ache?"

"No Mom, I didn't think of that. And besides, I just couldn't help myself, they were so good," replies Susie.

Daniel was always getting in trouble for fighting with his brother, Milt. It was easy for Milt to push his brother's buttons. Before dinner one evening Daniel's younger brother, Jason, asked if he would play a game of chess with him. "Sure," Daniel responded, "set up the chess board and pieces on the coffee table."

Just as Daniel was ready to sit down, Milt squeezed into the seat and said to Jason, "I'll play with you, Jason. Daniel sucks at chess. Besides, you don't want to take advantage of this whimpy nerd." Before Jason had a chance to feel smug over this comment, Daniel had flipped the chess pieces on the floor and tossed the chess board at his brother like a frisbee.

"Didn't hurt a bit, butt wipe," exclaimed Milt, running up the stairs, two at a time, heading for his bedroom.

"You're dead meat, jerk," yelled Daniel as he bounded up the stairs after his brother. Daniel got in one good kick to Milt's calf before his brother slammed and locked his bedroom door. For his trouble, Daniel was grounded by his parents for one week.

Many of the problems of self-control are similar to the problem faced by Susie and Daniel. They involve self-restraint—learning to decrease excessive behaviors that have immediate gratification, such as excessive eating or becoming aggressive with a sibling. Other problems of self-control require behavior change in the opposite direction—responses that need to be increased, such as studying, exercising, being assertive and performing household chores.

Many people speak as though there's some magical force within us—called *willpower*—that is responsible for overcoming such problems. In part, we probably believe this, because parents often tell their children things like, "If you had more willpower you could restrain yourself from eating too much." Or "If you had more willpower you could simply ignore your brother when he bothers you." Or "If you had more willpower you would study harder and get better grades." Most children have heard such advice many times. Unfortunately, it's usually not very helpful advice, because the parent offering it almost always neglects to tell the child how to get more of this so-called "willpower."

I alluded previously to the various ways authors have described self-control. Teaching self-reliance, self-discipline, goal-setting, values and responsibility are some of the ways self-control has been conceptualized. Unfortunately, there are as many definitions of self-control as there are books written to teach it. I would like to discuss two different concepts of self-control that I think contain useful information. The first focuses primarily on the consequences of behavior and performance, the other views feedback as the major component of self-control.

The Consequences of Self-Control

In their book *Behavior Modification*, Garry Martin and Joseph Pear describe a model of self-control that focuses on the impact of short-term versus long-term positive and negative consequences of engaging in particular behaviors. For example, why is obesity one of the major health problems facing Americans today? In part, it's because eating is a behavior for which the immediate consequences are positive—food tastes good. Although potential delayed consequences of overeating are clearly negative, immediate consequences bring about a response much more strongly than do delayed ones. Thus, when the immediate consequences are reinforcing and the delayed consequences are punishing, the immediate reinforcers frequently win out. That's why Susie ate too many cookies and Daniel hit his brother. The immediate gratification each received outweighed the delayed consequences of getting a stomach ache, or being grounded.

Many self-control-related problems experienced by adults in addition to overeating stem from this fact. For example, the immediate consequences of smoking are positive for most smokers. Punishers such as shortness of breath, sore throat and coughing, not to mention possible lung cancer and coronary disease, are long delayed. Similarly, the immediate enjoyable consequences of drinking alcohol override the delayed punishing consequences of a hangover. The immediate reinforcing consequences from having a sexual liaison with your best friend's spouse may override the delayed hurt and emotional anguish when your friend finds out and is no longer your friend.

The effect of immediate versus delayed consequences can be observed in other self-control problems. Why are some children so hesitant to learn how to dive? To take up a new sport? To make new friends? To try something different? This type of self-control problem occurs because learning new skills frequently involves minor, but immediate, punishing consequences such as looking foolish, not knowing what to do, or experiencing "put-downs" from onlookers. The potentially reinforcing consequences, on the other hand, are delayed. After all, it takes a while to get good enough at an activity that you can really enjoy. Other self-control problems involve immediate weak punishers that are more desirable than delayed, but stronger punishers. For example, many people postpone going to the dentist. The immediate weak punisher is that it can hurt. So many people avoid going even though the delayed consequences are much more aversive, such as getting teeth pulled or having a root canal.

A model of self-control that examines the short-term versus the long-term positive and negative consequences of a child's behavior must take into account several factors. The first two considerations have been described in Chapters 2 and 3: clear specification of the target behavior to be controlled and application of reinforcement techniques to manage the problem behavior. On the surface, this approach to self-control seems deceptively simple: self-control consists of doing something (applying reinforcement techniques) to increase the chances that a child will do something else (exhibit a new behavior). A child must behave in some way that arranges the environment to manage subsequent behavior. But here is where the process becomes messy: it means a child must emit a controlling behavior to effect a change in a behavior to be controlled.

This process presents the problem of controlling the controlling behavior. That is, since this model of self-control implies that some components of a child's behavior control other components of his behavior, the question arises: What is to control the controlling behavior? If the answer is that the child is to control his own controlling behavior, we are really saying that the controlling behavior is itself to be controlled by controlling behavior. But then the question is: What is to control that controlling behavior? Thus, with self-control, the problem of controlling the controlling behavior is always present and must be taken into account. If this description sounds like the chicken-and-egg argument, then you're beginning to see the difficulties involved in teaching children self-control. Not all conceptualizations of self-control, however, are concerned with the problem of determining an initial behavior or response to control the targeted behavior. One model, in particular, views self-control as a closed system that is based on the child's giving himself feedback about his performance.

Self-Control as Feedback

In order for a child to obtain feedback about her performance, she must go through a process of observing her own behavior, evaluating her performance against some standard, and providing consequences for her behavior in accord with her performance. Since this process is believed to occur covertly, this model of self-control is not bound by environmental consequences.

Self-monitoring

The first step in this process is for the child to become aware of her behavior. In essence, the child must self-monitor her performance, asking herself if she engaged in a certain behavior and making a mark on a piece of paper to indicate whether the behavior occurred or not. Techniques for using self-monitoring will be described shortly. Suffice it to say here that we all engage in various forms of self-monitoring. A golfer who keeps score is self-monitoring. Health clubs commonly display charts where their members can record the number of exercises they have completed and the time spent doing them. Dieting guru Richard Simmons incorporates aspects of self-monitoring in his Deal-a-Meal program. In this program, when an individual eats something from one of the food groups, she must remove a card representing that food group from a pocket on one side of a folder and place it in a pocket on the other side of the folder to indicate that no more food from that group can be consumed for that day. Other public figures have described how they have practiced self-monitoring. The noted author Irving Wallace related the following about his work habits:

> I maintained work charts while writing my first four published books. These charts showed the date I started each chapter, the date I finished it, and the number of pages written in that period. With my fifth book, I started keeping a more detailed chart, which also showed how many pages I had written by the end of every working day. I am not sure why I started keeping such records. I suspect that it was because, as a free-lance writer, entirely on my own, without employer or deadline, I wanted to create a discipline for myself... A chart on the wall served as such a discipline, its figures scolding me or encouraging me.

In my private practice, I occasionally work with individuals who want to quit smoking. One of the first "tasks" I ask these individuals to do is to keep a small piece of paper between the cellophane wrapping and the cigarette pack itself. They are to pull out this piece of paper and make a tally mark on it every time they smoke a cigarette.

The interesting aspect of self-monitoring is that by simply doing it, one can change one's behavior. Individuals *react* to recording the type of food they eat, the number of cigarettes smoked or the number of pages written by changing these behaviors. In the first two examples, the behavior change involves decreasing inappropriate behaviors and, in the last example, increasing an appropriate behavior. The technical term for this phenomenon is *reactivity*, since the individual's reaction to self-monitoring consists of changing the behavior being self-monitored.

There are three reasons why the simple act of keeping a record of our behavior has a positive impact upon changing the behavior being monitored: (1) it changes the consequences of the behavior, (2) it results in our feeling guilty, and (3) it sets in motion a process of evaluating and reinforcing our self—the feedback process described above.

The first explanation I offered for self-control problems was that individuals engage in certain behaviors because the delayed consequences are much weaker than the immediate consequences. In the case of smoking and overeating, the short-term consequences of experiencing pleasure are much stronger than the long-term negative consequences to one's health. However, when a person records daily the number of cigarettes smoked or the amount of food eaten, she is providing herself with short-term negative consequences in the form of a repeated awareness of the behavior, in addition to the short-term pleasurable consequences.

Similarly, children who play instead of studying or cleaning their room are doing so because the short-term consequences are positive—it's fun to play—whereas the long-term negative consequences of getting a bad grade or being grounded are too far off in the future to impact upon their behavior. Having children keep track of the time they study daily, however, provides them with immediate feedback to combat the short-term pleasure they receive from not engaging in the desired behavior. The greater attention given to short-term than to long-term consequences is why it is usually ineffective for a parent to say to a child, "I'll give you $20 at the end of the semester if you can get a 'B' in math." The positive long-term consequences of receiving money are too far removed from the short-term pleasure of engaging in activities other than studying. However, recording every grade received on a math assignment, quiz and test on a chart gives a child immediate feedback.

The second reason why self-monitoring works is that it produces feelings of guilt. When a child records on a chart that he did not complete his chores, for example, he expresses a private covert guilt that can be escaped only by better performance. Learning to feel guilty when doing something wrong and limiting one's rewards to occasions when they are deserved are crucial ingredients in helping children develop self-control and ultimately achieve a degree of successful socialization.

Children begin learning to feel guilty at an early age. Most of us think of guilt as an unwanted emotion—one that our mothers are good at eliciting. Obviously, feeling too much guilt can become debilitating—the old saying "guilt is the give that keeps on giving" being an example of its negative connotations. Yet guilt can serve a positive function in teaching children self-control. Because misbehavior typically is followed by some sign of parental displeasure, either a disapproving look, application of punishment or withdrawal of attention for a period of time, children come to experience anxiety in the form of guilt. The anxiety often can be elevated by verbalizing self-critical remarks. In addition, when children begin to empathize with another's distress and believe they are somehow responsible for that distress, they will begin to feel guilt. Thus, in order for a child to feel guilty over a completed or a contemplated transgression, he must be able to respond empathically to the plight or distress of someone who might be harmed by the transgression and realize that he could be the cause of the other person's negative state.

At the risk of falling back into a chicken-and-egg explanation, we must try to answer how children develop empathy toward others and feel distress over their misfortunes. Just receiving their parents' disapproval for transgressing is not sufficient. In fact, there is no research evidence to suggest that children whose parents rely on punishment and love-withdrawal techniques demonstrate the most guilt after transgressing. Instead, it is children whose parents spell out to them the causal role they can play in producing harmful outcomes for others who display the most guilt and who apologize, confess and accept responsibility. By being exposed to positive, proactive child-rearing practices, children develop clear conceptions of what is and is not expected of them and, consequently, develop standards of conduct that they compare to their actual behavior. The process of comparing one's behavior to some standard of conduct is referred to as "self-evaluation."

Self-evaluation

According to the feedback model of self-control, children are more likely to evaluate their performance against socially accepted standards when they are confronted with information regarding their performance. Consequently, self-monitoring is considered a prerequisite for children to engage in self-evaluation. That is, self-evaluation involves a comparison between self-monitoring information and the child's standard for the behavior. In essence, the child is forced to examine the degree to which a match exists between what is done and what should be done. Children are observing their behavior and deciding whether or not their behavior is satisfactory. A judgment that one's behavior reaches or exceeds a desired level leads to covert self-rewarding verbalizations (e.g., "I did a good job cleaning my room") that serve to reinforce chore completion. In fact, when children observe that their progress is satisfactory, they tend to adjust their self-evaluative standards upward, requiring greater levels of self-control before rewarding themselves the next time. When, on the other hand, children fall short of a desired behavior, they try to improve their behavior or else lower their standards. Interestingly, children would rather have adults impose standards and evaluate their performance than lower the standards they apply to themselves.

The noted psychiatrist William Glasser discussed the importance of children evaluating their own performance in his book *The Quality School.* By evaluating their performance, children begin to see that what they do—their behavior—has quality. For example, a parent may ask his child to evaluate how well she cleaned her room. Each behavior involved in cleaning her bedroom could be rated on a 1 to 10 scale. The child is told to circle the number across from each task to indicate how well she performed that task. In addition, the child could rate the overall quality of how well she cleaned her room. An example of such a scale is provided in Figure 4.1, using the behaviors appearing in the star chart in Chapter 3.

Task	Evaluation Criteria 1 = Poor, 5 = Average, 10 = Excellent									
Make bed	1	2	3	4	5	6	7	8	9	10
Fold clothes and put in dresser	1	2	3	4	5	6	7	8	9	10
Put toys on shelf	1	2	3	4	5	6	7	8	9	10
Throw away trash	1	2	3	4	5	6	7	8	9	10
My overall evaluation	1	2	3	4	5	6	7	8	9	10

Figure 4.1. Example of having child evaluate how well she cleaned her room.

Obviously, the child's and the parents' evaluations of the cleanliness of the room may differ. A child might rate putting clothes away as a 10 because the clothes are off the floor, whereas a parent may rate this behavior as a 5 since the clothes were merely stuffed into the drawer. The reverse may also happen. A parent could rate the child's overall job of cleaning her room as an 8 because everything was off the floor and put either in the dresser drawers or in the closet. The child, however, may rate the job she did as a 5 because the clothes were not arranged neatly. Where there are differences between the child's and the parents' evaluation of the quality of performing a task or behavior, these differences can be discussed. In this way, the child becomes a partner in the process of setting criteria for determining what constitutes a clean room and the amount of effort required. The child will come to view her input as important, thereby becoming better at evaluating the quality of her work. As a result, the child develops self-control. Even when parent and child evaluate the quality of the child's performance or behavior in the same way, it is still important to discuss each person's evaluations since the reasons behind the same evaluation could be different.

Through the process of evaluating their own behavior, children start reaching the conclusion that it is worth working hard because they are in control and it feels good. Unfortunately, most interactions with children are based on the parents' evaluation of the child's behavior. In turn, the child evaluates (or more accurately, criticizes) her parent's behavior rather than evaluating her own. Consequently, children exert a great deal of energy trying to outwit their parents. Think of all the time and effort your child has spent trying to make his room "look" clean by rearranging things. Many children go to great lengths to hide clothes under their bed or stack toys in the closet rather than putting them away properly. We throw up our arms in a combination of amazement, disbelief and exasperation at these behaviors. Yet our efforts to convince our children that they could have spent half the time cleaning their room if they did it correctly in the first place fall on deaf ears. Why? Because a child is not interested in her parent's point of view; besides, her point of view has not been asked.

Let me give a further illustration of the goofy thinking and behavior that children engage in when they focus on blaming us for the standards we set. My friend's daughter is a typical teenager in terms of her cleanliness—it's nonexistent. I'm not referring to her personal hygiene. Like other teenagers, she is hypervigilant about her appearance. In fact, a good indicator of how meticulous she is at any given time with her make-up, hair and clothes is to examine the condition of her bathroom and bedroom. I've come to the conclusion that there is an inverse relationship between the two—the better she looks, the messier are her bathroom and bedroom. In the past, both my friend and his wife have tried every known method to get their daughter to clean her room—with varying degrees of success. Regardless of the success they achieved, they never seemed to get her to be consistently neat on her own—that is, to demonstrate self-control in keeping her room clean. Their coercive lectures and platitudes about the virtues of neatness were met with resistance. After all, as she constantly reminded them, it was her room. Therefore, she could keep it in any condition she liked.

I told my friend to ask his daughter to evaluate the neatness of her room on a daily basis using a system similar to the one presented in Figure 4.1. That night my friend called and told me that his daughter hated the idea of evaluating the condition of her room. This response is not uncommon. Most children dislike having to evaluate their own performance and would rather blame their parents. Blaming their parents is easy and takes little effort. Besides, it releases the child from assuming any responsibility for her behavior—the absence of self-control. In contrast, when children evaluate their performance honestly, they have to work much harder since they are not being coerced. In essence, their need for control makes it difficult for them to evaluate their behavior poorly. As long as children do not evaluate their own behavior, they can blame their parents.

In response to the unwillingness of my friend's daughter to evaluate the condition of her room, I developed a simple plan. I told my friend to inform his daughter that before she could use the phone, she needed to take one minute to scan her room—specifically to determine where her clothes, schoolbooks and trash were. She then would evaluate the condition of her room. On a 3 x 5 card she was to rate its condition as "poor," "average," "good" or "excellent," and then sign and date it.

I told my friend to begin by discussing with his daughter how she would describe the advantages and disadvantages of having a clean room. Simply by making a list of the advantages and disadvantages of having a clean room, my friend's daughter has begun the process of evaluating her standards for cleanliness. By evaluating her standards, she might begin to see the disparity between her standards and the condition of her room.

Of course it is quite possible that my friend's daughter could see through this technique and list no advantages of having a clean room. There are two ways to handle this situation. First, you can ignore it. By taking the time to write down all the advantages of not having a clean room, the child nevertheless engages in self-evaluation—a process that can have the desired effect. Second, you can move back from having your child evaluate the advantages and disadvantages of having a clean room, asking her instead to make a list of the positive qualities or traits she looks for in others. Either way, the child begins the process of self-evaluation, which is necessary for developing self-control.

Self-administered consequences

The last component of the feedback model of self-control is self-administered consequences—either positive or negative covert statements directed at ourselves. Once children have developed personal standards of appropriate behavior, they anticipate self-rewards for adhering to their prescribed course of action while expecting self-punishment for breaking their rules. The key phrase in the preceding sentence is "*their* rules." In essence, once children formulate personal standards of appropriate and inappropriate behavior, they come to anticipate positive self-reactions (feelings of pride or self-satisfaction) to conforming to these standards and to expect negative self-reactions (guilt or self-punishment) to violating their standards. The more children perceive their self-evaluation as voluntary and as originating within themselves, the more effectively their self-evaluations affect their behavior. Children who decide for themselves how much they should be punished for a transgression are more likely to resist temptations, at the same time they also accept more responsibility when they misbehave. Children who commit themselves to a rule by writing it down or by verbalizing it will adhere to it more faithfully. We are now ready to consider specific techniques for promoting this process.

Recommendations for How to Promote Self-Control

The aim of most techniques for promoting self-control is threefold: (1) arrange the environment to promote appropriate behavior or stop inappropriate behavior if it occurs; (2) monitor and evaluate behavior; and (3) engage in either positive self-statements (e.g., pride and accomplishment) for exerting control or negative self-statements (e.g., self-criticism, feelings of guilt) for failing to exert control.

Parents can help children arrange the environment to either increase or decrease a given behavior. Behavior monitoring can involve charting procedures, such as tallying the number of times one talks politely, or such activities as practicing relaxation when confronted with a stressful situation. Evaluation requires children to compare their current behavior or performance to some standard. Self-statements refer to subvocalizations based on children's evaluations of their behavior. Specific recommendations can be made for each of these three areas.

Arranging the Environment

Certain environmental conditions are more likely to elicit certain behaviors than others. Thus, a person, situation or physical arrangement can serve as a cue for children engaging in certain behaviors. For example, the mere presence of an antagonistic sibling may elicit aggressiveness from her brother. A child who is normally quiet in the classroom may become loud and obnoxious on the playground during a game of four square. Eating at a restaurant can serve as a cue for using better table manners than those normally displayed at home.

These people, situations or physical arrangements provide us with cues on how to behave in certain ways. Sometimes they provide incentives for behaving well, sometimes for behaving poorly. We typically think that we have very little control over environmental conditions that confront us. However, it is possible to rearrange them to increase or decrease the occurrence of certain behaviors. When this occurs, self-control is enhanced.

Three common sense techniques, based on the writings of Cooper, Heron and Heward, for arranging the environment can be used to help children gain self-control: (1) providing extra cues; (2) altering the environment to make the inappropriate behavior less likely to occur; and (3) restricting the conditions for engaging in an inappropriate behavior.

Provide extra cues for appropriate behavior

Messages on sticky notes are perfect examples of providing extra cues for appropriate behavior. My office is cluttered with these little slips of paper as reminders to call a person, pick up groceries or drop off clothes to be cleaned on my way home from work. Of course, I quickly learned that placing notes in my office to remind me to pick up groceries or take clothes to the cleaners was ineffective because I'd forget them. Instead, when I keep sticky notes on the dashboard of my car, they serve as much more effective cues for controlling my behavior. And that is the most important aspect of providing extra cues in the environment—they must appear in a place where they are likely to control the behavior.

One of the techniques I use in my private practice to help individuals quit smoking involves making up a card that states how many people die from tobacco-related deaths each year. I then have the person insert this card in the cellophane wrapper around her cigarette pack. Next to the card in the cellophane I ask her to keep a stick of gum. This procedure serves two purposes. First, the card with the number of tobacco-related deaths is placed where it is seen every time the person goes to pull out a cigarette from her pack. Second, seeing this card can set the occasion for other positive controlling responses. In this case, I've orchestrated the situation so the person has a positive controlling response handy—the stick of gum next to the card. I have used another technique to increase the number of times I exercise during the week by placing my workout clothes in my car each morning. When I leave work, my workout clothes serve as a reminder to drive to the health club.

A common family problem that I have alluded to in previous chapters is dealing with siblings' behavior at the dinner table. It seems that in families with at least two children, one child is particularly good at getting the other upset. And the child who's getting upset gladly obliges with some form of reciprocal antagonistic behavior. Sibling fighting is like a personal foul in a football game—the referee only sees the end of the altercation; consequently, the instigator is rarely flagged for the infraction. Similarly, the sibling who learns how to get a quick reaction from his brother rarely receives the same punishment as the brother who retaliates.

One way to help prevent the sibling on the receiving end of the teasing from retaliating is to provide him with a reminder note. I have seen parents write a note saying "Ignore your brother when he teases you" and place it next to the child's placemat at the dinner table. The advantage of this note is that it gives the child an instruction—ignore your brother. Besides, it appears at a place where the inappropriate behavior needs to be controlled—the dinner table. However, the disadvantage of this note is that it doesn't specify how to ignore the sibling. A better note is one that provides the child not only with a cue to control the inappropriate behavior, but also specifies the particular appropriate behavior in which he is to engage. A note could read "When your brother begins to tease you, count to 10 silently." Or "When your brother begins to tease you, ask Dad how his day went." Or "When your brother begins to tease you, think of how much trouble he'll get in if you don't say anything back to him." These notes serve as cues to control the behavior and provide a suggestion for engaging in other controlling behaviors.

I have used this approach with parents to help them increase the amount of praise they provide their children. I instruct parents to make reminders and place them around their house where they are likely to see them. I frequently have parents place such reminders by the placemat at the dinner table, by the bedroom lamp, in the bathroom and next to the television. Each time parents see one of the cues, they are reminded to catch their child being good and praise him.

Alter the environment to make the inappropriate behavior less likely to occur

This suggestion is straightforward and utilizes common sense—change the environment so it becomes harder to engage in the inappropriate behavior. An obvious example is the smoker who throws out her cigarettes or the dieter who removes all the junk food from the house.

Returning to the case of the child being teased by his sibling at the dinner table, a parent could simply sit between the child and his sibling. This simple alteration changes the physical environment, making it less likely for the sibling to tease his brother when seated next to a parent. In this case, he would have to lean in front of his parent to tease. And the other sibling would have to lean in front of his parent to retaliate. Sometimes it is helpful to use extra cues as a reminder for the sibling to sit between a parent and his brother.

Restrict the conditions for engaging in an inappropriate behavior

Put quite simply, this recommendation requires that children do what they are already doing but under different conditions. In essence, by restricting or changing the conditions or context under which a behavior occurs, that behavior loses its meaning and, consequently, its reinforcing value. I once worked with a married couple whose chief complaint was that they fought too much. They fought over typical subjects such as finances, perceived inequity in shared household responsibilities, and methods for dealing with their children. Many therapists would help such a couple increase their level of meaningful communication, learn to argue constructively, be more empathic toward each other's position, and clarify their values and areas of agreement.

My approach was different. I told the couple to continue arguing as often and as intensely as they had been doing, but with one stipulation: They were to have their arguments in the garage! That was the extent of my recommendation. I dismissed the couple and asked them to make another appointment in a week. A week later the couple each took a seat in my office and looked at me sheepishly. They both reported that the number of arguments had decreased dramatically. The reason for this improvement is amazingly simple: I had changed the conditions under which their arguing occurred. Once the conditions were changed, the meaning of the behavior also changed.

Remember, the premise behind this recommendation is that every behavior has meaning in some, but not all contexts. A perfect example of this comes from a personal triumph. I had a seven-year cigarette smoking habit which I kicked at the young age of 21. Like most smokers, there were certain situations in which I enjoyed smoking the most—having a morning cup of coffee, after meals, and at a bar having a beer with friends. The last situation was the one in which it was the most difficult for me to refrain from smoking. As a college student in the mid-1970s living in a town where the drinking age was 18, much of my recreation focused around playing foosball at local bars. I could have a cigarette going almost continuously for hours at a time. But I reduced the number of cigarettes I smoked while at bars by restricting the conditions for engaging in this behavior. Quite simply, I only would smoke a cigarette in the bathroom. As a result, cigarette smoking was no longer associated with the fun of interacting with others and playing a game. Instead, it became associated with a stinky bar bathroom. With this change in context, the meaning of smoking in a bar changed for me. Consequently, I was able to quite smoking in an environment—the bar—that in past efforts had exerted a great toll on my "willpower."

Much of our ability to help children gain self-control depends on our ability to appreciate the context in which a given behavior occurs and help children select another context. For example, a common and annoying problem many parents encounter from children between the ages of 3 to 8 is screaming outbursts. For a child, screaming is a highly effective behavior for getting what she wants. Children quickly learn that screaming is highly aversive to their parents. Parents also learn that giving in to their child terminates the screaming. In Chapter 2, I described principles of reinforcement that parents can use to eliminate this problem. We can also use the technique of restricting the conditions for this behavior to teach the child self-control. Here's how I used it with a 6-year-old girl who had a screaming problem.

Mr. and Mrs. Wilson entered my office accompanied by their daughter, Felicia. The parents' chief complaint was the number of screaming tantrums in which their daughter engaged. Felicia sat looking coyly from me to her parents as they described the nature of her loud, high-pitched screaming. I turned to her and asked her if she could really scream as loud and in such a high-pitched voice as her parents claimed. Her reply was that she guessed so. At this point, I asked her parents to wait in the outer office. On the way out I told them that I would help Felicia control her screaming, but that they probably wouldn't like my recommendation. They looked at each other suspiciously, but agreed to whatever I recommended as long as it would help Felicia gain control over her screaming.

I returned to my office, sat down and faced Felicia. "Now," I began, "you obviously have a very nice scream. It is loud and high-pitched. 'High-pitched' means that your scream sounds like a siren or jet airplane taking off. In fact, if your scream gets very high-pitched, it could even shatter glass." Felicia became quite interested and started smiling when I described her scream and its potential. "Yep, that scream of yours is quite strong. I bet you're very proud of it. And I know your parents are very aware of your scream. But I wonder if you could make your scream even louder—crank it up a notch. Are you interested in being able to scream even louder?" Felicia nodded enthusiastically. "Well then, we'll have to come up with a plan for helping you scream even louder. Screaming louder will require a lot of concentration. 'Concentration' means you'll have to put all your attention and effort into just screaming and not pay attention to anything else going on. I have just the thing that will help you concentrate so you can scream even louder—a screaming chair. What you need is a special place where you can put all your effort into screaming like a special chair where you can sit and try to scream even louder than you have been. So, whenever you feel like screaming at your parents, go over to the screaming chair, sit down, and really try and scream louder than you ever have before."

Felicia was very enthusiastic about her screaming chair. I called her parents back into my office and explained the screaming chair and its purpose. During my explanation, Felicia had a smile from ear to ear while her parents' brows furrowed more and more as I continued. When Felicia was satisfied that I had explained the purpose of the screaming chair sufficiently to her parents, I asked her to go and wait in the outer office for a couple of minutes. I could see from the look on Mr. and Mrs. Wilson's faces that they regretted agreeing with whatever recommendation I would make as long as it would teach Felicia to control her screaming. I began by asking them if it was possible for Felicia to scream much louder than her current level. They both agreed that seemed unlikely. However, they were concerned that Felicia would scream more often now that she had a designated place to scream. I tried to alleviate this fear by explaining to them how the meaning of a behavior is tied to the context in which it occurs and that when the context or situation changes, so does the meaning of the behavior, and consequently its reinforcing value.

The three methods described for arranging the environment can help children gain self-control. However, additional techniques often are needed to get the child to emit the controlling response that modifies the inappropriate behavior. For example, in order to provide myself with a sticky note as a cue to pick something up on my way home from work, I have to write the note. Writing the note is the controlling response for remembering the task. A smoker who wants to stop smoking must be willing to throw away all his cigarettes—this controlling response is often difficult for a smoker to perform. Even if he does throw away his cigarettes, a quick trip to the local drugstore can replenish his supply. In the previous example, the controlling response I wanted Felicia to emit was sitting in a designated chair. Yet for this intervention to be effective, she had to actually go over and sit in the chair. I tried to make sitting in the chair fun by framing it as a way to scream even louder. However, the success of this technique could wear off early. Therefore, additional self-control strategies based on the feedback model also must be employed.

Feedback Techniques

I previously introduced the three components of the feedback model: self-monitoring, self-evaluation and self-administered consequences. Self-monitoring was described as the process of observing and recording one's own behavior. The act of self-monitoring leads to self-evaluation in which the child compares his behavior to some standard that is either externally imposed (e.g., parent sets standard) or internally applied (e.g., child compares current performance to past performance). Once a child makes a personal evaluation, she will either engage in positive self-statements of pride and accomplishment if the standard has been achieved, if the standard has not been met, engage in negative self-statements such as experiencing guilt or attributions of needing to try harder next time.

The use of these three components to teach children self-control can be illustrated with the case of a 12-year-old girl, whom I'll call Kathy. Kathy came to see me with her parents, who related two major complaints.

First, Kathy refused to comply with parental requests. Specifically, she had to be asked repeatedly to get ready for school in the morning, often having to be dragged kicking and screaming out the door by her mother. She was late for school several mornings a week, and it was not unusual for her to miss one day of school a week. In the latter circumstance, she would simply refuse to go to school, stating that she was sick. Evenings were no better. Her parents had a terrible time convincing Kathy to get ready for bed. She would either procrastinate taking a shower, brushing her teeth, or washing her hands and face, or would refuse to do them altogether. It became so bad that hygiene was a major concern to her parents.

I initially approached these problems using a star chart like the one described in Chapter 3. We developed morning, afternoon and evening expectations. Kathy needed to complete these behaviors correctly before she had access to any rewarding activities including watching television, talking on the phone, playing with her toys or games, or having a friend visit or going over to a friend's house. The star chart proved to be successful in getting Kathy to engage in appropriate behaviors, such as getting ready for school, leaving for school on time, and getting ready for bed in the evening.

The second major complaint expressed by Kathy's parents was that she became extremely frustrated over what appeared to them to be the most trivial matters. If Kathy got a tangle in her hair while brushing it, she would throw the brush and hit her father if he was close by. If she had trouble selecting clothes to wear to school the following day, she would yell and find some object to throw or break.

Upon questioning, her parents reported that Kathy had plenty of clothes she liked in her closet. But when she tried on an outfit at night, it had to "feel right" or else she wouldn't want to wear it the next day. After going through two or three outfits, she would become frustrated and then act out. Kathy would become very frustrated when she accidentally hurt herself, as when she would stub her toe against the wall or door. Kathy would also become frustrated if she encountered homework problems for which she did not know the answer. Interestingly, Kathy enjoyed doing homework. But when she got stuck doing math problems or couldn't get the correct spelling of a word during a practice test her mother would administer, she would become frustrated and act out by yelling or throwing and breaking objects.

When the star chart was introduced, Kathy's parents reported some improvement in her ability to react positively when frustrated. Even though the star chart did not focus on frustration, it had a positive "spill-over" effect: When children learn that a particular behavior consistently brings a reward or, conversely, that a certain behavior results in a reward being withheld, they are motivated to regulate their behavior so that it brings the desired outcome. Nevertheless, I felt the need to use feedback techniques to enhance Kathy's ability to control her frustration.

Self-monitoring

The first step was to determine exactly what behavior I wanted Kathy to self-monitor. Initially, I was faced with the dilemma of deciding whether it would be better to have her self-monitor situations when she became frustrated or when she successfully controlled her frustration. There are always two sides of a behavior that can be monitored—the negative and the positive. Sometimes it is beneficial to have the child monitor the side of the behavior she cares most about changing. At other times it seems that one side is more important for self-monitoring than the other. Asking a child who is suicidal to self-monitor her depressive thoughts may only lead the child to persevere in feeling depressed and suicidal.

In Kathy's case, I was concerned that having her self-monitor her frustration might increase the number of times she became frustrated. Yet I was willing to take that chance for the following reason. Many times, children who lack self-control are not aware of their behavior. They perform the behavior automatically because it has become such an ingrained habit. Therefore, my overriding concern was getting Kathy to increase her awareness of the situations in which she became frustrated and the way she behaved in those situations. After self-monitoring had become a part of Kathy's daily activities and her awareness of situations in which she became frustrated increased, I would have her shift to self-monitoring situations in which she successfully controlled her frustration.

The second step was to select an appropriate medium for Kathy to record the situations in which she became frustrated. I had two options: I could have her keep an open-ended diary in which she would write down three situations during the day when she was frustrated. This approach takes a good deal of effort because of its unstructured nature. Or I could create a self-monitoring sheet specific to Kathy's problem—frustration. I decided on the latter method because it offered more structure. Figure 4.2 shows the self-monitoring sheet I developed for Kathy. This sheet is easy for upper elementary grade school children to comprehend. It is straightforward and uncomplicated.

The third step was to provide Kathy with a rationale for self-monitoring. This was necessary to increase the likelihood that Kathy would follow through with the assignment. In other words, I needed to get her to buy into the value of completing the frustration action sheet. A rationale answers the question "What's in it for me?" *Reactivity*, or the ability of self-monitoring to produce a change in behavior, is affected by the value one assigns to the response to be self-monitored. However, coming up with a rationale children

---

Frustration Action Sheet

---

1. Today I was frustrated when:

2. What I wanted was:

3. I reacted by:

4. This did/did not satisfy me because:

Figure 4.2. Frustration action self-monitoring sheet.

will buy into is not an easy task. Remember, many children resist efforts to develop more self-control because it is easier to blame their parents for their difficulties.

The first approach to developing a rationale is to enlist the child's support using noncoercive means. Here's how I went about enlisting Kathy as a willing participant.

"Kathy, you described three situations where you become frustrated. You said that it happens when you are brushing your hair and hit a tangle, trying to select clothes to wear to school, and running up against homework problems for which you don't know the answer. Are there any other situations when you get frustrated?"

"Yeah, my sister frustrates me a lot. She's always teasing me."

"What exactly does she do that frustrates you?" I asked.

"Well, I'll be watching TV and she'll come up and change the channel. Or she'll go into my room and take something without asking. Or sometimes when I ask if I can borrow something like a shirt or music tape she'll say yes and then change her mind. That last one really gets me frustrated."

I nodded empathically and said, "You told me that when you get frustrated you'll start to scream, throw whatever is handy like a magazine if you're in the family room, or even hit your father if he's around. Is that right?"

"Yeah, I guess so," Kathy responded.

"When you say 'I guess so,' does that mean you do scream or throw or break things when you're frustrated, or not?" I asked. It is important to ensure that children and adults alike take a position on an issue. Responses such as "I don't know" or "I guess so" are unacceptable. We want to nail down a child's position so we are operating at a factual, observable level. It is perfectly acceptable for children to change their positions, but clarity must be preserved.

Kathy responded to my question stating, "Yeah, you're right. That's what I do when I get frustrated."

"Well, Kathy, I can understand how those things would get you frustrated. Let me ask you this question: Do you like feeling frustrated?"

"No way," Kathy responded. "Who would like to feel frustrated?"

"So it's not any fun to feel frustrated," I summarized. "Well, would you be interested in learning some ways to feel less frustrated?"

"I don't know," Kathy replied.

"But Kathy," I went on, "you just told me that you don't like feeling frustrated."

"Yeah, but it's the things that happen to me that get me frustrated, not myself. If my sister would just leave me alone I'd get a lot less frustrated."

"I can't guarantee that your sister will never do anything to frustrate you," I replied sympathetically. "Also, unless you lived at a clothing store, you're still going to have to select an outfit to wear to school from your closet. And I don't know how to guarantee that your hair will never get tangled when you brush it. But I can show you some ways for dealing with those things that frustrate you. Do you want to try some things that will help you control your frustration?"

"Well, would the things you're going to show me be hard to do?" asked Kathy.

"Not at all. We'd start with something easy."

"Well, in that case, yes, I'd like to learn some things to control my frustration."

At this point, Kathy bought into the rationale for trying a technique to control her frustration. I kept confronting her with the discrepancy between her not liking to feel frustrated and wanting to do something to alleviate those feelings. Eventually, Kathy had no choice but to agree to try something if she stood by her position of not liking to feel frustrated. She could have told me that she didn't mind feeling frustrated. In that case, I would have had to develop a program to motivate Kathy to perform self-monitoring.

Often, developing a contract with a child to try self-monitoring for a specified period of time is effective. In this type of contract, I specify that after a certain amount of time—say a week—the child can stop self-monitor-ing. At the end of a week, most children are pleasantly surprised with the results of self-monitoring and desire to continue. In a few situations, self-monitoring must be included in a star chart as a behavior expected to be performed in the evening along with getting ready for bed, doing homework, or taking a shower. In Kathy's case, she bought into trying self-monitoring without having to develop a contract or incorporating self-monitoring into her evening chores on her star chart.

The fourth step was to ensure that Kathy was able to identify when she was in a frustrating situation and observe her own behavior during that situation. Therefore, Kathy needed a definition of "frustration." Remember from Chapter 2 that the first step in changing any behavior is to ensure the behavior we select passes the stranger test. The stranger test refers to specifying a behavior in enough detail so that a stranger could walk into your house and observe the same thing. In Kathy's case, we needed to come up with a definition of frustration that she would find personally relevant. Kathy volunteered the following definition: "Anything that doesn't work out the way I want it to." Although this behavior did not exactly pass the stranger test as I described it in Chapter 2, it seemed to be a definition to which Kathy could relate. Besides, in the case of self-monitoring, the child observes her own behavior and is not dependent upon external observation.

Nevertheless, we still want the definition of frustration to be as concrete as possible. In Kathy's case, we decided to go with her definition, but also to list all the examples of "when things don't work out the way she wanted them to." Kathy was able to list the five things described previously by her parents: brushing hair and hitting a tangle, trying to select clothes to wear to school, completing difficult math problems and spelling words, and several of her sister's annoying behaviors including turning the TV channel, going in her room, or saying she could borrow something and then changing her mind.

I used this list as a starting point for Kathy and her parents. Her parents could remind Kathy of an incident of becoming frustrated based on these examples. Also, Kathy would be focused on them. I stressed that these examples were not exhaustive and that any time Kathy was in a situation "when things don't work out the way she wanted them to," she could self-monitor.

The fifth step was to have Kathy chart the results of her frustration action sheets. A mechanism that allowed Kathy to visually inspect her progress set the occasion for her to engage in self-evaluation and, subsequently, self-ad-ministered consequences. There are two common ways of charting self-mon-itoring data: (1) a line graph or (2) a bar graph. Figure 4.3 is an example of a line graph used to chart progress. As this figure illustrates, Kathy charted the number of times she became frustrated each day over a two-week period and connected the numbers. She initially reported getting frustrated about eight times a day. By the end of the second week, she was reporting about two episodes of frustration.

Some children find the line graph too complicated or not visual enough for self-evaluation. In these cases, a bar graph can be used (see Figure 4.4). Here a bar is constructed for each day of the week and the child simply colors in the portion of the bar up to the number of times she engaged in the behavior for that day. This type of graph is analogous to a thermometer. As the temperature rises, more of the tube appears red; and as the temperature drops, less of the tube appears red.

The sixth and final step of self-monitoring is to display the graph in a prominent area. I asked Kathy and her parents what would be a good place to display her graph. They all responded that the refrigerator door would be fine. So, every day, Kathy would take the graph off the refrigerator door, enter that day's data, and return it to the door. Displaying the chart publicly served as a reminder to both Kathy and her parents of her progress, or lack

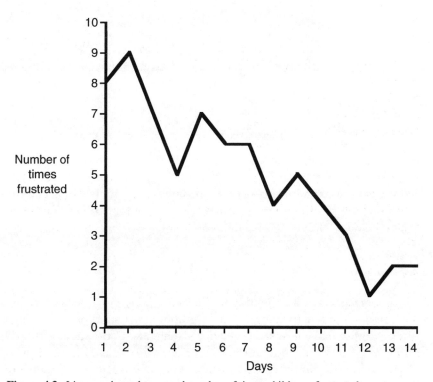

Figure 4.3. Line graph used to record number of times child was frustrated.

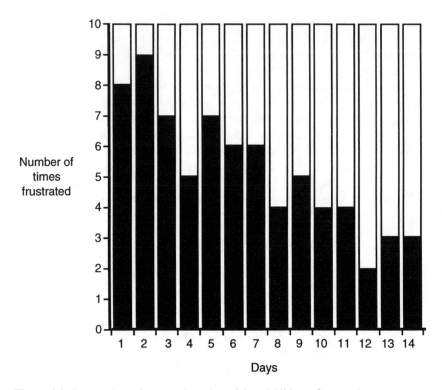

Figure 4.4. Bar graph used to record number of times child was frustrated.

of progress. When progress was noted, the graph served as a prompt for Kathy's parents to praise her—a necessary component for teaching children self-control. Also, the graph provided a visual cue for Kathy to engage in self-evaluation—the second feedback technique.

Self-evaluation

The importance of self-evaluation in the feedback model of self-control was previously described. In many instances, graphing self-monitoring data leads directly to the making of self-evaluative statements. Consequently, there is little else to do to promote self-evaluation. In other situations, the process of self-monitoring does not seem to have as big an impact on self-evaluation as one would like. In Kathy's case, I decided to be proactive and include additional techniques to promote self-evaluation from the beginning.

First, I modified Kathy's frustration action sheet by adding an additional component, which can be seen in Figure 4.5.

Number five on this sheet asks Kathy to rate how well she handled the specific frustrating situation. I provided her with a numerical scale for accomplishing this task. The question prompts Kathy to self-evaluate her performance while the numerical scale provides her with an objective method for making an evaluation. When I added this component to Kathy's self-monitoring sheet, I realized that I needed to solicit her personal stan-

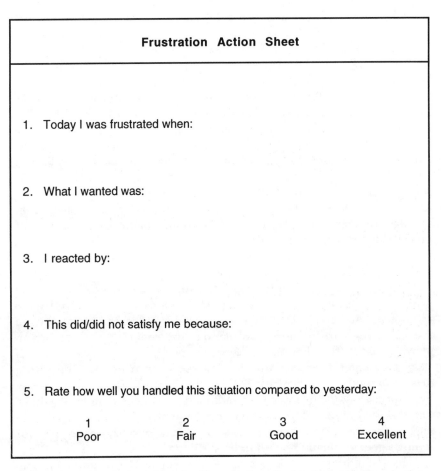

Figure 4.5. Modified version of self-monitoring sheet to include self-evaluation component.

dards, which would form the basis for evaluating her performance. Generally speaking, children develop and apply more stringent standards than do adults.

I did not want Kathy's standards to be so high that she could not meet them. On the other hand, I did not want her standards to be so low as to cancel out any benefit she would gain from evaluating her performance. Therefore, we set about coming up with a definition for the four descriptors: excellent, good, fair and poor. We came up with the following criteria: "Poor" was used when Kathy's performance was worse than the previous frustrating incident. "Fair" was used when she handled the situation in a way comparable to the previous situation. "Good" was used when Kathy's performance was better than that described on the previous frustration action sheet. Finally, "excellent" was a special category that we did not specifically define. Instead, I told Kathy she could use this category whenever she thought she did an extra good job handling her frustration. However, knowing that children tend to be critical of themselves, I told her to use the excellent category at least once a week.

The second modification designed to encourage Kathy to self-evaluate was made to her graph. Besides having her evaluate "how well" she handled frustration as previously outlined on her self-monitoring sheet, I also asked her to evaluate her daily improvement in the number of times she was frustrated. Therefore, on the bottom of her graph I added the following statement: "Compared to yesterday, how would you rate the number of times you were frustrated today?" I listed the same categories: excellent, good, fair, and poor, but we did not discuss the criteria for applying them. Since Kathy was objectively comparing her numerical total for a particular day against the previous day's total, I wanted her to assign a descriptor based on her own numerical criteria. An example of the modified graph is presented in Figure 4.6.

A third technique I used to help Kathy self-evaluate was to have her set two goals for the next day based on the modifications made in her frustration action sheet and graph. Depending on how she evaluated her handling of the frustrating situation on a particular day, she would have to set a performance goal for the following day. For example, based on an evaluation of "fair" for her performance on Monday, she needed to come up with a descriptor for the next day. I told her that she did not always have to increase her expectations. If she was content with a rating of fair, then fair could be the goal for the next day. However, if she wanted to improve her performance, she needed to set a higher goal. The same explanation was given for setting a goal for the number of times she became frustrated in a day.

Having children establish clear goals is essential for teaching them self-control. Goals can be long-range, short-range, specific or general. Goal setting helps the child identify the specific behaviors that lead to goal

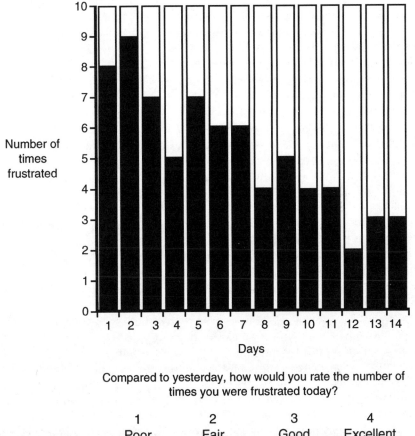

Number of times frustrated

Days

Compared to yesterday, how would you rate the number of times you were frustrated today?

| 1 | 2 | 3 | 4 |
| Poor | Fair | Good | Excellent |

Days

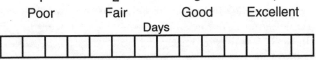

Figure 4.6. Modified graph including self-evaluative component.

attainment. In Kathy's case, I asked her what type of behaviors she would need to exhibit in order to handle a frustrating situation effectively. This type of question sets the stage for engaging in a problem-solving process whereby each behavior and its possible consequences are evaluated by the child to determine whether they will lead to successful completion of the goal or interfere with its attainment. At one point Kathy mentioned that hitting her sister would get her to stop changing the TV channel and, consequently, alleviate Kathy's frustration. I responded by saying, "Well Kathy, that certainly may work. What has happened in the past when you have hit your sister when you felt frustrated by her?"

"She will stop bugging me," Kathy responded.

"Does anything else ever happen? Will she ever do anything different than stop?"

Kathy began to smile and said, "Sometimes she will hit me back or turn off the TV altogether."

"Is that what you wanted your sister to do?" I asked.

"No!" Kathy responded sharply.

"Do you feel less frustrated when your sister hits you back or turns off the television?" I probed.

"No way. I just get more frustrated and want to hit her harder or find something to throw at her," Kathy said with more than a little irritation in her voice.

"What happens if you hit her back or throw something at her?" I asked.

"Usually, I'm also yelling at her by this time and my mother or father comes into the room to break up the fight."

"What happens next?" I asked.

"I usually get into a fight with my parents," Kathy responded somewhat dejectedly.

"You don't seem to be happy getting into a fight with your parents over becoming frustrated about your sister bugging you?"

"No, I just end up getting punished," Kathy admitted.

"Well, maybe we can think of some more successful behaviors for you to try when your sister gets you frustrated. Would you be willing to try to come up with some more behaviors?" I asked. "I'd be glad to help you."

"Yes, that's probably a good idea," Kathy concluded.

In this way I helped Kathy analyze the potential positive and negative consequences of selecting the behavior of hitting her sister as a goal when she feels frustrated. Kathy was able to generate other behaviors such as ignoring her, telling her parents, asking her to stop and leaving the room. I then asked her to rank these behaviors in terms of which ones she thought would be the most effective and which she would be willing to try. These behaviors then became the goal to strive for when Kathy became frustrated with her sister. Successfully meeting this goal leads to the third component of the feedback model—self-administered consequences.

Self-administered consequences

Children typically self-administer rewarding or punishing consequences depending on whether their performance falls short of, matches or exceeds their self-prescribed demands. Substantial evidence suggests that most patterns of self-reinforcement and self-punishment are acquired and modified through learning. At least three conditions must exist in order for a child to engage in self-reinforcement: (1) the child (rather than the parents) determines the criteria for adequacy of her performance and for resulting reinforcement; (2) the child (rather than the parents) controls access to the reward; and (3) the child (rather than the parents) acts as her own reinforcing agent and administers the rewards.

Note that self-reinforcement involves both self-determination and self-administration of a reward. This distinction is at times overlooked. Consequently, self-reinforcement is not always used effectively by children. Another distinction must be made between *external* and *internal* self-reinforcement.

External reinforcement parallels the type a parent presents to a child for performing a particular behavior. Parents who allow their child to stay up an extra 30 minutes if her homework is completed by 8:00 p.m. are using external reinforcement. This same type of reinforcement can be used by the child. The child may want an extra 30 minutes of playing Nintendo if she completes her homework by 8:00 p.m. This is also an external reinforcer, but the child determines it and must also administer it.

Self-reinforcement can also be internal. In this instance, self-monitoring and self-evaluation lead to self-reinforcing statements if the child's performance meets or exceeds her standard. The child may tell himself, "I did a really good job finishing my homework on time tonight."

I wanted to promote both self-determination and self-administration of external and internal self-reinforcement when Kathy successfully met or exceeded her goals. I used the following procedure to promote external self-reinforcement: I asked Kathy to make a list of 10 things she likes to do around the house. Her list included baking cookies or brownies, renting a movie, staying up an extra hour to watch television and eat popcorn, and several other similar activities. Since these reinforcers were not the type of things that typically could be administered on a daily basis, we decided on using them at the end of every five days if Kathy met her goals, based on her self-evaluative criteria. Specifically, she came up the with the condition that if she reached her goal four out of five days, she would treat herself to one of these rewards. The first criterion for external self-reinforcement was met—Kathy self-determined the rewards.

The second step was to have her self-deliver the reward. This was relatively simple. I asked Kathy and her mother to go to the store and buy two boxes of brownie mix, the ingredients for making chocolate chip cookies (Kathy's favorite), and two packages of microwave popcorn. Then I asked Kathy where she would like to store these things. She replied that there was some room in a cabinet in the utility room closet. She wanted to put these things in a box and place them in this closet. Everyone agreed that this place was acceptable. I told Kathy that if at the end of five days she met her goal for at least four of the previous days, she could treat herself to one of these items.

Many parents are concerned that children will cheat when self-adminis-tering rewards. Generally, however, cheating is not as big a problem as one would suspect. Because children are holding themselves responsible, they are less likely to cheat since the only person they would be cheating would be themselves. On occasion, however, children do cheat. In such instances, it helps to develop a contract with the child specifying the conditions for self-administering the reward, including the time and amount. Also, the consequences for not complying with the contract should be specified. For example, if Kathy took one of her reinforcers without earning it, she would lose the opportunity to self-reinforce for a day. In Kathy's case, such a contract was not necessary since her reinforcers involved baking in the kitchen or making popcorn in the microwave, limiting the opportunities to cheat because her parents would most likely know if she was baking in the kitchen.

In order to promote Kathy's use of internal self-rewarding statements, I made yet another modification on her frustration action sheet. As can be seen from Figure 4.7, I added a self-administered consequence section as number 6. In 6a, Kathy was to write a positive self-statement if she reached or exceeded her self-evaluative criteria. In 6b, she was to write a self-statement aimed at helping her reach her goal for the next time she was frustrated.

Notice that in 6b, I worded the item so as not to ask Kathy for negative self-talk. Children and adults alike are very good at criticizing themselves. In some instances, criticism can have a positive value. A young boy playing little league may say to himself upon striking out, "That was a really dumb pitch to hit." Such self-criticism may serve as a motivator to be more selective the next time at bat. However, for other children, this can lead to self-defeating behavior or just plain giving up. Since it is difficult to determine how self-criticism will affect a child's performance, I phrased 6b in a way that encouraged Kathy to try harder next time.

Finally, I'd like to make a comment about self-delivery of punishing consequences: Avoid them! I described the problems with children admin-istering self-critical covert statements. In addition, problems occur when children administer external punishing consequences. First, all the prob-lems associated with punishment I described in Chapters 1 and 2 apply here as well. For example, I explained that punishment is most effective when delivered at maximum intensity continuously. How many children are going to self-deliver really aversive consequences? And would you really want children to deliver them even if they were effective?

I worked with a 13-year-old boy who engaged in a lot of overt negative self-statements about his performance on almost any task—whether school-related or recreational. I had the boy wear a rubber band around his wrist. Whenever he expressed a negative thought about his performance, he was

---

Frustration Action Sheet

---

1. Today I was frustrated when:

2. What I wanted was:

3. I reacted by:

4. This did/did not satisfy me because:

5. Rate how well you handled this situation compared to yesterday:

1	2	3	4
Poor	Fair	Good	Excellent

6. Based on the above rating, write down either:

   (a) what you told yourself that was good about the way you handled the situation

   or

   (b) what you told yourself that could help you improve your performance next time.

Figure 4.7. Frustration action sheet with internal self-administered consequences component.

to snap the rubber band which delivered a brief but painful sting to his wrist. The initial success the boy experienced in decreasing his negative self-talk was quickly offset by his unwillingness to inflict pain on himself by snapping the rubber band. As he put it: "Why would I want to inflict pain on myself when I'm already beating myself up with my negative thoughts." I agreed.

Controlling Emotions and Behavior

Up to this point, I have provided specific strategies for improving children's self-control by modifying the environment and teaching feedback techniques. Now, I would like to change gears a little.

Although this next section still focuses on methods for teaching children self-control, it also is meant to teach adults how to control emotions and behavior. Sometimes our ability to deal effectively with children is impaired by our own inability to exert control over our emotional reactions and behavioral responses. Children are very adept at finding and pushing the right buttons that get a reaction from us. Of course, children are no different from us: We are quite good at pushing those buttons with the significant others in our own lives. When our buttons are pushed, we tend to push back—one way or another. In many instances, we feel guilty or upset at having responded to our children, or spouse, in the way we did. We are saying, in essence, that we wish we were better able to control our emotions and behavior when confronted with certain situations. Although children may not engage in the same introspection, there are situations where they overreact emotionally and behaviorally. Like many adults, children often do things impulsively that turn out to be counterproductive. Therefore, the system I am going to present is intended to help you, the parent, gain more control over your emotional reactions and behavioral responses to children. Once you understand and can practice this system, you will be able to teach it to your children.

The key element in learning how to control our emotions and behaviors and our children's involves examining our covert beliefs or self-statements in any given situation. Remember from the previous section that the purpose of having children self-monitor is to give them data to make covert evaluative statements. When children's performance reaches their standard, they are likely to engage in positive self-statements; the opposite is true when their behavior fails to reach the standard. We all talk to ourselves. As adults we are more aware of this through our ability to be introspective.

Children do the same thing. All one has to do is visit a preschool and watch toddlers learning a new task. You will hear them talk themselves through the activity out loud. As they become more proficient, their talk becomes less audible and more covert. When teaching children how to control their emotions and behaviors, the key is to help them understand that they talk to themselves and that their self-talk affects how they react emotionally and behaviorally. Changing one's self-talk represents a powerful technique for controlling undesirable emotions and behaviors. The remainder of this chapter is devoted to developing emotional and behavioral control in children and adults.

The Underlying Model

The model I am going to describe for developing emotional and behavioral control is based on rational-emotive therapy, or RET for short. The techniques and procedures I will present are based on the work of psychologist

Tom Miller. Dr. Miller has developed an informative, highly motivating and practical system for learning and using Albert Ellis' principles of RET.

More than just a series of techniques for developing emotional and behavioral control, RET is a unique philosophy of life which can be used to help both adults and children develop better emotional and behavioral control. By developing better emotional and behavioral control, parents will ultimately be better able to deal with their children. Children who develop emotional and behavioral control will be better able to deal with a variety of situations they encounter at home, at school and in the community.

In a nutshell, RET teaches people how to live more satisfactory lives by applying logical, rational thinking. RET is a re-educative model which emphasizes individual accountability and self-evaluation. Individuals who overreact emotionally and exhibit counterproductive behavior patterns do so because of their internalized negative beliefs, referred to as "self-talk." Irrational, illogical thoughts are believed to distort reality and serve a self-defeating purpose. In his seminars, Dr. Miller tells a story of a 4-year-old throwing a temper tantrum in a grocery store at the checkout line. He wanted his mother to buy him a candy bar. This kid was really going at it. He was dusting a 10-foot radius of the floor with his flailing arms and legs. Here is what the kid was probably telling himself: "I need my mommy to buy me the candy. If she doesn't buy me the candy, that may mean she doesn't love me. And the one person in my life that's supposed to love me is my mommy. If my mommy doesn't love me, then maybe I'm an unlovable slug. Nobody's going to care about me, I won't have any friends, and I'll have a terrible life." Of course, the child is not consciously aware of these thoughts because they have become habitual and activated automatically. Nevertheless, thoughts similar to these drive his emotional state and behavioral responses.

Suppose there is a second boy in line who asked his mommy to buy him a candy bar. Only this child has learned the techniques I will be describing shortly. He is standing quietly, not liking the fact that his mother won't buy him the candy bar, but nevertheless not throwing a tantrum. The boy throwing the tantrum turns to the second boy and says, "What's wrong with you? Don't you know what it means when your mommy won't buy you a candy bar?"

The second boy responds, "Well, I know it doesn't mean that she doesn't love me. All it means is that she's cheap!" Of course, their failure to buy the desired candy bar could mean that both mothers are concerned about their children's teeth, or that it is too close to dinner for eating candy, or a variety of other reasons—none of which have anything to do with not loving their children. Although this scenario is a caricature of what the boy was actually thinking, it does illustrate the main point of RET: our interpretation of an event, rather than the event itself, results in our emotional reaction and behavioral responses. The goal of RET is to challenge a person's belief system, point out irrational beliefs, and show how to correct mistakes in reasoning, thereby eliminating undesirable emotions and behaviors. So, if I was working with the boy having the tantrum at the grocery store, I would have asked him to list all the things his mother does that demonstrate that she cares about him. This list would serve as a first step in pointing out the irrationality in the boy's belief that if his mother doesn't buy him the candy, it means she doesn't love him.

The Formation of Irrational Beliefs

There is no firm explanation of how people form and attach irrational belief to situations. Albert Ellis, the developer of RET, suggests that early childhood experiences and a biological predisposition contribute to the way we interpret events. Ellis never states exactly what this "biological predisposition" is. However, he does view children, in terms of the role of early childhood experiences, as gullible and suggestible because of a basic need for love and attention. Consequently, the way parents, family members, peers and teachers treat a child becomes a pattern that contributes to a child's habitual way of responding to situations. I view the basic mechanism of how we acquire and attach irrational beliefs to situations as based on past experiences. Through past experiences we develop *schemas*, or packets of information, that help us interpret, or make sense of, new experiences. As we are exposed to new situations, we try to match these new situations to established schemas by utilizing the concept of consistency. It is to these processes that I now turn.

The nature and purpose of schemas

Every situation we encounter is composed of a variety of stimuli that correspond to five senses: visual (sight), auditory (sound), olfactory (smell), kinesthetic (touch), and proprioceptive (balance). That is, every experience is composed of some combination of these senses. For example, if I am watching people hang glide for the first time, that experience is composed of visual stimuli (I can see the hang glider, its colors and the pilot), auditory stimuli (I can hear the wind passing over the wings) and perhaps olfactory stimuli (I may be able to smell any vegetation in the area). If I were hang gliding for the first time, rather than just observing others, that experience would most likely include incoming kinesthetic stimuli (I would be able to feel the glider) and proprioceptive stimuli (I would experience attempts to maintain my balance).

The experience of hang gliding for the first time is obviously made up of a variety of other sense stimuli. But we selectively attend to what past experience has told are important stimuli. So, while I am hang gliding for the first time, there are a variety of other stimuli around me: clouds in the sky, the position of the sun, the number of people on the ground watching me. However, if I attended to those visual stimuli, I would most likely be distracted from the task at hand: remembering and practicing all the necessary skills for successfully flying and landing the hang glider.

The stimuli that we deem important in a situation are selectively attended to. If we attended to all the stimuli we would feel overwhelmed, confused and unable to make sense out of situations—a state described by many individuals with schizophrenia. Once we decide what stimuli are important to attend to, they must be organized in our brain in such a way that they give the experience meaning to us. Meaning is a function of context and past experiences. We try to match new experiences to similar experiences in the past, using schemas. A schema is simply a packet or a structure of knowledge. Schemas help us represent concepts that are stored in our memory. They are arranged in a hierarchical system.

The best analogy I have found to explain schemas is to picture a metal file cabinet with two or three drawers—the type in which most of us store important documents. Think of the file cabinet as our brain. Inside the file cabinet are our files. Because my wife and I are so obsessive-compulsive, we have two distinct types of files. First, we have hanging files that designate a general topic. For example, we have a hanging file labeled "gasoline charges." That hanging file contains two manila files labeled "Amoco" and "Phillips 66." Think of those files as analogous to schemas: The hanging files can be considered *general schema* while the manila files can be considered *specific schema.* Consider also that when we receive a monthly bill from Amoco, this is analogous to a "new experience." In order to make sense of that new experience, the general file (schema) must be located (activated). Once that schema has been located (activated), the specific file (schema) must be located (activated). That is, once the Amoco file (specific schema) is located (activated), the bill (new information) can be placed into the correct file.

Here is a real-life example of how general and specific schemas operate. We all have a general schema for "restaurants." If we are traveling across the country and pull into a strange town hungry and tired, we can identify buildings that are restaurants, even though we may have never seen a particular restaurant in that town. When we see a building with a certain name or the words "eat," "diner" or "restaurant," we automatically match that information to our general schema of "restaurants" to give the new information meaning. The meaning we attach to the new information is that the building represents a place where we can get a meal prepared for us. However, we also have specific schemas for "restaurants," such as "fast food," "cafeteria" and "sit-down." So, if we pass a building with yellow arches on a sign, we first activate our general schema of restaurants to tell us that this building will serve us food, then we activate the specific schema for "fast food." It is extremely important to activate the correct specific schema. For example, if I went into McDonald's with a friend from a foreign country who has never experienced a "fast food" restaurant, he would not possess an appropriate specific schema. Instead, he might activate the only schema he has for restaurants: go in, sit down and wait for a waiter or waitress to take your order and bring your food. The consequences of mismatching schemas are readily apparent in this example: my friend will go hungry.

Here is another amusing, albeit somewhat morbid, example of mismatching an experience and schema. A friend of a friend, Sally, had a fairly obnoxious German shepherd, who spent most of the time in a fenced-in back yard. The fence is of the typical four-foot chain-link variety. The dog had a history of jumping it and causing general havoc in the neighborhood. Sally's constant concern focused on the neighbors directly on the other side of the fence who had a white rabbit, affectionately named Fluffy, living in a hutch in the corner of the yard. Every day the little neighbor girl would go outside to play with the rabbit. Sally was afraid that her dog would get hold of the rabbit. Her worst fears came true one day. The family who owned the rabbit had gone on a weekend vacation. On Saturday afternoon, Sally went into the back yard to play with her dog. To her mortification, she found the dog with the rabbit in its mouth, shaking it back and forth. She grabbed her dog and pried its jaws open, but alas, the rabbit was dead. The poor little creature was covered with dirt and dog saliva and its fur was all ruffled.

In her highly upset state, Sally came up with a bizarre plan that, had she been thinking more rationally, she would have abandoned as sheer folly. She took the dead rabbit into the house, gave it a bath, and took the blow dryer and made Fluffy as fluffy as possible. Sally waited until it was dark and placed Fluffy on the ground next to the hutch. It was her hope that the neighbors would think Fluffy died while they were away on vacation.

The next day the neighbors came home. The little girl went into the back yard with her brother to play on the swing set. Sally saw them playing, and began wondering why the girl did not immediately go over to see her rabbit. But before she could finish this thought, she heard the girl scream. This is it, Sally thought. Just stay calm and eventually the girl will get over it and maybe her parents will buy her another rabbit. The girl's parents ran outside when they heard her scream. The girl turned to her parents and said, "Mommy, Daddy, someone dug up Fluffy!"

The rabbit had died of natural causes several days before the family went on their weekend vacation. Apparently, Sally's dog jumped the fence and dug up Fluffy. Sally, however, interpreted the situation differently. She applied a schema that did not match the reality of the situation. The moral of this story is that when we encounter situations, we tend to activate the schema that we have used in the past. As mentioned, this practice arises from the concept of *consistency*.

The concept of consistency

All humans strive for consistency in their interpretations of situations and in their interactions with others. Consistency breeds predictability which, in turn, leads to feelings of comfort and a sense of self-assurance. However, interpreting different situations using the same schema, as illustrated in the previous two stories, can lead to inappropriate emotions and behaviors.

Different individuals can view the same situation in different ways. When my wife and I go to a movie, she may like it while I may not. Obviously, we were both exposed to the same stimuli, yet we viewed the situation quite differently. My wife tends to like movies with a lot of dialogue between individuals. My taste runs more toward Steven Seagal action movies. I don't generally like movies that are heavy in dialogue and light in action because, in the past, I have found those types of movies to be boring. I respond consistently when my wife asks me if I want to see such a movie. My emotional reaction is irritation or disappointment; my behavioral reaction usually involves rolling my eyes, sighing and asking if there is some other movie she'd like to see. For example, my wife dragged me to see *Steel Magnolias*. I just knew I wouldn't like that movie because it didn't have enough action. But I was pleasantly surprised: I enjoyed the movie very much. Sometime later my wife asked if I wanted to see *Fried Green Tomatoes*. Even though I had a positive experience seeing *Steel Magnolias*, do you think I wanted to see *Fried Green Tomatoes?* No way! I activated my schema that said high on dialogue, low on action. And that's exactly how the concept of consistency works. The more we activate a certain schema to interpret a situation, the more ingrained it becomes. Consequently, the schema continues to be activated even when we are confronted with evidence that is contrary to our interpretations. Also, and most damaging, schema that are activated often in one situation tend to be activated in situations that become increasingly dissimilar to the original situation in which it was employed. That is how dysfunctional schemas are formed.

Formation and activation of dysfunctional schemas

I described how schemas help us interpret situations. Sometimes, however, the normal matching of an appropriate schema to a particular situation is upset: The matching is overridden by a dysfunctional schema. This is nothing more than activating a schema that is inappropriate for a given situation and, consequently, gives us an interpretation of the event that is illogical. An illogical interpretation results in an overreactive emotional response and counterproductive behaviors. But how does a mismatching between schema and situation occur in the first place? I think the best explanation is that mismatching is a *learned process*. Although there is no perfect explanation for this phenomenon, here is my best hypothesis:

A person initially attaches a correct, but negative, schema (interpretation) to a particular situation. For example, a child may overhear his teacher say, "Billy really did poorly on that addition facts quiz." Because children generally look up to teachers, they tend to believe what they say. So, when Billy gets his math quiz back and sees he missed half the problems, he may say to himself, "Yep, my teacher was right, I did poorly on this quiz." In reality, this would be a correct matching of schema (interpretation) and situation (score on the math quiz). However, the interpretation, albeit accurate, is negative— poor performance is not usually considered a positive experience. This is where learning takes over. If Billy scores poorly on several more arithmetic quizzes, he will continue to activate the schema that he is no good at addition. At this point, the schema is not dysfunctional since it correctly, albeit negatively, matched to the situation. However, the more this schema is correctly activated, the more automatic and habitual it becomes. This is no different than learning any skill. After you practice a skill enough times, it becomes automatic. It's like learning how to ride a bicycle—you don't have to think about it.

If the schema proves to be correct in one situation, there is a greater chance it will be activated in other situations. In addition, when a schema becomes automatic and habitual, it is likely to be activated in situations that are slightly different from the original one to which it was matched correctly. So, when Billy is confronted with his first subtraction quiz, he may tell himself upon seeing the quiz placed on his desk, "Since I'm lousy at addition, I'll probably be lousy at subtraction." This interpretation leads to feelings of inadequacy and anxiety and, consequently, inappropriate behavior, such as experiencing a loss of concentration. Therefore, Billy's performance on the subtraction quiz is likely to be impaired; thus, his interpretation becomes a self-fulfilling prophecy.

Because of the concept of consistency, Billy is likely to activate that schema in situations that are increasingly different from the original one. Eventually, the schema will be activated in situations that are so dissimilar from the original that it becomes dysfunctional or completely mismatched. Perhaps Billy will activate that particular schema when faced with any mathematics content. Then it can be activated to apply to any academic content. In other words, just because Billy does fine in other areas of mathematics, reading, science or history, it does not mean that the schema will not be activated any more than the positive experience I had seeing *Steel Magnolias* transferred to *Fried Green Tomatoes*.

The Four Parts of Any Experience

Throughout my discussion of schema and the concept of consistency, I have been interweaving the four parts of any experience, according to principles of RET: (1) event, (2) meaning/interpretation, (3) feeling and (4) behavioral response. Understanding how these four parts operate is essential for enhancing adults' and children's emotional and behavioral control for the following reason: the events that happen to us do not cause the emotional and behavioral reactions you experience. We do! No one has the power to determine your emotional and behavioral reactions but you. This statement is quite radical, given that we all have been brought up to think in the opposite way. How many times have we told our children, "You make me so mad," "You really try my patience," or "You drive me crazy." How many times do we say things about our boss such as, "My boss really hurt my feelings," or "My boss really gets me nervous when she asks for my opinion at a meeting."

We are conditioned to think that others are responsible for creating our feelings. This type of thinking leads to only two options. First, we try to find a way to make people stop whatever it is they are doing. This approach makes sense if you think they upset you in the first place. However, I would venture to say that most of us have failed miserably at that task. Second, we find a way to get away from people or get them away from us. A common way to accomplish this task is divorce. Unfortunately, that solution is not always feasible when we are dealing with children. The point that *we*, rather than others, get us over upset is well made in the hypothetical story of Robert and Karen.

Robert and Karen have been dating for several months. The courtship is progressing nicely as both of them move toward a more intimate and meaningful relationship. Robert's line of work requires him to be out of town several days a month. Upon returning after a business trip, he goes to Karen's apartment. When she answers the door he presents her with a dozen beautiful roses. Karen looks at the roses and then at Robert. A big smile creases her face as she joyfully gives Robert a big hug and kiss, saying how much she loves him. We can break this interaction down into the four parts of any experience as follows:

1. *Event:* Robert gives Karen flowers.
2. *Meaning/Interpretation:* Karen tells herself Robert cares about her.
3. *Feeling:* Karen feels happy.
4. *Behavioral Response:* Karen tells Robert she loves him, gives him kisses and hugs.

Now, let's change the story between Karen and Robert just a little. The beginning of the story remains the same: Robert shows up at Karen's door with a dozen beautiful roses after being out of town for several days. Karen looks at the roses and then at Robert, only this time her face remains expressionless. She does not accept the flowers; instead she asks Robert whom he was sleeping around with while out of town. Robert is stunned, but before he can reply, Karen pushes him toward the elevator and tells him she never wants to see him again. As above, we can break this interaction down into the four parts of any experience as follows:

1. *Event:* Robert gives Karen flowers.
2. *Meaning/Interpretation:* Karen tells herself Robert was cheating on her.
3. *Feeling:* Karen feels suspicious and angry.
4. *Behavioral Response:* Karen pushes Robert toward the elevator, telling him she never wants to see him again.

How can the same event, Robert giving Karen the flowers, result in different feelings and behavioral responses? The answer is that it can't! Events, or more precisely people, never cause our emotional and behavioral reactions. We cause them through the meaning we assign to events. We assign meaning by activating a schema that gives us our interpretation of the event. Why might Karen feel suspicious and angry in the second story? Because she could have experienced this problem with previous boyfriends. If Karen receives flowers enough times from boyfriends who cheated on her, that schema will be activated in situations with different boyfriends even though Robert was not cheating on her. It doesn't matter whether Robert cheated on her or not. If Robert really did cheat on Karen, but she interpreted receiving the flowers as an indication of how much he cared for her, she would still feel happy and, consequently, engage in the behaviors described above. Conversely, if Robert did not cheat on her, but Karen's interpretation was that he did, her emotional reaction will be suspicious and angry, which leads to the behaviors described above. Robert's motivation does not have anything to do with how Karen feels or behaves—only she controls the feeling and behavior through her interpretation.

If you can believe that whenever you or your children get over upset and exhibit counterproductive behavior, you—rather than someone else—caused it, you have become atypical. Very few people understand this concept. Yet it is one of the most powerful and fundamental principles behind governing your own life and helping your children govern theirs: Nobody but you has the power to determine your emotional and behavioral reactions. All people do is give you stuff to deal with. Sometimes people don't give you very nice stuff to deal with. By "stuff," I mean their behavior. And people need to be responsible for their behavior. However, they do not control how you feel or behave.

Expressing and Changing Your Emotions: A Myth

It is difficult for most of us to understand our emotions. Therefore, most counseling with children and their parents focuses on getting people to describe how they feel. During family therapy sessions, many therapists have family members communicate with each other through "I feel" statements: "I feel hurt when you ignore me," for example. In most instances, both children and adults misuse "I feel" statements. The common misuse is to say "I feel" when you are really expressing a thought. If Nancy says, "I feel you give Annie more attention than me," she is not expressing a feeling but rather a thought. If you can substitute the word "think" for "feel" and the sentence still makes sense, then you are expressing a thought rather than a feeling. In the above example, Nancy could easily say, "I think you give Annie more attention than me" without changing the meaning.

In general, I believe we place too much emphasis on having both children and adults express their feelings. First, emotional or psychological feelings can be very confusing compared to physiological feelings. For example, if the water level in your body is low, you feel thirsty. Thirst is not a good feeling. If thirst were a good feeling, we would all die of dehydration because we would want to prolong the good feelings associated with thirst. However, thirst is a bad feeling. Most importantly, because it is a physiological feeling, it tells us what to do—it's instinctive. If we feel thirst, that feeling tells us to get a drink. I have not yet had a person come to me for counseling because she felt thirsty and didn't know how to handle it.

Contrast how easily we can interpret and act on physiological feelings with the way we react to psychological feelings. Negative psychological feelings such as hurt, inadequacy, depression, anxiety, guilt and anger tell us something is wrong. And we are aware of negative feelings much more frequently than positive feelings. How many people wake up in the morning and say, "Boy does my arm ever feel good this morning." Yet, if we slept with our arm in an awkward position, we certainly are aware of that bad feeling in the morning. The problem with bad psychological feelings is that, unlike physiological feelings, they don't tell us what to do. Feeling depressed doesn't tell us what to do—feeling thirsty does.

One of the first experiences I had while working as a counselor on an adolescent psychiatric unit illustrates the difficulty of understanding feelings like depression. In one of my first counseling sessions, a patient commented how depressed she was feeling. In my naiveté, I responded by telling her to cheer up.

"I can't cheer up," she retorted. "Don't you know I'm depressed!"

"Well, are you going to be depressed the rest of your life?" I asked.

"Of course not," she said.

"Then cheer up now and stop wasting time being miserable," I exclaimed.

If only it were that easy to understand the feelings associated with depression. Most importantly, I believe that focusing on getting people to understand their feelings and, ultimately, getting them to "control" those feelings is a misplaced goal. Here is the reason why. In discussing the four parts of any experience, I stated that it is our interpretation of an event that results in our emotional and behavioral reaction. Therefore, every emotion is logical and correct for your interpretation. However, not every interpretation is logical and correct, as we saw with Karen's two interpretations of receiving flowers from Robert. This point is very important and deserves some elaboration, which I will provide through a personal experience.

Both my wife and I are "clean freaks"—real Felix Unger types. Generally, we have the same standards for cleanliness. However, every now and again my wife gets very upset if things are not perfectly clean. For example, I may drop a crumb on the floor or leave several drops of water on the bathroom sink after I finish washing up before going to bed. In response to those two situations, my wife will say things like, "John, you've dropped crumbs *all* over the floor," or "Did you know that the bathroom counter top is *soaking* wet?" She will make these comments in a way that indicates to me that she is *really* upset about them. I used to ask myself how anyone could get that upset about a few crumbs on the floor or drops of water on the counter. However, my wife's emotional reaction was very appropriate for her interpretations: crumbs were *all* over the floor and the counter was *soaking* wet. I too would be very upset if crumbs were *all* over the floor and the counter was *soaking* wet. The point is that my wife's interpretation resulted in her emotional reaction. It doesn't matter that her interpretation may be faulty, because once someone activates a particular schema, that interpretation is elevated to factual status—the belief becomes reality.

We can't always trust our emotions because they may be based on faulty interpretations. And the way we behave is directly influenced by how we feel. Therefore, the key for gaining choice and control over our emotions is to apply more *reasonable* interpretations to events in our lives. We can do so by training ourselves and our children to think in a more precise fashion. Now, the same bad event can happen to us or our children, but instead of getting overly upset, we can just get reasonably upset. Then we have choice and control of how to respond behaviorally in more appropriate ways to a situation. This is not as easy as I may make it sound, however. We have to exert an incredible amount of power to change the way we interpret events. The schemas we activate have become habitual through repetitive use and, consequently, are applied unconsciously. It is important to understand how the unconscious part of our brain makes it difficult to change our interpretations.

The Horse-and-Rider Analogy: Understanding How Our Conscious and Unconscious Work

A useful analogy for how the conscious and unconscious parts of our brain work was developed by Tom Miller. He divides our brain into two sections.

The outside part is called the neocortex. This is the conscious part of the brain where we can hear ourselves think and where we can intellectually control our behavior. Miller refers to this part of the brain as the "rider." The rider is responsible for learning new skills. This part of the brain is only the first step in gaining emotional and behavioral control. The inside part of the brain is called the limbic system. This is where we store and use learned, unconscious information and actions and control our feelings. This part of the brain allows us to perform a task without consciously thinking about it because the information has become habitual and automatic. Miller calls this the "horse." Through conscious repetition of new and desired learning, the horse takes over ("eats" the thought) from the rider and generates a new, automatic response (both feeling and behavior).

Here is how the horse-and-rider analogy works. Imagine a circular riding arena. About six feet in from the fence of the arena 10 barrels are spread evenly. Imagine also a horse trainer who teaches a horse to trot around the barrels, starting by going to the outside of the first barrel, the inside of the second, the outside of the third, and so on all the way around the inside perimeter of the arena. At first the trainer has to guide the horse by using the reins. However, after a while the horse learns the routine and goes around the barrels correctly without the trainer using the reins at all. In fact, after the horse has learned the routine very well through repetition, any rider could get on it and the horse would respond by going around the arena the way it was taught. However, if a new rider wants the horse to trot straight down the middle of the arena, go around the barrel at the other end, and trot back down the middle of the arena, the horse will resist. It will want to go back to the initially learned path. And to get the horse to travel a new path, the rider must exert an incredible amount of energy to break it from its old pattern.

The unconscious part of our brain works in the same way. We use our rider when we learn new information, such as learning how to drive a car. Think back to when you were learning to drive a car. Remember how aware you were of driving. You literally talked yourself through the process: it was initially a highly conscious one. Your self-talk may have gone something like this. "Okay, I need to adjust the seat and put my seat belt on—damn, I hate that buzzer. Now, make sure I put the right key in the ignition; did I adjust the mirror and seat? Okay, the car is started, now I need to look both ways before I pull out into traffic. Here I come up to a four-way stop sign—take my foot off the accelerator and apply pressure to the break—not too much pressure, I don't want other people see me come to a sudden stop. Now, two of us got to the stop sign at the same time. Let's see, I think the person on the right gets to go first. Okay, it's my turn to go, take my foot off the brake and apply even pressure to the accelerator."

When was the last time you were aware of those thoughts? If you are like most people, probably not for a long time. Through repetition acquired from driving for so many years, those thoughts were driven deeper into your brain until they were eaten up by your "horse" (your unconscious). You no longer had to think about those thoughts. Who drives your car now? The horse. Your "rider" (your conscious awareness) can drink coffee, read the paper, talk on the cellular phone, or put on makeup in the meantime.

Both children and adults have developed ingrained, habitual ways of interpreting situations that lead to ingrained, habitual feelings and ways of behaving. In order to gain emotional and behavioral control, our rider needs to exert a tremendous amount of power to change our horse—just as it literally took the rider to change the way the horse trotted around the arena. Although it takes a lot of power to change your horse, or your child's horse, the good news is that it is possible to behave differently than you feel.

Remember, the feeling is generated in our unconscious based on our interpretation of the event. However, we can consciously force ourselves to behave differently than the feeling generated in our unconscious. Here is an example: Imagine you accept a promotion and are transferred to England. Among other things, you will have to get accustomed to driving on the left side of the road. This will be a new experience initially requiring considerable concentration on your part. Therefore, your rider (your conscious mind) is going to instruct you on how to drive. And you probably will do a fairly good job driving with your rider. But alas, your horse (your unconscious mind) comes along to England with you. Your horse gets into the car and freaks out. Would you want your horse to drive the car? Obviously not. Your rider is intellectually driving the car correctly but how are you feeling? Probably nervous, scared or upset. Those feelings are generated by your horse through its interpretation of driving on the other side of the road. Yet you are able to drive with your rider even though it feels bad to your horse. That is, you can force yourself to behave (consciously) differently than you feel (unconsciously).

There are some important facts you need to know about your horse. First, whenever your horse runs into something new, such as driving in England, it codes it as wrong and ultimately dangerous. Second, you can have opposing thoughts in your conscious and unconscious mind at the exact same time. Going back to the example of learning to drive in England. Your rider can be saying, "Stay calm, you know the rules for driving in England. If you just drive slowly and carefully, you will do fine." However, your horse may activate a schema based on driving rules in the United States, since that is where you have spent most of the time driving, and tell you something like this, "I'm going to get into a wreck. There's no way I can drive on the wrong side of the road. How in the heck can I make turns and avoid other cars?" Third, you will always experience the emotional reactions that are logical for the way your horse is interpreting a situation. However, the horse's interpretation is not always logical and correct. Fourth, your horse's goal is to remain unchanged until you die. That goal is based on the concept of consistency described in the previous sections. Fifth, horses almost always win. Any pattern that becomes habitual and automatic is extremely difficult to change—witness people trying to quit smoking or lose weight. Sixth, your horse's thought processes never improve, due to the concept of consistency. Seventh, the only thing that will change your horse is power exerted by your rider.

Our horse, or unconscious, is where we get our interpretation of events. Consequently, that is also where we get our emotional reactions and behavioral responses. The way to change our emotions and behaviors, therefore, is to give our horse new interpretations of events. Those new interpretations come from the rider. But giving our horse new interpretations is not easy. As I mentioned, changing any habitual pattern is difficult. It requires that you exert a lot of power in your rider. In addition, the horse has developed four extremely powerful, yet irrational thinking styles that you must combat. I will now describe these thinking styles and how to combat them.

Irrational Thinking Styles

We engage in a variety of irrational thinking styles that interfere with our generating reasonable emotional reactions and behavioral responses to situations. However, four particularly insidious irrational thinking styles have been developed by our unconscious over the years: *Demandingness, Awfulizing, I Can't Stand It-It's,* and *Condemning and Damning.* Because we engage in these thinking styles automatically, we are rarely aware of them at a conscious level. In fact, when we encounter an event which makes us overreact emotionally and exhibit counterproductive behavior patterns, we tell ourselves something like this:

> That event (whatever is was) shouldn't have happened; it's awful that it did; I can't stand it, and somebody around here needs to be condemned and damned as rotten and worthless—let's see, is it me, is it you, or is it the way the world works?

This sentence represents the general nonsense our unconscious tells us. It also contains all four irrational thinking styles in the order we unconsciously tell ourselves. I will give examples that will make this sentence more specific. The point is that when our unconscious issues this sentence, our interpretation will lead to overreacting emotionally and exhibiting counterproductive behavior. In order to gain self-discipline so we can control our emotions and subsequent behavior, we need to replace the irrational thinking styles represented in the sentence with more rational interpretations or schemas. By using more rational interpretations, we will only get reasonably upset rather than exclusively so. Therefore, our behavior will reflect a more reasonable emotion. When this occurs, emotional and behavioral control have been established. Based on the work of Tom Miller, I will now explore how we can combat those four irrational beliefs.

Demandingness

Demandingness is the most difficult irrational thinking style to get rid of because your unconscious will tell you that the methods for removing it are wrong. Yet demandingness is the major reason we get overly upset and exhibit counterproductive behavior. Removing demandingness requires an incredible amount of conscious effort. Remember, your unconscious will take information that is different and code it to mean "wrong," "bad" and ultimately dangerous. However, just because something feels wrong doesn't mean it is wrong.

Several words are synonymous with "demand" and, therefore, reflect demandingness. The first word is *must*. According to the *American Heritage Dictionary*, the definition for must is "imperative requirement." The words *have to* also describe an imperative requirement. When we use the words *must, have to,* or their companions *ought, need to* or *got to*, there is absolutely no choice involved. An additional demanding word I will address shortly is *should* and its opposite *shouldn't*.

But for now, there is a simple rule for not engaging in demandingness: When using words like *must*, make them live up to their definition. That is, if something is a *must* then there is absolutely no choice involved. You will be compelled by forces beyond your control to do something. However, if there is any choice at all, then what you're about to do is not a *must*. Below is a list of demanding words and phrases:

1. must
2. should
3. have to
4. need to
5. got to
6. ought

Here is the problem with using words like *must* or *have to*. If we believe we cannot live up to or are failing to live up to the imperative requirement explicit in the use of these words, then we are going to become overly upset and engage in counterproductive behavior. Therefore, if there is any choice involved in what you are about to do, it is not a *must*. Let's take the sentence "I must be on time." Ask yourself this test question: "Is it possible not to be on time regardless of the consequences?" If we begin to train our rider to think in literal, precise and accurate thinking styles, we will begin to refrain from engaging in demandingness. Then the demand of being on time is turned into what it really is—a desire or want. You would prefer to be on time or it would be better if you were on time. Because these words are not demands, you will get an emotional reaction far more reasonable than the one experienced when demanding words are used to interpret a situation.

There are some musts that are true. Dying is a must—you can't live forever. If you jump off the roof of your house, you must fall to the ground because of the law of gravity. The simple guideline for using the word *must* is to make sure it only describes *reality*. If you only use the word *must* to describe reality, you are less likely to get overly upset and exhibit counterproductive behavior patterns. Let's see how well we can use the word *must* to describe reality. What *must* you be doing right now? Reading this book. Why *must* you be reading this book? Because you are. How long *must* you read this book? Until you stop. If you said as long as you want to, that would be incorrect. There may be some of you, for whom this book is assigned reading, who have read it longer than you wanted to. What do you tell yourself when you put this book down? I *must* be putting this book down.

Let's try one more example of the demanding word *must* before moving on to the big demanding word, *should*. To make a point to my students about the word *must*, I will be talking and then drop an eraser on the floor. Then I'll ask them some questions: "Where is the eraser?" "On the floor." "Where must it be?" "On the floor." "Where does it have to be?" "On the floor." So far, my students are responding correctly to the use of the words *must* and *have to*. Then I ask them this question: "Where does it need to be?" And they uniformly answer "On the chalk tray." That answer is wrong, because it does not use the demanding word *need* to describe reality. The correct answer to this last question is "On the floor." Don't you think the eraser needs to be wherever it is? Remember, we are just describing reality. But your unconscious is saying something like this: "Well, having the eraser on the floor sure isn't a very useful place for it to be. It's not sensible to keep it on the floor. Therefore, it *needs* to be on the chalk tray." But by engaging in this demanding sentence, we set ourselves up to become overly upset and exhibit counterproductive behavior. Now, I'm not suggesting that everyone overreacts to dropping an eraser on the floor. Nevertheless, the example proves my point. When something happens we do not like, our unconscious immediately uses a demanding word—as if all the demandingness in the world will transport the eraser back to the chalk tray. If, instead, we consciously say, "The eraser needs to be on the floor because that's where it is," our unconsciousness cannot elevate that reality into a demand. If the situation is not elevated into a demand, we will only get reasonably upset rather than overly upset.

Now here is the most wicked demanding word of them all: *should*. We use the word *should* or *shouldn't* unconsciously all the time to interpret situations in a demanding way that leads to overreacting emotionally and exhibiting counterproductive behavior. Interestingly, your unconscious will start out with a nondemanding word and then elevate it into a demanding interpretation. Let's say your teenage son wakes up in the morning, looks in the bathroom mirror and sees a big zit. The first thing his unconscious will say is, "I wish that zit wasn't there." However, since he wishes the zit was not there, his unconscious elevates the interpretation into demandingness by saying, "That zit *shouldn't* be there." If the zit shouldn't be there, then it's awful that it is and somebody around here needs to be condemned as rotten or worthless. If you happen to be walking past the bathroom when your son looks at the zit, he may just overreact emotionally and exhibit counterproductive behavior by saying to you, "You don't ever give me space. Just get out of here. Can't you see I'm in the bathroom now. I can't get any privacy around here." Of course, your unconscious then will reciprocate with a demanding interpretation, saying, "My son *shouldn't* talk to me like that." Yet, if we use the word *should* correctly, we would say, "My son *should* have talked to me like that because he did." In the last interpretation, you would be using the word *should* correctly. Therefore, it becomes much more difficult for your unconscious to elevate the interpretation into a demand.

Using the words *should* and *shouldn't* correctly gets rid of a lot of demanding interpretations. However, it is hard to train ourselves to think in these terms. One of the reasons is that if we say, "My son *should* have talked back to me," we automatically assume that we approve of that type of verbal behavior. However, that is not the case at all! What you're doing is simply saying that you accept that a reality occurred; you do not have to approve of it. To combat the use of demanding interpretations of events, you only have to accept that a reality has occurred. For example, while Jimmy Carter was president, the Iranians took some Americans hostage. This incident was considered a nail in the proverbial coffin of Carter's re-election. Now, here's the question: Should the Iranians have taken the Americans hostage? The factual answer is yes, because they did. But it wouldn't have set well with the American public if President Carter had come on television saying that the Iranians *should* have taken hostages. In our culture, we are brought up to use the word *should* in a demanding way. However, using *should* in a demanding way leads to overreacting emotionally and exhibiting counterproductive behavior patterns. Witness our failed attempt to rescue the hostages and how much further President Carter's popularity plummeted. Instead of saying *should*, we can use a nondemanding word such as *ethical*. Therefore, we can ask, "Was it *ethical* for the Iranians to take the Americans hostage?" Then we can answer no, unless we are Iranians. But because *ethical* is a nondemanding word, it is less likely to result in our overreacting emotionally and exhibiting counterproductive behavior.

The real issue in not engaging in demandingness is to separate acceptance from approval. The word *should* will not lead to demandingness when used to acknowledge that a reality occurred. However, from years of learning imposed by our parents and culture, our unconscious confuses acceptance with approval. If our unconscious can't approve of something, then it is difficult for us to accept that some reality occurred. That is why we continue to stay stuck in demanding thinking styles. The goal is to prevent our unconscious from elevating nondemanding thoughts. We do this by accepting things for the way they are and then deciding whether or not we like that—two very different issues. If we use the word *should* correctly, it basically has two meanings: the *should* of probability and the *should* of obligation.

The *should* of probability is easy to get rid of—simply drop the word *should* from the sentence in which it is used. For example, I could say to my secretary, "If you *should* see Bob, please tell him to come into my office." Since we are talking probability, I can simply drop the word and engage in less demandingness: "If you see Bob, please tell him to come into my office." Although this difference is subtle, it is nevertheless very powerful. When I say, "*Should* you see Bob," I'm setting myself up for disappointment and blaming my secretary. Of course, she should see Bob, since we work in the same office suite. Yet, if I stopped to think of all the places Bob could be, the probability is actually great that an entire morning could pass without my secretary seeing Bob. However, if I drop the *should*, then if Bob doesn't come into my office, I know my secretary hasn't seen him yet.

The *should* of obligation is much more difficult to stop. The first way to approach this use of the word is to answer the following question: Do humans always live up to their obligations—no matter how small they may be? The answer is obviously no. Therefore, living up to obligations is not a *should* or *must*. It's just a pipe dream our unconscious pulls on us. Therefore, do not use *should* the old way—just use it to describe reality. After using *should* to describe reality, ask yourself, how bad is it? Say you leave work, go out to your car and find your windshield smashed in. The first thing your unconscious will tell you is that your windshield is smashed in. However, it will then instantaneously elevate the interpretation by telling you that your windshield *shouldn't* be smashed in. We say *shouldn't* because we don't approve of the windshield being smashed in. Yet you can stop the demandingness by saying, "My windshield *should* be smashed in, because it is." Saying this statement feels funny to people because they think it means that they don't care if their windshield is smashed in. But that's not the case at all. Of course, you don't approve of it, but how bad is it? Asking yourself this last question is a way to combat the second irrational thinking style: Awfulizing.

Awfulizing

Other terms for awfulizing are *catastrophizing, making mountains out of mole hills,* or *blowing things out of proportion.* Awfulizing is a logical consequence of engaging in demandingness. If we say that something *should* or *shouldn't* have happened, the next interpretation will be that it's *awful* that whatever happened happened. In order to understand how we engage in awfulizing, it is important to understand two fundamental assumptions. First, 100 percent equals *all.* It means we got *all* of whatever we're talking about. It is not possible to get more than 100 percent of anything. Therefore, when sports announcers say that Joe Montana gave 110 percent on that last drive, that is impossible. It is not dealing with reality. To gain emotional and behavioral control for ourselves and teach these things to our children, on the other hand, we must be precise, factual and literal. Second, whenever something negative happens to us, we describe it as bad. The logical deduction of these two assumptions is this: Bad (negative) things that can happen to us range from approximately .00001 percent of "badness" up to the maximum of 100 percent bad. Bad things cannot go over 100 percent.

In order not to engage in awfulizing, we need to get an idea of the types of bad things that happen to us on a daily basis. I am not referring to bad events that happen physically to our bodies, since we have less control over those incidents. I am referring to psychological, social or emotional bad things that happen to us. Here are three scenarios.

First, imagine that someone stole your purse or wallet while you were at the mall. The person took all your money, as well as the checks and credit cards, which must be canceled; pictures of the kids are gone with no back-up negatives; and any other items of sentimental value are also gone; furthermore, you'll incur the cost of replacing the purse or wallet. Second, imagine someone with whom you don't get along well at work. This person could be your boss or supervisor, your co-worker, or someone you supervise. Third, think of a person from your family with whom you occasionally have a hard time. This can be one of your children or an extended family member like your mother-in-law. Fourth, imagine going out to your car after a hard day at work only to realize that you have locked your keys in the car. Fifth, imagine eating lunch out with several friends. You order a steak sandwich cooked medium rare and it comes very well done.

Now we are going to try to transform awfulizing by using the body scale that Dr. Miller developed and the five scenarios I provided above. The body scale appears in Figure 4.8. The body scale helps you measure how bad things are; this allows you to decide that an event is a certain percentage bad. After you train yourself to use the scale, your unconscious will automatically give you a response that's logical for the percentage you select. As a result,

The Physical Injury Scale	
100% —	worst
95% —	4 limbs cut off
90% —	3 limbs cut off
85% —	2 limbs cut off
80% —	dominant arm cut off
75% —	nondominant arm cut off
70% —	1 hand cut off
65% —	1 foot cut off
60% —	3 fingers cut off
55% —	big toe cut off
50% —	3 broken limbs
45% —	2 broken limbs
40% —	dominant arm broken
35% —	nondominant arm broken
30% —	broken nose
25% —	badly sprained ankle
20% —	laceration (6 stitches)
15% —	cut
10% —	bruise
5% —	small bump
1% —	gnat bite
0% —	

Figure 4.8. Physical injury scale designed to transform awfulizing.

because you won't be over- or underreacting, your behavior will be reasonable for a given situation.

Think of the first scenario I described above: losing your purse or wallet including all its contents. Remember, you are going to have to make that wonderful trip to the Department of Motor Vehicles to get a new driver's license, cancel your credit cards, and put a hold on your checks. Now, assume that I can magically get your purse or wallet back for you with all its contents. Your job is to look at the body scale in Figure 4.8 and go high enough to get me to use my magic. You obviously do not want to go too high; it isn't worth it. Conversely, if you go too low, I won't use my magic. So, start at 20—would you go through stitches to get your purse or wallet back? Going through stitches means sitting in the emergency room of a hospital for about an hour with kleenex against your laceration. Then the doctor will give you a shot of Novocain right into the laceration. Then you get the stitches.

If you answered yes, then go up to 25—badly sprained ankle. Those who have had a badly sprained ankle can testify that it's no fun. You can't wear a shoe on that foot, your foot must be elevated, the pain is intense for 10 to 14 days and your mobility is very limited. Also, you aren't too much fun to be around.

If, on the other hand, 20 was too high, then go down lower to the point where you are willing to make the trade. On the right side of the body scale, across from the percentage you selected, write "lost purse/wallet."

Most people typically do not go higher than a cut or a laceration requiring stitches. Now, you can use the test question to transform awfulizing: "How bad is it?" If it's only 15 percent bad, then you should get an emotional reaction commensurate with 15 percent, and your behavior should consequently reflect an emotion of 15 percent bad. However, most of us usually get much more upset than 15 percent when we're looking for a lost purse or wallet. The difference between how upset you say you are now and how upset your unconscious actually gets you when the event happens represents emotional overpayment. You can apply the body scale to the other four scenarios I provided, or to any of your own, in a similar fashion. In addition, you can modify the body scale to include any hierarchy of items that make sense to you.

Now we have two methods for developing emotional and behavioral control. First, in order to combat demandingness, whenever an event happens we tell ourselves that it should have happened. In the purse/wallet scenario, we would initially tell ourselves, I should have lost my purse or wallet. We tell ourselves this to prevent our unconscious from elevating the event into a demand. We are *not* trying to convince ourselves that we don't care. We are only acknowledging that a reality occurred. Then we can ask ourselves how bad is it? This scenario was about 15 percent bad. Then you tell yourself you can stand a 15. By telling yourself you can stand a 15, you are combating the next irrational thinking style: I can't stand it-it's.

I can't stand it-it's

How many people have you heard say, "I can't stand this anymore"? This irrational thinking style is a gross exaggeration that results in inappropriate emotional and behavioral responses. Saying "I can't stand it" is a complete fallacy. You are living proof that you've stood everything that has ever happened to you. And you are going to be able to stand and handle everything that is going to happen to you except the one thing that will kill you. And, as the noted psychiatrist Milton Erickson was fond of saying, "I don't worry about dying. In fact, it will be the last thing I do." Death is the only thing you can't stand. However, when we tell ourselves we can't stand something, we are destined to engage in the fourth irrational thinking style: Damning and condemning.

Damning and condemning

Damning and condemning directs the other three irrational thinking styles to three possible places: yourself, others or the world. When you think, I must and if I don't I won't be able to stand it, you are making yourself the target of your irrational thinking. The most frequent target of our irrational thinking styles is ourselves. As Albert Ellis suggested, we are a gullible species. If someone tells us something we don't like, we assume it's the truth—otherwise why would we be told? Feelings of hurt and inadequacy result when we put ourselves down. The second target of our irrational thinking styles is others. When you think, Nancy must clean this house, and if she doesn't I can't stand it, you are targeting others. Targeting others can lead to feelings of frustration and anger. Essentially, you are giving up all your control to others. Your own happiness, consequently, becomes dependent upon others living up to your expectations. Finally, when you think, The world must...and when it doesn't it's awful and I can't stand it, you are making everything the target of your irrational beliefs. Making the world the target for your irrational thoughts leads to feelings of depression, hopelessness and helplessness. If the world is to blame, how much control could you possible have? No one can change the entire world. Those types of beliefs lead to the feelings of hopelessness and helplessness associated with suicide.

Putting It All Together

Remember the general sentence we tell ourselves based on the four irrational thinking styles:

That event (whatever it was) shouldn't have happened; it's awful that it did, I can't stand it, and somebody around here needs to be condemned and damned as rotten and worthless—let's see, is it me, is it you, or is it the way the world works?

We can now develop a more appropriate sentence to tell ourselves when some event happens to us:

That event (whatever it was) should have happened, and it's about ___ percent bad, and I can stand a ____.

With this general sentence, you can insert any event to make the sentence specific to that situation. For example, if you ask your child to wash the dishes and she says, "No, I won't. It's not my turn, and you can't make me," you can counter by telling yourself this sentence:

My daughter should have just talked back to me, and it's about 10 percent bad, and I can stand a 10.

Remember, you say *should* to stop your unconscious from elevating the situation into demandingness, then you apply the body scale to give yourself a rational, factual idea of how bad the situation really is, and then you tell yourself you can stand the situation. By practicing this sentence you are more likely to get a reasonable emotional response—that is, you will not overreact emotionally. If you do not overreact emotionally, you still have control over your choice of behavioral response. Consequently, you will be better able to deal with your child constructively without overreacting.

I mentioned at the beginning of this section that this information was meant for both parents and children. I hope the benefit to parents is obvious. We interpret many of the behaviors our children present as a direct challenge to our authority. Since we are the adults, our authority *shouldn't* be challenged by children who don't have the years of experience we do. So we engage in demandingness, thereby losing some of our emotional and behavioral control. However, I did not present the RET system just for parents to gain better emotional and behavioral control. I presented this system so you can teach it to your children.

Think of the ages of your children and figure out how many more years they have ahead of them. Think of all the tough events they will be facing. Now, visualize using the RET system in your own life. Once your emotional and behavioral control is enhanced through practice, start teaching the system to your children. They won't understand it at first, but with a little help and patience from you, they will begin to catch on. Think of the amount of pain you may save both your children and yourself. Maybe the next generation will perform better than ours has. At least it has the chance to do so with a lot less pain.

5

Diagnosis and Behavior Problems

In the previous chapters, I have tried to present techniques that can be used to address a wide range of difficult behavior children can present. I have purposely avoided labeling any one technique as specific to a particular behavior problem. The reason for this is simple: When we focus too much attention and energy on a particular problem, we begin to view the child as the problem rather than as a person who is exhibiting a difficult behavior. Although this semantic difference may seem trivial, it has a profound effect: focusing attention on the label muddles efforts at dealing effectively with a child's behavior. For example, it is common for schools to say they have special services for learning disabled or behaviorally disordered students. Notice how the label "learning disabled" or "behaviorally disordered" becomes the student. As a consequence, schools expend a lot of effort developing learning disabilities or behavioral disorders interventions. The problem is that there are very few, if any, interventions specific to any given label or diagnosis. Therefore, instead of spending time looking for more effective ways to teach reading or math to students with learning difficulties, schools expend much effort in labeling students. Consequently, parents of children with disabilities can become extremely frustrated with schools that they perceive are not "properly labeling" their child.

Ironically, when I talk to parents in the situation described above, what they are really after is more effective programming for their child. I receive numerous phone calls from parents who are displeased with the "label" their child received from the school. One parent, Mrs. Christenson, was disturbed that her son, who had been diagnosed by a child psychiatrist as having an attention deficit disorder, received the label "learning disabled" from the school in order to qualify him for special services. Mrs. Christenson disagreed with this label. However, since attention deficit disorder is not currently a federal category of disability, she wanted her child reclassified as "other health impaired," expending considerable effort toward this end. The school was even willing to have an outside evaluator come in and reevaluate her son.

Upon meeting Mrs. Christenson, I let her vent her frustration at the school for quite some time. Then, when she paused, I said, "Mrs. Christenson, what exactly do you want the school to do?"

"I want them to reclassify my son as 'other health impaired,'" she said.

"Why do you want your son reclassified?" I asked.

She looked at me sardonically. "If my son is reclassified, then he'd finally get a more appropriate education. I just don't like the approach the school uses to teach my son and manage his behavior. I have been through the wringer with the principal, the school psychologist and his teachers. They all think I don't know what I'm talking about. They have this condescending attitude. And I can't believe that they won't even consider my suggestions. I mean, they're talking about *my* son. Who should know him better than his mother!"

After acknowledging her concern, I asked, "Do you think schools hold back certain interventions to use only with children who receive a particular label?" She looked somewhat puzzled at hearing this question, so I continued by asking, "Do you think your son's behavior would automatically change if he was reclassified from 'learning disabled' to 'other health impaired'?"

"Well, of course not," she replied.

"Okay then, what I suggest we do is come up with a list of the specific behaviors your son is exhibiting at school and how the school is currently dealing with them. Then we can generate some intervention techniques to address those behaviors that the school is not currently employing. I'll contact the school and see if we can set up a meeting to discuss your concerns."

The point of this conversation is that parents often want to search for the correct "diagnosis" or "label," believing that the label will somehow lead to a new treatment approach. Unfortunately, when it comes to behavior problems, a diagnosis or label has limited usefulness. I have seen parents spend hundreds of thousands of dollars taking their child to special clinics around the country trying to get a correct diagnosis. Many of these clinics are ethically suspect and are out to make a buck preying on parents' desperation. Even if a correct diagnosis is made, the behaviors a child exhibits still have to be addressed.

What a Diagnoses Does for Managing Behavior Problems

Many children who exhibit difficult behaviors eventually find their way into the mental health system. It is becoming increasingly common for parents to take their child to a psychiatrist when they are having trouble managing her behavior. Because psychiatrists are trained in medicine, they approach a problem in terms of trying to correctly "diagnose" it. A diagnosis usually is based on listening to parental reports of a child's behavior, interviewing the child and obtaining information from a child's teachers. A psychiatrist will then consult the *Diagnostic and Statistical Manual of Mental Disorders,* the psychiatric handbook that classifies mental disorders, in order to make a diagnosis.

Labeling a child with a particular disorder is based on the belief that the label provides useful information for treatment. Unfortunately, there are very few diagnostic labels applied to children's difficult behavior that have treatment relevance. The notable exceptions are attention deficits and depression which can be treated with medication. And these "disorders" are being treated with medication at an astronomical rate. More and more children are being placed on Ritalin for attention problems and hyperactivity or Prozac for depression. Not surprisingly, there is concern in some circles of the psychiatric community that medications for attentional problems and depression are being overprescribed for difficulties that could be easily treated through nonpharmaceutical approaches.

We probably should not be surprised by the trend toward prescribing medication for relatively minor behavior problems. Our society is preoccupied with drugs. Many people drink coffee to jump-start themselves in the morning, smoke cigarettes to manage daily stress, and drink alcohol to relax in the evening. One of the biggest advertising markets is for licit drugs: rugged men smoke Marlboros while attractive young women smoke Salems. If you are a young adult and looking for a good time, Bud Light and Coors Light are for you. Sexuality sells everything from aspirin to laxatives. It should not come as a surprise that children in the United States who have attention- and hyperactivity-related problems are 50 times more likely to be placed on medication than in Britain and France. In these countries, behaviors associated with inattention and hyperactivity are viewed as conduct problems, and therefore treatment is primarily psychological. I seriously doubt that some unknown but insidious biochemical or hereditary factors are making British and French children more immune to attention deficits than children in the United States. I do concede that the equivalent European diagnostic criteria for attention deficits are somewhat more restrictive than those used in the United States. Nevertheless, my point is that the treatment implications of having children receive a diagnosis based solely on the difficult behavior they exhibit are limited by the fact that disorders are largely socially defined and socially negotiated.

The Social Construction of Childhood Mental Disorders

The irony of diagnosing a child with a mental disorder, based on the behavior he exhibits, is that diagnostic standards are really determined socially rather than medically. The psychiatrist Thomas Szasz wrote a controversial yet influential book in the early 1960s entitled *The Myth of Mental Illness.* Szasz begins by stating that the words "illness" and "disorder" imply that such phenomena result from some, perhaps subtle, neurological or biochemical deficit. If no physical anomaly can be found, it is only because the technology does not yet exist to identify it. Therefore, mental illness or disorder is regarded as basically no different than other physical diseases such as measles or hepatitis.

Szasz sees several problems with this conceptualization. First, maladaptive behavior, such as a person's bizarre verbalization that "bugs are crawling out of scabs on my body" cannot typically be explained by a defect or disease of the nervous system. In fact, this type of thinking is only considered bizarre because of our current societal values. In *The Divided Self,* R.D. Laing analyzed the language of individuals with schizophrenia and found that even the most bizarre language had meaning for the person using it. Therefore, just because people are saying or doing something that society believes to be out of the norm does not necessarily mean they suffer from a mental "illness" or "disorder."

The second problem Szasz has is that making a diagnosis requires a person to compare a child's observed behavior to some societal standard. These standards, of course, can vary from context to context within and across a culture. A child who yells and runs around her school classroom may lead her teacher to believe she has a behavior problem. But if the child was playing basketball in P.E. class, this teacher may think she was being appropriately aggressive. So who has the behavior problem—the child or the teacher? The judgment that a child is exhibiting behaviors severe enough to warrant receiving a diagnostic label is based on matching his past experiences to the society and culture in which he lives. In other words, the concept of "disorder" implies a deviation from some clearly defined norms. In the case of physical illness, the norm is the structural processes of the physical body. There is universal agreement that normal body temperature is 98.6 degrees. A temperature of 103 degrees indicates a fever. That diagnosis won't vary from physician to physician or from one part of the country to another.

In terms of behavior problems, however, the standards for acceptable and unacceptable behavior are socially and ethically based. And societal standards vary across context and time. Imagine watching a sitcom from the 1950s, say the *Andy Griffith Show.* Think of the types of situations Opie found himself in and the behaviors he exhibited. Now think about the three kids on *Roseanne* and the type of situations they are in and the behaviors they exhibit. Imagine taking those kids and placing them with Opie on the *Andy Griffith Show.* Would Opie's behavior look bizarre and aberrant? Of course it would. The standards and norms for appropriate child behavior in the 1950s were far different than the standards today—for better or worse. Therefore, if Opie behaved then in a way that the children on *Roseanne* do now, he probably would have been referred to a psychiatrist and, most likely, would have been diagnosed as having some disorder. The irony is that his problems can be reduced to nothing more than a case of bad timing—being three decades behind the now-accepted societal standards for child behavior.

The third problem Szasz has with the concept of mental "illness" or "disorder" is that although a diagnosis is made on the assumption that some neurological or biochemical deficit exists, treatment is usually nonmedical. To reiterate, the reason for making a diagnosis is to inform treatment. If a diagnosis of "oppositional-defiant disorder" is made, then in theory this label should provide us information on how to treat the child. Yet there is no medical treatment for oppositional-defiant disorder. I have listed the symptoms below. An examination of these "symptoms" may lead one to wonder if all children around the time of puberty do not have an oppositional-defiant disorder:

1. Often loses temper
2. Often argues with adults
3. Often actively defies or refuses adult requests or rules
4. Often deliberately does things that annoy other people, e.g., grabs other children's hats
5. Often blames others for his or her own mistakes
6. Is often touchy or easily annoyed by others
7. Is often angry and resentful
8. Is often spiteful and vindictive
9. Often swears or uses obscene language[*]

The fourth problem Szasz sees is that the professional—psychiatrist, psychologist, psychotherapist—is making a judgment about whether a child's behavior reaches the diagnostic criteria for a particular condition. But don't the professional's beliefs concerning religion, ethics, politics, philosophy and other value-laden topics influence his judgment? If the professional's judgment is affected by these or similar factors, what should we make of it? Psychiatrists who believe that attention deficits have a neurological or biochemical basis are more likely to prescribe medication than psychiatrists espousing a more holistic view. In fact, parents readily become aware of the differences in values between psychiatrists and will seek out one they feel holds beliefs congruent with their own. Therefore, can we really claim that diagnosing a child as having a mental illness or disorder is as real

---

[*] The only function a diagnosis of oppositional-defiant disorder serves is to state the obvious: a child is demonstrating undesirable behaviors and a robust intervention is required. But to focus on the diagnosis rather than the specific behaviors is misleading and nonproductive.

and objective a process as identifying a child with hepatitis? And because human values and behavioral interactions are so diverse, should we not expect some children to have difficulty fitting into the societal norm simply because of inherent differences between individuals?

Individuals differ on a wide range of characteristics—both physical and psychological. Because of hereditary, and to an extent environment, some people are tall, while others are medium or short. The same can be said for other physical features such as the size of an individual's nose, ears and lips. When do we decide that individuals are too short and, consequently, label them dwarfs? Can any cutoff be anything but arbitrary? Let's examine intelligence as an illustrative example. Normal intelligence, as measured by intelligence tests, is indicated by a score of 100, plus or minus 15 points. Therefore, a child with an intelligence quotient (IQ) between 85 and 115 is considered normal. But what about the child with an IQ of 84? He could be considered mildly mentally retarded by some accounts. But is this child's functioning likely to be that different from the child with an IQ of 85 or even 90? In order to determine any differences, we must examine each child's behavioral functioning in the context of the home, community and school. And that is what I'm advocating in the case of mental disorders, such as attention deficits or depression. But before I turn to those two specific "disorders" of childhood, I would like to end this discussion by providing some insights into the social implications of labeling.

The Social Implications of Labels

Individuals, whether children or adults, are likely to be viewed differently by society depending on what diagnosis they receive to label their problems. Any behavior in which individuals engage takes place in a context of societal values. In this broad sense, no human activity is devoid of social implications. When certain values are widely shared by members of a society, they become easy to lose sight of altogether. However, when the behavior of an individual is at odds with societal values, then society tries to explain them. For example, extremely aberrant behaviors such as those engaged in by Jeffrey Dahmer need to be explained so that society can feel good about its members. Jeffrey Dahmer was a member of our society. But his behavior brought into question the functioning of our society. If he could act in so aberrant a fashion, then maybe other humans can do likewise—an unsettling thought. Therefore, society needs to create a place for people like Jeffrey Dahmer to exist without disturbing the balance of society.

The places we create for people like Jeffrey Dahmer are called *niches*. A niche is the role or relationship a person plays and its function in society. Jeffrey Dahmer's niche was "crazy." Although he was not found insane (a legal term to describe culpability), he certainly was considered to be crazy in some way. The label "crazy" is a niche because it defines Jeffrey Dahmer as different from the rest of us. By defining him as different, we feel better about ourselves as a species. The deviant person is shunted into these niches. A variety of labels that have negative connotations serve as niches where deviant individuals can function without disturbing the mainstream of society. What I mean by *function* is that the individual's behavior can be explained away by the label. And as members of a society, we view individuals with certain labels very differently from those with other labels.

Society attributes problems associated with the label *emotional disturbance* to people's unwillingness to behave appropriately, which brings into question their moral character. The diagnosis of "conduct disorder" describes children who steal, run away from home, deliberately engage in fire-setting, break into buildings or cars, deliberately destroy others' property, are physically cruel to animals, force someone into sexual activity, or use a weapon in a fight. Although these behaviors are illustrative rather than inclusive, they imply that a child with this disorder is aware of what he is doing and, in fact, chooses to engage in the behaviors. Words like *deliberately* and *force* imply conscious awareness and choice of behavior. Because of the connotation of these words, we view individuals with labels—emotionally disturbed, conduct disordered, juvenile delinquent—much more negatively because we believe such persons could behave differently if they wanted to.

Contrast the negative view society holds toward individuals with the pejorative labels described above with labels that are believed to have a physical origin, such as "mentally retarded" or "learning disabled." Because these labels convey a medical condition, they are viewed in a way similar to other medical disorders such as diabetes, epilepsy or asthma. With all these labels, society tends to hold "afflicted" individuals in high esteem when they are able to overcome or compensate for their disorder. These views are vividly portrayed in the media. For example, a television show that aired several years ago, *Life Goes On*, had as one of the main characters a young man with Down syndrome. This young man was endeared to us through his struggles and accomplishments. His problems were not considered to be of his own making but rather an unfortunate byproduct of some neurological, biochemical or genetic defect. Several very affirmative television documentaries have focused on people with learning disabilities, most notably the reading disorder dyslexia.

Contrast this view with the case of someone that society has given a more insidious label. It would be difficult to imagine a person running for political office coming forward and stating on television that he is seriously emotionally disturbed. Society would view him as weak and unfit to hold political office. We would assume he suffered from some character flaw, that he could overcome the problem if he wanted to, and that the root of the problem must reside in a lack of will power or self-control. In fact, George McGovern was forced to replace Thomas Eagleton as his running mate during the 1972 presidential campaign because the media discovered that Eagleton had been hospitalized for depression. Even though Eagleton "recovered," he was still viewed as weak for having emotional difficulties in the first place.

My point in making this distinction is that societal factors may not only drive definitions of whether someone has a "disorder," but also the type of label the person receives. Take the term learning disabled, which has become one of the most frequently applied labels for children over the past 20 years. The history of learning disabilities is an interesting one. Briefly, a learning disability refers to a condition in which a child possesses normal intelligence (IQ score between 85 and 115) but is at least two years behind his same-age peers in academic achievement (as measured by scores on standardized achievement tests). In the case of learning disabilities, there is almost never any neurological, biochemical or genetic cause. We simply can't see what causes learning disabilities. Here is how the label evolved.

Before the enactment of federal legislation in 1975 (PL 94-142) that mandated free, appropriate and individualized education services for children with disabilities, few public school special programs existed. The notable exceptions were programs for children who were mentally retarded or emotionally disturbed. Most of the children in these two programs were from poor, minority families. However, there seemed to be a growing number of children who were not mentally retarded and did not have severe emotional disturbances, but nevertheless had difficulty performing academically. Most importantly, these children came from intact, middle- to upper-middle class families. Parents of these children did not want them placed in classes for the mentally retarded or emotionally disturbed because of the negative connotations associated with these labels. Specifically, parents did not want their children's academic problems perceived as stemming from negative environmental factors commonly associated with poor or minority children—many of whom were labeled mentally retarded or emotionally disturbed. And during the first 10 years since the enactment of PL 94-142 that designated learning disability as a category for children to receive special services, the children in these classes were predominantly white and middle-class. To legitimize this new category, it quickly became synonymous with various physiological theories to explain its existence.

Given public support for the label "learning disability," it quickly became the largest category of disability. The label had both intended and unintended results. The intended result was obvious: to serve children who did not seem to fit any other label. The unintended results were less obvious, but nonetheless quite telling. Physicians now had a socially acceptable "diagnosis" with which to label children for whom no physical problems existed. Concerned parents could then be assured by physicians and teachers that problems were organic and that they were not responsible for the child's academic failures. Teachers were also relieved of responsibility because these children, by definition, were *supposed* to be underachievers. Finally, children with learning disabilities could have their low-achievement test scores excluded from district-wide averages, which made the school district appear in a more favorable light to the community who holds the purse strings on allocating money for public education.

Labels based on medical classifications appease everyone because they relieve physicians, parents, teachers and public servants of responsibility. Medical labels are, in essence, "no fault" labels. Even the child cannot be held responsible because his problems can be attributed to some neurological, biochemical or genetic defect. Unfortunately, this emphasis on diagnosing and labeling takes the focus away from how to address the difficult behaviors children exhibit. Therefore, as our discussion turns toward two disorders that have garnered considerable interest from the public media, attention deficits and depression, keep in mind that the focus remains on behaviors rather than labels.

A Prelude to Attention Deficits and Depression

Perhaps no other conditions have received as much attention in the professional literature and popular press as have attention deficits and depression. Children with these two conditions primarily are seen by psychiatrists, since medication is a common treatment. Nevertheless these conditions are conceptualized quite differently.

Attention deficits are primarily thought of as an *externalizing* condition. The behaviors of a child with an attention deficit exhibits bring him into conflict with his environment—namely parents, teachers and peers. Because the behaviors are generally viewed as disruptive, this condition is largely diagnosed through parent and teacher reports. Remember from Chapter 2 how observing a child's behavior often is a subjective process that is affected by an observer's biases and beliefs about a child. In addition, there is no neurological or biochemical criteria for making a diagnosis of an attention deficit.

In contrast, depression is considered an *internalizing* disorder. The problems are not particularly bothersome to others, but rather are troubling internally to a child. Specific behaviors associated with depression include changes in sleep and eating habits and withdrawing from peers. Because they generally do not bring a child into conflict with the environment, these behaviors are easily overlooked. Remember, the squeaky wheel gets the grease: behaviors associated with attention deficits are squeaky while those associated with depression are not.

The purpose of the next two chapters is to provide the reader with an alternative perspective on two common behavior problems that have been grouped and labeled as "disorders." My intent is not to discredit the medical profession—to the contrary, psychiatrists play a valuable role in diagnosing and treating attention deficits and depression. Instead, I want to point out that, in terms of what parents can do to help their child, it is more beneficial to focus on the specific behaviors a child exhibits and apply the principles and techniques described in this book.

The following two chapters are by no means the definitive statement on attention deficits and depression—literally hundreds of books have been written on these conditions. My intent is to present a no-nonsense, nonmedical approach to these conditions that is free of psycho-babble. In terms of attention deficits, it has been my experience that one of parents' chief concerns is how the school accommodates to their child's needs. I think parents will find information on this aspect helpful. With depression, I want to highlight specific common-sense techniques that parents can use with their children who may be experiencing depression.

I hope that the information presented in the next two chapters will convince parents to look beyond the specific label a child may receive and instead examine the behaviors a child exhibits and make those behaviors the target for intervention. There are too many hucksters selling therapeutic "snake oil," and parents who have children with behavior problems are often an easy mark. To the best of my knowledge, there are no nonmedical techniques that are specific to any one diagnostic label. With this information in mind, I believe parents can effectively work with children who have attention deficits, are depressed, or have received some other label from psychiatric or educational professionals.

6

Attention Deficits

Perhaps no one problem of childhood has received more attention in the past several years than attention deficits. Some national data indicate that as many as 23 percent of U.S. children have attention deficits; although a more widely accepted figure is 5 percent. Even applying this conservative figure means that about two million school-age children have attention deficit disorder (ADD). Of this number, approximately 90 percent are being treated with some form of medication—the most common being Ritalin. Unfortunately, medication alone often is insufficient for managing the behaviors that children with attention deficits exhibit. In fact, the average length of time such children are on medication is between two and three years, although this time span is increasing. Therefore, procedures for managing the behavior of children with attention deficits become an integral component of an overall treatment program.

It has been my experience that when a child has been diagnosed with an attention deficit, parents expect some "cure." Sometimes medication can manage the symptoms in a fashion similar to the way insulin manages the symptoms of a child with diabetes. However, not all children who have been diagnosed with an attention deficit respond positively to medication. In these instances, parents are left frustrated and some begin the endless search for "the treatment" that will "cure" their child. This quest is fueled to a large extent by the view that attention deficit is a medical condition. Therefore, parents continue to look for the definitive "answer" to their child's problems through medical solutions. This view can obscure efforts to employ nonmedical techniques for managing a child's difficult behavior related to an attention deficit.

There are literally hundreds of books written on the topic of ADD for parents. In fact, the *A.D.D. WareHouse* publishes products for children with attention deficits including technical books for professionals, nontechnical books for parents and teachers, audio and videotape programs, training programs, and books for kids. My intent here is not to replicate this information. Instead I would like to propose an alternative perspective for conceptualizing attention deficits, provide information on the school's responsibility for meeting the educational needs of children with attention deficits, and describe the effects of medication.

Reconceptualizing Attention Deficits: From Deviance to Variance

Attention deficits have been conceptualized almost exclusively from the biochemical and neurological orientation taken by psychiatry. Psychiatry is based on a medical-disease model that posits that behavior problems are clinical entities much like physical diseases that exist *within* persons. This perspective was typified in a report by G.E. Still who, in 1902, wrote about children he described as having "morbid defects in moral control." Still's article appeared at a time when the behavior problems we now view as characteristic of attention deficits began to be linked to traumatic brain injury. Early investigators unknowingly laid the foundation for what was to become an almost single-minded approach to examining attention deficits that is based on the medical-disease model. Consequently, the history of attention deficits is laced with such medically oriented terms as brain damage syndrome, minimal brain dysfunction and hyperkinetic reaction of childhood.

The 1980s and early 1990s saw psychiatry take steps to operationalize attention deficit disorders in three versions of the *Diagnostic and Statistical Manual of Mental Disorders* (DSM). In 1980, the DSM-III broke down attention deficit disorders into two distinct categories: ADD with hyperactivity and ADD without hyperactivity. Seven years later, the DSM-IIIR combined the two categories into one disorder designated as attention-deficit hyperactivity disorder (ADHD). In 1994, the DSM-IV kept the term ADHD, but split the disorder into three subcategories: predominantly inattentive type, predominantly hyperactive-impulsive type and combined type. The DSM-IV conceptualization is amazingly similar to that appearing in DSM-III.

Problems with the Deviance Approach

Despite changes in nomenclature and criteria over the past 30 years, the medical-disease model remains the primary paradigm for understanding the etiology, diagnosis, assessment and treatment of ADHD. Yet the focus of this disorder remains on an ill-defined constellation of symptoms that do not take contextual factors into consideration (see Fig. 6.1). For example, what is actually meant by "often fidgets with hands or feet or squirms in seat"? which is one of the diagnostic criteria. I often play with the two rings on my

---

ADHD Diagnostic Criteria

- Often fidgets with hands or feet or squirms in seat (in adolescents, may be limited to subjective feelings of restlessness)

- Has difficulty remaining seated when required to do so

- Is easily distracted by extraneous stimuli

- Has difficulty awaiting turn in game or group situations

- Often blurts out answers to questions before they have been completed

- Has difficulty following through on instructions from others (not due to oppositional behavior or failure of comprehension), e.g., fails to finish chores

- Has difficulty sustaining attention in tasks or play activities

- Often shifts from one uncompleted activity to another

- Has difficulty playing quietly

- Often talks excessively

- Often interrupts or intrudes on others, e.g., butts into other children's games

- Often does not seem to listen to what is being said to him or her

- Often loses things necessary for tasks or activities at school or at home (e.g., toys, pencils, books, assignments)

- Often engages in physically dangerous activities without considering possible consequences (not for purpose of thrill-seeking), e.g., runs into street without looking

---

Figure 6.1. Diagnostic criteria for attention-deficit hyperactivity disorder. (Reprinted from *Diagnostic and Statistical Manual of Mental Disorders*, 3rd Ed., Rev., Washington, DC: American Psychiatric Association, 1987.)

fingers—spinning them, taking them off and flipping them in between my fingers. I also have the habit of playing with my pen when I am in meetings or seeing a client. I couldn't even begin to count the number of times students in my courses tap their feet or twirl their hair.

Or take another criterion: "has difficulty awaiting turn in game or group situation." Have you ever been at a meeting or social gathering where someone just continues to interrupt others? And what exactly is meant by "often talks excessively"?—still another criterion. When I come home from a long day and I'm tired, my wife seems to talk excessively, although she doesn't think so. How many times have you been introduced to someone and they ask you a question, only to appear uninterested in your response, as if they were staring out into space, or thinking of what they wanted to say next? Could we say this person meets the criterion of "often does not seem to listen to what is being said to him or her"?

My point is that these criteria are extremely subjective and can vary depending on the context or situation in which they are applied. Remember the discussion of Test 5 from Chapter 2 that dealt with determining the purpose and desired outcome of a child's behavior. I said that all behavior is purposeful and intentional—it is directed toward achieving a perceived outcome. The specific type of behavior a child exhibits is shaped by the desired outcome. Let us consider some possible outcomes for a child engaging in the ADHD criterion "often loses things necessary for tasks or activities at school or at home." As I discussed earlier, adults have a tendency to expect good behavior and react to bad behavior. Children who are behaving well tend to be ignored while children who cause trouble get teacher attention, even though that attention is negative. But remember, negative attention is better than no attention at all.

So, returning to the above-mentioned criterion, a child may "lose things" because of the attention he receives from the teacher. Some teachers are very understanding and take time to talk to the student individually, maybe to set up a program for keeping track of work or just to offer encouragement. In this instance, the purpose or desired outcome for "losing things" is getting teacher attention. Here is another possible outcome: Realizing that he will be unable to complete an assignment correctly, the child fails to bring it to school, or "loses it," thus avoiding possible ridicule from the teacher or classmates regarding his performance. There are a myriad of other possible contextual factors that could contribute to a child "losing things." The point is that current diagnostic criteria fail to address these factors in a meaningful way. The only consideration when making a diagnosis of attention deficit is whether the clinician is convinced that a child exhibits the particular symptom. And there are a lot of possible combinations of symptoms that could lead to a diagnosis of attention deficit disorder. In fact, using the DSM-IIIR criteria requiring the presence of 8 of 14 symptoms, over 3,000 possible combinations exist on which a diagnosis of ADHD could be based. Consequently, there is no "typical" child with ADHD. Therefore, it makes more sense to focus on the specific behaviors a child exhibits, analyze them for the purpose they serve, and develop an intervention based on the principles presented in Chapters 3 and 4. After all, we have identified, and can literally see, the chromosome aberrations that cause Down syndrome. Yet this knowledge has not had a particularly large impact upon developing appropriate interventions for afflicted children.

An Argument for Normal Variation

The behaviors exhibited with children who have received the label ADHD are generally considered to be abnormal. It is illustrative to examine the meaning of the word *abnormal*. *Ab* means "away" or "from," while *normal* refers to the average or standard. Consequently, *abnormal* simply means something that varies from the average, although when it comes to children's behavior, we assume that the variation is in the negative direction. The pertinent question in regard to attention deficits is this: When does a variation from the average become a deviation? Or put differently, when does problem behavior become a distinct disorder with well-established boundaries? The answer to this question is not easy. Any answer will be based on societal standards and cultural norms which are fluid. Mental retardation provides a good example. In 1961 the American Association on Mental Deficiency (AAMD) defined mental retardation in terms of "subaverage intellectual functioning" which translated into an IQ score of either 84 or 85 (depending on the test). The average IQ score is 100 (plus or minus 15 or 16 points). In 1973 the AAMD revised the definition of mental retardation in two ways. The first was to add a component that viewed subaverage intellectual functioning in light of adaptive behavior. The second change was to redefine "subaverage intellectual functioning" as referring to an IQ score of 69 or 70 instead of 84 or 85. It is interesting to ponder what happened to the children labeled using the 1961 criteria who had IQs between 71 and 84 when the criteria was changed in 1973? Were they cured or were they not mentally retarded to begin with?

The example of mental retardation points to another important fact—IQ is an *evenly distributed* trait. Normal variation on any trait—psychological or physical—can be placed upon a continuum. That continuum is usually illustrated by a graph called the normal or bell-shaped curve because of its appearance (Figure 6.2). The vertical line in the middle of the curve represents the average on some trait. However, "average" is not just one case, but rather represents a range of cases. A case can be thought of as one person, number or score on a test of a trait or variable. I have indicated the range of average cases by the brackets appearing at the bottom of the figure. The top

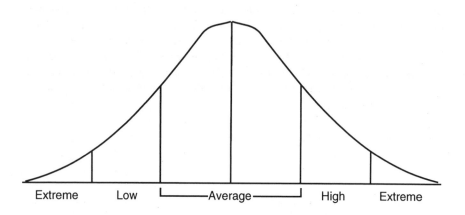

Figure 6.2. Normal curve applicable with any phenomenon.

of these brackets point to the two vertical lines directly to the right and left of the middle line. Notice that the vertical lines get shorter as they approach the ends, or tails, of the curve. The shorter the line, the fewer cases appear in that particular range. The opposite is also true. Therefore, the middle line—representing the exact average—will be longest since the most cases on any trait are average.

There are two implications about the normal distribution of traits. First, any cutoff score that serves as a demarcation for normal and abnormal is arbitrary. This is easily illustrated by returning to our example of the change in definitions for mental retardation. According to the 1973 AAMD definition, a child cannot be considered mentally retarded unless she has an IQ score of 69 or 70 (depending on the test). But what if a child has an IQ of 71? She would not technically be considered mentally retarded. But is this child's functioning likely to be that different from the child that has an IQ of 69 or 70? The second implication is that the "normality" of the normal curve is affected by the context in which the cases are drawn. For example, according the U.S. National Center for Health Statistics, the average height for a man 35 to 44 years of age is 5 feet 9 inches. Therefore, a man who was 6 feet 2 inches would fall in the extreme right tail of the curve—well out of the normal range. But what if this individual was a professional basketball player? A height of 6 feet 2 inches would be considered short when compared to other professional basketball players. Therefore, whether some trait is considered normal or abnormal depends on the standards applied to the sample of individuals being measured.

We can place any of the three defining characteristics of ADHD—inatten-tion, impulsivity and hyperactivity—on the normal curve since I believe any of these three traits are normally distributed through the population. That means that if we observe every child in the United States on these three traits, we could probably determine some average range. In fact, this is routinely done using behavior rating scales. A behavior rating scale consists of groups of statements about children's behavior that an adult, usually a parent or teacher, rates as *not at all, just a little, pretty much,* or *very much.* Points are usually assigned to the rating, for example, 0 points for *not at all* and 5 points for *very much.* A common item on these scales is "Often fidgets or squirms in seat." A parent or teacher then would select the appropriate descriptor based on their subjective opinion of a child. A total score is obtained by summing the responses to each item on the rating scale. Total scores are plotted on a normal curve. Based on some fairly simple statistical calculations, cutoff scores are developed. Children who obtain a score below the cutoff may be considered to have an attention deficit.

Unfortunately, where the line is drawn between whether a child is *hyper-active* or just *highly active* is arbitrary. If a child's level of motor activity is interfering with her ability to complete school work, would a parent be content with a school psychologist who said that intervention was not necessary since the child did not reach a critical score on some behavior rating scale? Of course not. The reason is obvious: At some point, the parent does not care whether a child is diagnosed as anything, but rather wants to see the child receive the help she needs to succeed in school. Unfortunately, parents and professionals alike often believe the only way to get that help is through a diagnosis or label. Although there is some truth to this belief, focusing considerable attention on diagnosis pulls the focus away from the problem—a child's behavior.

There is another interesting trait relevant to attention deficits that can be plotted on the normal curve: teachers' ability to tolerate various types of classroom behavior. As with any other trait, tolerance level is probably evenly distributed. We can find an average range of tolerance for the majority of teachers and then proceed in both directions toward the extremes. Consider a teacher whose tolerance level is in the extreme right tail—that is, she is very tolerant of children's behavior. Now, let's take a child whose hyperac-tivity falls in the middle high range of the normal curve depicted in Figure 6.1. Given the interaction of these two traits one might ask: Is this child hyperactive? This question is tantamount to asking: If a tree falls in the forest, but no one is there to hear it, does it make a noise? In other words, it is our perception of an event that gives meaning to that event. But I can give you a real-life example of one boy and his third-grade and fourth-grade teach-ers—the former with a low tolerance level and the latter with a high tolerance level.

This boy had been previously diagnosed as having an attention deficit. He was having a very difficult time during third-grade due to his high activity level. Specifically, he had trouble remaining in his chair. His third-grade teacher was a real stickler for children sitting in their chairs. Therefore, his parents would receive at least one phone call a week asking if his medication could be increased since it obviously wasn't helping him remain in his chair. In this teacher's classroom, the boy looked very hyperactive. However, a different picture emerged when he started fourth grade. His fourth-grade teacher's tolerance level was very high. She did not try to stop him from getting out of his seat. Instead, she assigned him three desks—one in the middle of the room and one in each back corner. The boy could get up from one desk any time he wanted to and move to one of his other desks. This plan worked quite well. Regardless of where the boy was sitting, he was working and the teacher was not getting on his case about leaving his seat. This teacher did not once complain to the boy's parents about his restlessness, or about the ineffectiveness of his medication.

When we consider the tolerance levels of adults, the determination of which child has an attention deficit becomes much cloudier. The example above illustrates that some teachers impose regimentation and a single set of expectations on personal behavior and school performance rather than accepting the range of individual differences on a variety of traits children exhibit. Therefore, there are a range of factors—many of which refer to adult expectations and tolerance levels—that must be considered when developing an intervention for a child. In the example, I believe the third-grade teacher should have been the target of intervention efforts rather than the boy. Yet we very rarely accept the autonomy of a child. Children are easier to manipulate than adults. Children are truly the last underclass in our society. Therefore, we target children for intervention when, in fact, many adults should be targeted.

The School's Responsibility for Children with Attention Deficits

It has been my experience that a large part of parents' frustration with an ADD child stems from their perception of the school's unwillingness to address their child's specific needs. There is certainly more than a grain of truth to this perception. Many schools are baffled in making accommodations for children with attention deficits. I have already addressed part of the problem: Schools think a diagnosis of attention deficit means doing attention deficit-like things. However, the type of behaviors a child with an attention deficit exhibits are not that different from those of other children whose behavior is difficult to manage.

Regardless of what a parent may have been told by their child's school district, schools are responsible for making accommodations for children with attention deficits. There are two primary mechanisms for accomplishing this goal. The first is having a child receive special education services under one of the federal disability categories funded under the Individuals with Disabilities Act (IDEA). The second mechanism requires schools to provide educational accommodations to children with attention deficits under Section 504 of the Rehabilitation Act. I will discuss each of these mechanisms and how parents can use them to get proper services for a child.

IDEA and Attention Deficits

Currently, an attention deficit is not a disability category covered under IDEA. However, concerns about the adequacy of services for children with attention deficit disorders remain, and advocates for ADD children proposed adding attention deficits as a disability category during deliberations on the IDEA legislation in 1991. Two organizations spearheaded these efforts: the parent group for Children with Attention Deficit Disorders (CHADD) and the Professional Group for Attention Related Disorders (PGARD). The rationale for making attention deficits a category of disability is based on the belief that it interferes with educational performance and, because ADD children currently do not meet federal criteria for existing disability categories, they are being denied necessary special education services.

Primarily because of the efforts of CHADD and PGARD, Congress was motivated to require the U.S. Department of Education to issue a Notice of Inquiry. A Notice of Inquiry invites the public to send letters expressing their opinions about a topic being considered for legislative action. In this case, the Department of Education received over 2,000 comments, many of which echoed the belief that children with attention deficits were not receiving necessary services. However, two other professional groups, the National Association of State Directors of Special Education and the National Association of School Psychologists, spoke against making attention deficits a category of disability, arguing that existing categories adequately served these children's needs.

After reviewing these comments, the U.S. Department of Education developed a compromise position. Although attention deficits were not added as a category of disability, ADD children were made eligible for special education services under the existing Other Health Impaired (OHI) category if problems of limited alertness negatively affected academic performance. Conditions within the OHI category include fragile health; chronic diseases such as asthma, cystic fibrosis, epilepsy and cerebral palsy; deficits of the spinal cord such as spina bifida, polio, muscular dystrophy and multiple sclerosis; and communicable diseases such as HIV and cytomegalovirus infections. Ironically, an unintended byproduct of opening up the OHI category for children with attention deficits was further legitimizing attention deficits as neurological or biochemical disorders. Consequently, I have worked with many parents who are adamant about getting their child's label changed to OHI. Unfortunately, as I will discuss shortly, a change in label from one category of disability to another has little or no effect on the individualized educational program a child receives.

In addition to the OHI category of disability, the U.S. Department of Education stated that children with attention deficits were eligible for special education services under other existing categories of disability if the child met that category's criteria. For example, many children with attention deficits currently are receiving special education under the Learning Disability (LD) category. Children can qualify for this category if they possess average or above-average intelligence but their scores on standardized achievement tests are at least 20 points below their score on intelligence tests. Generally speaking, this means a child who possesses normal intelligence but is about two and a half years below grade level academically will qualify for the LD category and, consequently, can receive special education services for his academic problems. In a study conducted by Robert Reid and his colleagues, about 20 percent of children with attention deficits who receive special education are served under the LD category.

Parents generally have a favorable reaction to their child with attention deficits receiving special education services under the LD or OHI categories because these are, in essence, no-fault labels. On the other hand, parents dislike having their children placed in the federal category of Seriously Emotional Disturbance (SED), which they feel carries very negative social connotations. However, because many children with attention deficits engage in inappropriate behavior, Reid and his colleagues found about 40 percent of ADD children who receive special education are served under this category.

For many children with attention deficits, receiving special education services can have a positive impact upon their academic performance and interpersonal behavior. However, as many parents can attest, simply having a child qualify for special education is no guarantee that an appropriate education program will be developed. Many parents have expressed their frustration to me about the inappropriateness of the school program developed for their child. As I mentioned earlier in this chapter, most parents think the answer to their frustration is to have the school reclassify their child under some other category of disability. However, there are no interventions specific to a disability category. The only purpose of disability categories is to ensure that a child is eligible and, consequently, receives special education services. Therefore, parental efforts to have a child reclassified are misplaced. Reclassification has very little to do with the program a child receives.

The mechanism for parents getting changes in their child's education is the Individual Education Plan, or IEP for short. Every child who qualifies for special education services, regardless of the category of disability, must have an IEP. The IEP offers parents a way to ensure that their suggestions are incorporated into their child's educational program. It spells out just what teachers plan to do to meet a child's educational needs. By law, the IEP must include the following: (1) the child's present levels of academic performance; (2) annual goals for the child; (3) short-term instructional objectives related to the annual goals; (4) the special education and related services that will be provided and the extent to which the child will participate in regular education programs; (5) plans for starting the services and the anticipated duration of the services; and (6) appropriate plans for evaluating, at least annually, whether the goals and objectives are being achieved.

Teachers are not legally liable for reaching IEP goals. However, teachers and other school personnel are responsible for seeing that the IEP is written to include the six components listed above, that the parents have an opportunity to review and participate in developing the IEP, that the IEP is approved by the parents before placement, and that the services called for in the IEP are actually provided. In essence, teachers and other school personnel are responsible for making a good-faith effort to achieve the goals and objectives of the IEP. An IEP must be reviewed, and revised if necessary, at least once each year. Therefore, parents who have concerns with the appropriateness of their child's IEP have an opportunity to have it modified. Parents must consent to the IEP and receive a copy of the document. If parents do not think the IEP is appropriate for their child's needs, they can refuse to sign it until changes are made. If the school district refuses to make the necessary changes, or if they make the changes but are not carrying them out as specified in the IEP, parents can initiate a due process hearing.

A due process hearing represents a legal safeguard for children and parents. Basically, parents and children have the right to challenge or examine the decisions a school district makes regarding the appropriateness of a child's educational program before an impartial party. A due process hearing officer assumes the role of impartial party. This individual is not a judge but also is not employed by the school district. At this level, no action is taken by the judicial system. A due process hearing is an initial step before filing a suit in court. During the due process hearing, the school must give parents adequate time and information to prepare a defense and must allow them to be represented by lawyers or other advocates if they so desire. Following the hearing, parents and the school district must have a written statement that specifies the facts that were considered and the conclusions that were drawn. In this case, the adequacy of the IEP would be decided by the hearing officer. If parents are not satisfied with the results of the impartial hearing, the decision may be appealed to the state department of education and to the courts for official legal action.

It has been my experience that schools are very receptive to modifying an IEP once parents notify them that they will otherwise initiate a due process hearing. Schools want to avoid due process hearings because they may lead to bad publicity. Unfortunately, most parents do not understand how the system works and, consequently, fail to wield the considerable power they possess.

The threat of initiating a due process hearing usually is sufficient to get desired changes in a child's IEP. Common modifications parents desire for their child with attention deficits include: (1) provisions for having more time to take tests or to be able to take them in an isolated room that is relatively free of distractions; (2) the use of positive proactive behavior management methods, such as those discussed in Chapter 3, rather than punitive methods; (3) provisions for seeing that homework gets sent home; and (4) teaching social skills.

Unfortunately, the safeguard of due process extended to children who receive special education services does not apply to children with attention deficits who do not receive these services. According to Reid and his colleagues, about 50 percent of children with ADHD do not receive any special education services. However, there is another legal mechanism for assuring children with attention deficits receive appropriate educational accommodations: Section 504 of the Rehabilitation Act.

Section 504 and Attention Deficits

Section 504 of the Rehabilitation Act of 1973 was originally intended to do three things: (1) prohibit discrimination against people who are handicapped; (2) remove steps and other barriers that limit the participation of people with disabilities; and (3) mandate the provision of auxiliary aids (e.g., readers for children who are blind, interpreters for children who are deaf) for those with impaired sensory, manual or speaking skills. This last provision does not mean that a school must provide these services at all times; it simply means that it cannot exclude students for failing to have an appropriate aid. Section 504 is not a federal grant program. Unlike IDEA, it does not provide any federal money to assist children with disabilities. Therefore, some school administrators counsel parents not to push for services for a child under Section 504. This advice, however, is misleading in the case of children with attention deficits. Section 504 imposes a duty on every recipient of federal funds not to discriminate against persons with a disability, which includes public school districts, since they receive federal support. In addition, Section 504 is administered by the Office of Civil Rights, which conducts periodic compliance reviews and acts on complaints when parents contend that a school district is violating Section 504.

With this brief overview, I will now turn to how Section 504 can be used to ensure that school districts provide accommodations to children with attention deficits. Under Section 504, a child is considered disabled if he or she (1) has a physical or mental impairment that substantially limits one or more major life activities; (2) has a record or history of such an impairment; or (3) is regarded as having such an impairment. In the case of attention deficits, the most frequently mentioned major life activity that is impaired is learning. Because Section 504 eligibility makes no mention of specific categories of disability or condition considered as disabling, any child who has been diagnosed as having an attention deficit by a health professional should be considered for eligibility under this law. Consideration for eligibility can be based on parent report, review of discipline or academic records, or teacher report. A school district cannot refuse to evaluate a child for Section 504 eligibility solely on the basis that the child received a prior diagnosis of an attention deficit. A violation of a child's right to a free and appropriate public education may occur if a school district either does not address the needs of children with disabilities not covered by IDEA or fails to consider the education needs of children previously diagnosed as having an attention deficit.

Children with attention deficits are not automatically entitled to services under Section 504. Eligibility for services requires that an impairment in a major life activity be substantial. Depending on the severity of the condition, a child with an attention deficit may or may not qualify for services under Section 504. However, the issue of severity tends to be a moot one. If a child with an attention deficit is performing adequately in school, neither parents nor the school district will push for services under Section 504. It is only when parents become exasperated with the school system for their perceived lack of attention to ADD children that parents push for Section 504 services. Usually, a child's academic difficulties are severe enough that Section 504 action would be likely. However, if a school does decline to evaluate a child for Section 504 eligibility, they must inform parents of their due process rights under Section 504. Parents' due process rights are basically the same as those described above under IDEA.

The ultimate purpose of Section 504 is to ensure that children receive a free and appropriate public education. The emphasis for children with attention deficits is on the word *appropriate*. Therefore, a school district cannot refuse to provide special services to children with attention deficits simply because they do not otherwise meet eligibility criteria for a category of disability under IDEA. Specifically, Section 504 requires "the provision of regular or special education and related aids and services that are designed to meet individual educational needs of handicapped persons as adequately as the needs of nonhandicapped persons...."

One area of confusion in interpreting the last sentence is in the use of the term "special education." Special education in the context of Section 504 is not the same as in the sense of services provided under IDEA since no federal funds can be allocated for children with attention deficits who qualify only under Section 504. For example, a child with an attention deficit could not be placed in a resource room for several hours a week to receive remediation from a certified special education teacher. However, children with attention deficits are entitled to receive services under Section 504 in the form of accommodations and related services in the general education setting. One of the difficulties children with attention deficits experience is taking and completing homework assignments and turning them in the next day. Parents can get children to complete homework assignments using the star chart or contract described in Chapter 3, but they become especially frustrated trying to get teachers to send home the assignments. Also, parents are often miffed when their child will complete an assignment, only to lose it or forget to hand it in the following day.

A common strategy for dealing with this problem is to have a child carry a spiral notebook with pockets. A teacher would write down the assignment to be completed that night and place it in a pocket of the notebook. When a child finished the assignment, he would place it in a pocket labeled for that particular subject. Then a teacher would write a brief note in the notebook to the parents acknowledging that she received the assignment. Parents then can apply a variety of reinforcement techniques, as described in Chapter 3, contingent upon the child's completing the assignments. Although this process is fairly straightforward, a common and frustrating problem to parents is that teachers forget to write in a child's notebook or refuse to ask the child for the assignment—stating instead that it is the child's responsibility. At the junior high level, parents can find the task of getting each teacher to agree to this arrangement and follow through to be daunting. However, under Section 504, this accommodation must be followed through, or a parent can file for a due process hearing.

Also, if a child's needs require only adjustments in the regular education classroom, Section 504 mandates them. I have provided three examples which would fall under Section 504 protection. In Chapter 2, I gave the example of two boys with attention deficits. For one boy, who often fidgeted with classroom objects, I recommended that he be able to manipulate silly putty. One teacher agreed to this accommodation while another did not. Also in Chapter 2, I described another boy who talked excessively. I recommended that he be allowed to chew gum. One of his teachers agreed and his talking decreased substantially. Unfortunately, another of his teachers would not allow this accommodation. The talking continued to be a problem and, consequently, the boy was often receiving disciplinary action. In this chapter, I described how one teacher assigned a boy who had difficulty remaining seated three desks so that he could get up and move around. All these accommodations could be covered under Section 504.

Another important aspect of Section 504 relates to the use of stimulant medication to manage the symptoms of attention deficits. A high proportion (over 90 percent) of children diagnosed with attention deficits receive medication. Medication is considered a related service under Section 504 because it is prescribed in order to manage the symptoms of attention deficits. A school district may include medication in its accommodation plan if prescribed by a physician for attention deficits. However, a school *cannot* predicate services solely on the basis that a child is taking medication. Conversely, a school cannot compel the administration of medication as a prerequisite for providing a child with services under Section 504. Failure of a school district to administer medication violates the child's right to a free and appropriate public education. In some instances, children are made responsible for going to the nurse's office at a specified time to get their medication. Parents of children with attention deficits can attest to the frustration they experience when their child forgets to take his medication and discover that the school deems it the child's responsibility. However, if a child has difficulty remembering to take his medication, and this is stated in the Section 504 plan, then the school district must ensure that the child receives the medication or be in violation of Section 504.

A final area covered under Section 504 is the disciplinary practices a school district uses with children with attention deficits. School districts are required to develop a plan to address any behavior problems. It is unacceptable to administer punishment typically used with children without a disability. In one court case, a child with an attention deficit was repeatedly removed from class and sent to the principal's office because he yelled and hit other children and refused to obey his teacher. The school district was found to be in violation of Section 504 because it failed to develop a plan for addressing the child's misbehavior which was deemed to be *caused by his disability*. In essence, the disciplinary action practiced by the school district violated Section 504 because this action denied the child equal opportunity to participate in, and benefit from, the school district's educational programs. In addition, expelling a student for behavior related to an attention deficit or suspending a student for more than 10 consecutive school days also violates mandates of Section 504 as interpreted by the Office of Civil Rights. Sometimes school districts will try to get around the 10-day consecutive suspension by using a series of suspensions that are each 10 days or less. However, this constitutes a pattern of exclusions which also places the school district in violation.

I have found most parents and school districts to be unaware of the mandates of Section 504. Many common concerns of parents—entitlement to special services, ongoing communication with teachers, willingness of teachers to make classroom accommodations, evidence that the school is following through with administering medication and developing appropriate disciplinary practices—are covered under Section 504 of the Rehabilitation Act. Once parents are aware of this mechanism and convey this information to school districts, most are willing to develop a 504 plan and make the necessary accommodations in order to avoid a due process hearing.

Medication Effects and ADHD

The most common treatment for attention deficits is medication. More that 90 percent of children with attention deficits receive medication—the most common type being Ritalin. Parents' attitudes toward Ritalin range from considering it a "wonder drug" to "doing nothing at all." There is a lot of controversy over the use of medication for children with attention deficits. However, there is a trend, at least in the United States, of using medications such as Ritalin more frequently and for longer durations of time. Until recently, the average length of time a child was on Ritalin was about two to three years. However, the current trend is to have children on Ritalin for four years or more.

My position is not to advocate either for or against the use of stimulant medication such as Ritalin in the treatment of attention deficits. It is certain that medication will continue to be prescribed for children with attention deficits. My purpose here is to raise two points. First, there are a lot of misconceptions as to what stimulant medication does and does not do to help children with attention deficits. Therefore, I would like to present a summary of information gathered from research into the effect of stimulant medication on children with attention deficits. Second, there are a variety of nonmedical techniques that parents and teachers can use to help children with attention deficits. Many of the techniques have been described in Chapters 3 and 4.

My concern is that medication is viewed as such a panacea that nonmedical techniques are ignored. The research literature would seem to support my claim. There have been literally thousands of journal articles reporting on the effectiveness of stimulant medication on children with attention deficits. There have been less than 100 articles on the use of nonmedical treatments for children with attention deficits. This is unfortunate since, as I will show, stimulant medication has a limited effect on children's behavior. Therefore, I will present some of the more common nonmedical interventions that parents and teachers can use with children with attention deficits.

Given the large number of studies conducted on the effect of stimulant medication on children, the only way to draw generalizable conclusions is by examining researchers' reviews. There are several excellent reviews that summarize the effects of stimulant medication. James M. Swanson and his colleagues at the University of California, Irvine, Attention Deficit Disorder Center distilled and synthesized the findings of these reviews into a manageable set of generalizations. In essence, they conducted a "review of reviews" on the effect of stimulant medication. I would like to present the essence of their conclusions here.

Swanson's group begin their overview by discussing three influential reviews that were published in the 1970s—all of which agreed on the following points: First, in about 75 percent of children with attention deficits, stimulant medication produced immediate and positive changes in parent and teacher perceptions and improvement on tests requiring concentration and attention. Second, positive parent and teacher perceptions could be produced by placebo effects (i.e., having a child take a sugar pill instead of the actual medication without anyone knowing). Third, physiological and psychological profiles could not predict children's response to short-term positive effects of stimulant medication. Fourth, the documented long-range effects of stimulant medication on academic achievement or social competence were insubstantial.

Swanson and his colleagues go on to consider several other reviews, pointing out differences in the various methodologies, purposes and conclusions. Nevertheless, they provided the following generalizations derived from the reviews which I have summarized in Figure 6.3.

I would like to provide some comments on these conclusions. First, I am in total agreement that stimulant medication may well be overused in the United States—certainly when compared to other countries such as England and France.

Second, the positive effects of stimulant medication are relatively short term. By short-term, I mean that most studies of children's responses to stimulant medication are conducted for periods of only 10 to 12 weeks. Therefore, we have very little scientific evidence on the effects of stimulant medication over time. Also, in most cases, stimulant medication is discontinued within two years.

Third, children and adults who do not have attention deficits respond to stimulant medication in a fashion similar to children and adults who have such deficits. This finding contradicts the popular "paradoxical effect" which states that individuals with attention deficits probably have underaroused central nervous systems. Therefore, these individuals would seek extraneous stimulation (for example, by fidgeting, running around, or shifting from one uncompleted activity to another) in order to increase brain stimulation. Accordingly, it was believed that stimulant medication would increase the arousal in the individual's central nervous system, thereby alleviating the desire to seek extra stimulation externally. However, because children and adults without attention deficits generally respond to stimulant medication much as do children and adults with deficits, the so-called paradoxical effect has been discredited. Although there are several theories explaining why

What Should Be Expected from Stimulant Medication	
1. Temporary management of diagnostic symptoms	Improved ability to regulate motor behavior; increased concentration or effort on tasks; improved self-regulation
2. Temporary improvement in related characteristics	Increased compliance and effort; decreased physical and verbal hostility; decreased negative behaviors; increased amount and accuracy of work

What Should Not Be Expected from Stimulant Medication	
1. Paradoxical response	Responses of normal children and adults are the same as children and adults with ADHD; responses of children and adults with ADHD are similar
2. Prediction of response	Favorable response to medication cannot be predicted by neurological signs, physiological measures or biochemical indicators
3. Absence of side effects	Frequent problems with eating and sleeping; possible psychological effects on thinking; infrequent appearance of tics
4. Large effects on specific skills	No significant improvement of reading skills, athletic or game skills, or positive social skills; improvement on learning and achievement is less than improvement in behavior and attention
5. Improvement in long-term adjustment	No improvement in academic achievement; no reduction in antisocial behavior

Figure 6.3. What should and should not be expected from stimulant medication taken by children with ADHD.

stimulant medication produces some positive effects, the scientific evidence for any of them is not compelling.

Fourth, the most frequent side effects of stimulant medication are loss of appetite and difficulty in sleeping. Typically, the effects of stimulant medication, such as Ritalin, last four to five hours. Also, daily dosages often are given at breakfast and lunch times. Therefore, by the time the medication wears off, some children will engage in binge eating. To counteract the difficulties some children have in sleeping, the last dose of Ritalin is often given by or before 5:00 p.m. Although many parents understandably see these two common side effects as an easy trade-off for the improvement in their child's behavior, the long-term effects of stimulant medication remain unknown.

Fifth, when stimulant medication is discontinued, no residual effects should be expected. This is different from medications prescribed for other problems, such as depression. Although some individuals are on antidepressants for many years, the average length of time is 6 to 12 months. Often there are residual positive effects once an individual discontinues an antidepressant. No such effects occur with stimulant medication for attention deficits.

Sixth, although stimulant medication positively influences the symptoms diagnostic of attention deficits, it has no significant impact upon children's performance in specific academic areas or their social skills. Based on this conclusion, it should become increasingly apparent that nonmedical techniques are necessary to address specific academic and social behaviors of children with attention deficits.

Conclusion

By conceptualizing attention deficits as a normal variation, I hope you will be able to divorce yourself from the diagnostic label. Remember, the label "attention deficit" gives you no information on how to develop and implement any of the intervention techniques described in this book. I realize that it is difficult for parents to ignore the label when trying intervention techniques with a child with an attention deficit. In particular, when an intervention technique fails, there is a tendency on the part of parents and teachers to blame the failure on the "disorder." I often hear comments from parents and teachers such as these: "Reinforcement doesn't work because he has an attention deficit"; "I tried a contract and it didn't do a bit of good—he just can't remember long enough to do the behavior and earn the reward"; "star charts didn't work either—his attention span is just too short." These comments typify a belief that the disorder prevents intervention techniques from working. That is not the case at all. As long as you take the time to specify the behavior you want to change, demonstrate the appropriate behavior, provide a chance to practice the behavior, give specific instructions and use principles of reinforcement, children with attention deficits can learn to engage in appropriate behaviors.

7

Depression

Rachel Andersen was pouring herself a morning cup of coffee when she heard her daughter Carla's alarm go off. Carla is a tenth grader who turned 16 several months ago. Several minutes pass without Rachel hearing any activity that would indicate her daughter was getting ready for school. "Damn," Rachel said aloud, unaware that she had said this; although she was quite aware of her growing irritation at the difficulty her daughter was experiencing getting up and ready for school in the morning. She then burst out, "Carla, get up, or you're going to be late for school and make me late for work." Rachel typically would drop Carla off at school on her way to work. Carla usually liked to drive to school since she had her learner's permit. Rachel remembered how excited Carla had been to drive when she first got her permit and how she constantly pestered her to drive the car. Rachel thought back on the first time she let Carla drive. She, rather than Carla, had been the nervous wreck. But all that seemed like ages ago. Recently, Carla showed no interest in wanting to drive.

Rachel was brought out of her musings by the conspicuous lack of noise that would indicate Carla was getting ready for school. Setting her coffee cup on the kitchen table, Rachel stomped into Carla's bedroom only to find her curled up in bed with the sheets pulled up over her face. "Carla, get up," her mother said sternly, "this is becoming a habit and I'm sick of it!"

"I just don't feel like going to school today, it's boring," whined Carla from beneath the sheets in a voice that indicated she had been crying. "There's nothing to do there and my friends are all a drag."

Rachel's initial anger softened and was transformed into concern. "What do you mean, honey? You've always liked school and have gotten good grades. You're on the swim and debate teams and sing in the chorus. You're one of the most popular girls in school, if the number of times our phone rings Friday and Saturday night is any indication."

"Well, those things just don't seem to matter to me right now. Besides, I've never been that good a swimmer and people just wanted me on the debate team because I used to talk a lot. They don't know anything and my debate arguments are always lame."

"That's not what your debate coach told us," Rachel countered detecting a distinctly irritated quality to her daughter's tone of voice. Rachel has become more concerned about how infrequently her daughter seemed to smile lately. Carla used to be so bubbly and easygoing. Now, Rachel thought, she had become very irritable. Unable to come up with the words to convince her daughter that her perception of her skills and her friends was wrong, Rachel resorted to, "Look Carla, you need to get up now!"

"Fine!" Carla responded curtly.

Rachel returned to the kitchen where she heated up her cup of coffee in the microwave. Both thoughts of anger and concern regarding the recent changes in her daughter whirled around in her mind.

About 15 minutes later Carla appeared in the kitchen. She was wearing a pair of blue jeans, a t-shirt and sneakers. Although she had taken a shower, she wore no make-up and the normally meticulous way she fixed her hair was nowhere to be seen. Instead, it was parted in the middle and hung from her face like spaghetti noodles thrown against a wall to test whether they were cooked sufficiently.

Rachel hoped that her daughter was not going through one of those grunge phases, referring to the way she dressed, lack of make-up and disinterest in fixing her hair. Rachel thought how Carla had always been an easy child to raise. And maybe it was normal for a teenager to go through a period of rebellion.

"Do you want a bowl of cereal or a pop tart to take in the car?" Rachel inquired.

"Nope. You know I'm not hungry in the morning. And besides, I have a stomach ache."

"Well, you aren't eating much dinner either. And you haven't asked me for any lunch money in over two weeks. Are you eating lunch at school?"

Carla rolled her eyes. "What difference does it make? The food sucks at school anyway."

Ignoring this last comment, Rachel instead decided to pursue the stomach aches Carla was complaining about. "It seems like you've been getting a lot of stomach aches lately. Maybe you're allergic to something, or have that condition where some people can't eat dairy products. Let me think, what is that called…"

"It's called a lactose intolerance, Mom," Carla responded curtly. "And I don't have that. That's a stupid thing to say."

"I'm just concerned that you're not eating like you used to."

"Well, it's no big deal," replied Carla as she walked out the door to the car.

The silence between Rachel and Carla as they were driving was deafening to Rachel. Not wanting to start another argument with an increasingly sensitive and irritable daughter, Rachel opted to break the silence with what she considered a harmless question: "What are your plans tonight?"

"I don't have any plans. I guess I'm not going to do anything," replied Carla.

"But Carla, your friends always call to set something up on Friday nights."

"I don't care," said Carla nonchalantly. "And besides, I don't like what my friends want to do on weekends."

"Well, this is new to me," said Rachel sarcastically. She was immediately sorry she used this tone of voice, but she was becoming increasingly frustrated at her daughter's apparent apathy toward school and her friends. Nevertheless, she continued, hoping somehow to convince Carla to go out tonight: "Since when don't you like going out to eat with your friends, seeing a basketball game, going to the youth center, taking in a movie, or ..."

"Okay, I get the picture," Carla interrupted. "Those things just don't interest me anymore." Carla's tone softened as she continued: "Maybe I'll want to do them later, Mom. We'll see."

Understanding Depression

It is possible that Carla is suffering from depression—a condition that affects thousands of Americans every year. Yet depression can be a very perplexing condition. Unlike attention deficit disorder, depression represents an internalizing problem—the symptoms rarely bring an individual into direct conflict with others. In addition, depression is one of the few conditions whose symptoms have been felt by most people at some time. Symptoms of depression, such as feeling sad, are a common experience of everyday life. Therefore, for most people, to whom depression is a common and transitory feeling, it is difficult to understand how it can be so debilitating.

In fact, the clinical condition of depression is different from that of someone who occasionally experiences one of the symptoms. Clinical depression refers to a group of symptoms that occur together. The diagnostic criteria for depression are listed in Figure 7.1. Out of the nine symptoms, at least five must have been present during the same two-week period every day or nearly every day and represent a change from an individual's previous functioning. In addition, at least one of the symptoms must be either depressed mood or loss of interest or pleasure in activities. Finally, a person who displays these symptoms because of a normal reaction, for example, to the death of a loved one, may not necessarily be considered to be suffering from depression in the clinical sense.

Depression Diagnostic Criteria

- Depressed mood or irritable mood in children and adolescents

- Diminished interest or pleasure in all or almost all activities

- Significant weight loss or weight gain when not dieting

- Insomnia or hypersomnia

- Psychomotor agitation or retardation

- Fatigue or loss of energy

- Feelings of worthlessness or excessive or inappropriate guilt

- Diminished ability to think or concentrate, or indecisiveness

- Recurrent thoughts of death or suicidal ideation

Figure 7.1. Diagnostic criteria for major depressive syndrome. (Reprinted from *Diagnostic and Statistical Manual of Mental Disorders*, 3rd Ed., Rev., Washington, DC: American Psychiatric Association, 1987.)

Let's now return to the interaction Carla had with her mother and apply these criteria to Carla's behavior. First, when Rachel entered Carla's bedroom to get her up, Carla was crying with her head under her covers. In addition, Rachel noted that Carla had been becoming increasingly irritable. Consequently, Carla met the first criterion for depression. Second, we have some indication that Carla was experiencing a diminished interest or pleasure in activities. She no longer enjoyed driving and, most importantly, she did not want to be with her friends or engage in any activities with them. Third, her appetite was markedly diminished. Although we don't know exactly how much weight Carla has lost, based on her lack of appetite, it is reasonable to assume it could constitute a significant problem. Fourth, it seems likely that because Carla was having extreme difficulty getting up in the morning, she was either not sleeping well at night (insomnia) or was sleeping excessively (hypersomnia). Fifth, Carla seemed to have lost interest in dressing fashionably, putting on make-up and fixing her hair. These things could either be seen as more evidence of a diminished interest in activities, or they could indicate considerable fatigue or loss of energy. Sixth, there is some indication that Carla was experiencing feelings of worthlessness. Remember her saying that she really didn't believe she was a very good swimmer and didn't debate well, even though both her coaches thought she was quite good. Finally, although not an explicit part of the diagnostic criteria for depression, somatic (physical) complaints, such as Carla's stomach aches, also are an indication of depression.

Based on this information, it is possible that Carla is suffering from a major depressive episode. It would be immature to conclude that Carla was clinically depressed; for example, we don't know how long the symptoms have been present or whether they occur every day. Nevertheless, there is enough information for her mother to be concerned and to warrant an evaluation by a specialist, typically a psychiatrist, since medication has become an integral component for treating depression. However, even within the psychiatric community, there is concern that antidepressant medication is being prescribed for individuals who are experiencing normal feelings of sadness or anxiety.

It is important to remember that we live in a society that bombards us with commercials and advertisements that show young adults having fun. It is a natural tendency to compare our lives to those depicted in magazines and on TV. And by doing so, our lives often seem dreary and depressing. Include another common depiction in commercials—drugs can cure everything—and I think these factors begin to explain why some psychiatrists prescribe antidepressant medication for everyday problems. We have a tendency to believe we should be happier than we are—an observation insightfully made by Edith Weisskopf-Joelson:

> Our current mental-hygiene philosophy stresses the idea that people ought to be happy, that unhappiness is a symptom of maladjustment. Such a value system might be responsible for the fact that the burden of unavoidable unhappiness is increased by unhappiness about being unhappy.

My point here is not to discredit the use of medication in the treatment of depression. To the contrary, medication has been a life-saver for many individuals. And when antidepressant medication works for children, parents are understandably relieved. However, not every child who is experiencing depression responds favorably to antidepressant drugs. Therefore, I will describe some psychological treatment techniques that seem to work well for ameliorating depression.

Psychological Treatment Approaches

In order to examine the psychological and environmental causes of depression, I would first like to propose that depression in children and adolescents is similar to that experienced by adults. This is the position taken by the American Psychiatric Association. Because adults are generally more verbal than children, they are in a better position to provide an accurate verbal description of their depression. Some adolescents too can be fairly adept at describing their feelings. Children, on the other hand, often lack the cognitive and verbal skills to communicate their problems. Developmentally, children tend to be more motor-oriented so that their depression may be expressed through behavior, such as becoming oppositional, aggressive and antisocial.

This last observation has led some people to believe that depression in children is "masked." The term *masked depression* refers to a situation in which certain behavior problems such as enuresis, temper tantrums, hyperactivity, disobedience, truancy, running away, delinquency, learning problems and somatic complaints are overt indicators of underlying depression. Depression is believed to exist as an internal unobservable entity. The external behavior problems are believed to be the depressive counterparts. Consequently, these children may be depressed, but may only display the types of behavior problems described above. Although the concept of *masked depression* is intuitively appealing, it nevertheless remains logically indefensible. Considering the large number of behavior problems that could potentially be an indicator of some underlying depression, it becomes impossible to be certain these behaviors actually do "mask" depression rather than being a response to some other form of distress. Although the concept of masked depression has largely been discredited, it has alerted us to the importance of considering the developmental level of a child.

Development can have a profound impact on whether a child becomes depressed or not. Children's development can be characterized as a process that begins with the acquisition of general concepts and progresses to a state where they make finer discriminations between stimuli and begin integrating concepts when presented with and solving tasks. From a developmental perspective, depression occurs when children fail to organize and integrate social or cognitive competencies that influence solving developmental tasks. A child who does not develop the social skills necessary for positively interacting with and being accepted by her peers may be at risk for developing depression. Similarly, a child whose cognitive skills are impaired, for example, not possessing appropriate problem-solving skills, may begin viewing life as an endless parade of unsolvable tasks. This, in turn, can lead to feelings of helplessness and hopelessness—two important benchmark warning signs of depression.

As I now describe various problems depressed children can experience and provide recommendations for working with depressed children, it is important that parents also seek professional help. Depression can be an extremely debilitating condition and parents should not attempt to deal with it themselves. Nevertheless, there are many things parents can do to help their child who may be depressed, and it is to these things that I now turn. The following descriptions and recommendations are based on the writings of Nadine Kaslow and Lynn Rehm who both have studied depression extensively among children.

Provide Training in Social Skills

Some children who are depressed lack the social skills necessary to obtain reinforcement from their social environment—peers, parents and other adults such as teachers and coaches. Poor social skills result in what is called a low rate of *response-contingent positive reinforcement.* This long phrase actually makes a lot of sense. The word *response* refers to any behavior, or lack of behavior, a child exhibits. *Contingent* refers to the process whereby a behavior is followed by some response from another person. *Positive reinforcement* should be familiar to readers by now, and I do not believe it requires any further elaboration here. Therefore, a low rate of *response-contingent positive reinforcement* simply refers to a child whose social skills are so poor that other children either ignore him, thereby not providing him with positive reinforcement inherent in social interaction, or engage in negative social interactions, which a child finds punishing.

Social interaction is reciprocal. If I make an initiation toward someone, I expect a response. If the response is positive, then I have been reinforced for making the initiation and will be more likely to make initiations in the future. For example, a child may see a group of peers talking together on the playground at recess. That child may choose to go over and initiate a conversation with the group. He may say, "Hey, what are you guys talking about?" One of the peers could respond by saying, "This really scary horror movie Billy saw on television last night." This response, in essence, acknowledged the child's initiation and sets the stage for future interaction. The child could then say something like, "The scariest movie I ever saw was *The Thing.* In this movie these people had an alien popping out of their chest. It was really cool." If the peers in the group say, "Wow, that sounds really scary. Tell us more about that movie," then the child has been positively reinforced. Peer interaction is like a tennis match. I hit the ball to you. In order for me to hit it again, you must first hit it back to me. And so it is with social interaction.

Unfortunately, for some children who are depressed, they lack the necessary social skills to get positive social responses from their peers. These children may come to believe that they cannot control social situations and, consequently, withdraw from them altogether. In fact, children who are depressed are viewed by their peers as less likable and as engaging in fewer positive behaviors. This finding could be expected given the negative reaction children with poor social skills receive from their peers. In essence, it becomes easier for a child with poor social skills to just withdraw from peers to avoid the aversive interaction. Some children with poor social skills will nevertheless interact with peers even when it results in aversive peer responses. As I mentioned in Chapters 1 and 2, for many children, negative attention is better than no attention at all. The irony, however, lies in the fact that although some depressed children seek negative reactions from peers, they nevertheless feel unfulfilled from these interactions. This situation is almost analogous to a heroin addict needing a fix. He may crave the drug, but after a while, he no longer feels the euphoric high—only an empty feeling that the craving has been eliminated. Not surprisingly, researchers have found that unpopular and socially withdrawn children are more likely to experience depression than their popular and more sociable peers.

The most direct approach for dealing with social skill problems is simply to teach a child the necessary behaviors for interacting appropriately with peers or participating in an activity. In essence, we want children to acquire skills that effectively elicit consistent and enduring positive reinforcement from significant others. Teaching these skills is a fairly straightforward process. In fact, teaching children social skills is no different than teaching a child how to swim, play catch or hit a baseball, clean a bedroom correctly, or learn multiplication tables. Unfortunately, many parents appear astonished at the prospect of teaching a child social skills. I think the reason for this astonishment stems from parents' belief that learning social skills is analogous to learning to walk or develop language: children learn them automatically with little need for direct teaching. Therefore, when a child lacks certain social skills, there is a tendency on the part of parents to believe that there is little they can do to rectify the problem. This view could not be further from the case. Very simple procedures can be employed, such as identifying the target skill, providing a child with instructions, modeling the skills for a child, giving a child opportunities to rehearse the skill, setting up a role play for a child to try out the skills, and providing a child with feedback regarding performance. I will briefly elaborate on these steps.

Specify the behavior

Following the recommendations appearing in Chapter 2, the specific behaviors that are involved in the skills need to be identified and defined so the child knows exactly what he is to perform. For example, the skill of *initiating a conversation with peers* is an important area where children need to obtain reinforcement. I have broken down the specific behaviors for *initiating a conversation with peers* as follows:

1. Identify a peer group having a conversation.
2. Walk toward the peer group.
3. On approaching the peer group, say "Hi."
4. Stand an appropriate distance from the peer group.
5. Determine the topic of their conversation.
6. Think of something to say that is relevant to the topic.
7. Monitor the conversation to find an appropriate time to say something.
8. Look at someone and say something relevant to the conversation.
9. Wait for a response from peers.
10. Let other members of the group say something.
11. Respond to what they say.

Provide instructions

The second step is to provide a child with instructions on how to carry out these behaviors. For example, for the first behavior above, *identify a peer group having a conversation,* you could give the following instructions to a child: "When you are outside shooting baskets, look down the block to see if there are any kids that you know standing around talking." Here is another example of giving instructions for the sixth behavior above, *think of something to say that is relevant to the topic.* "Once you know that the group is talking about the basketball playoff game last night, you need to think of something about that game to say. I remember you telling me you saw an interview with Patrick Ewing after the game in which he said the Knicks try to play physical in order to intimidate other teams. That sounds like something interesting to add to the discussion."

Model the behavior

The third step is for the parent to model the behavior for the child. Modeling refers to the process of performing the behavior so the child can observe it. Modeling is an extremely important step in teaching children any skills, whether it be learning social skills or how to serve a tennis ball. Could you imagine taking tennis lessons only to find that the instructor "tells" you how to serve the ball but never shows you. You would most likely feel cheated out of your money. Much of the behavior we learn is acquired by watching others perform it. How many times as teenagers have we said to a friend, "There's no way I'm going to grow up to be like my parents!" We all chuckle at that statement now, knowing how similar to our parents we act. Of course, some of the similar behavior patterns between ourselves and our parents can be attributed to genetics. But a large portion of our behavior is a result of watching our parents act in certain ways.

There is an anecdote Albert Bandura, a Stanford professor who wrote extensively on the effects of modeling, would tell his students: It seemed that there was a parrot fancier who purchased a parrot and was trying to teach it how to say uncle. The parrot fancier spent many long hours at this task, but nothing he tried worked. Finally out of frustration the parrot fancier resorted to a stick. He would swat the bird on the wings while threatening, "Say uncle, you stupid bird!" Still the bird did not speak. This was the last straw. The man gave up on teaching the bird how to speak and placed it out in the hen house to live with the chickens. A couple days later the parrot fancier heard a commotion coming from the hen house. He ran out to see what was the matter. To his amazement he saw the parrot, with a stick firmly tucked in its wing, chasing the chickens around the hen house, hitting them on the back with the stick while squawking, "Say uncle, you stupid birds!"

The point of relating this anecdote is not only that the effects of modeling are profound, but also that adults sometimes model less than desirable behavior for our children to imitate. But is it simple to model appropriate behavior? Returning to the list of behaviors, we could model for a child behavior number six, *think of something to say that is relevant to the topic*, in the following way. "Okay, you just told me about the interview you saw with Patrick Ewing on television. Now I'm going to pretend to be you and tell the kids about that interview. I want you to watch me closely because I'm going to have you practice for me."

Rehearse the behavior

After modeling the behavior, a child is required to practice it. This represents the third step—rehearsal. It is insufficient to just have a child hear how to perform a behavior or watch someone else perform the behavior. In order to become proficient at a behavior, a child must actually perform it. Not only must he perform it, but it must be rehearsed repeatedly. Like learning anything new, a child will initially allocate a lot of conscious awareness to performing a new task. Therefore, any distractions from performing the task will negatively influence a child's performance. This is analogous to learning how to drive a car: It initially takes a lot of conscious awareness and you can't do much else except concentrate on the task at hand. However, after repeated practice, the behavior becomes unconscious and is performed automatically. So it is with social skills: The more a child practices them, the more likely they will be used even if the child is depressed or anxious, because the skills can be activated automatically. Therefore, you could say to a child: "Okay, I just showed you how to talk about the interview you saw on television

last night with Patrick Ewing. Now I want you to tell me about that interview."
In this way, the child begins to practice what was previously modeled.

Role-play the behavior

The fourth step, role-playing, requires a child to practice the behavior in a
real-life situation. A role play refers to what its name implies: Family members
can be recruited to play the role of peers having a conversation about last
night's basketball playoff game. Then the child goes up to them, as if they
were actually the peers, and performs the behaviors in the social skill of
initiating a conversation with peers. This process not only constitutes additional
practice, but does so under real-life conditions. It gives a child an opportunity
to practice the skill in front of people approximating the peer group.

Provide feedback

The last step in teaching social skills is to provide a child with feedback on
her performance. In reality, feedback can occur during any of the preceding
steps. For example, after giving a child instructions, you may want him to
paraphrase them back to ensure he was listening and understood them.
Similarly, you could give a child feedback when he is rehearsing the behaviors. Positive feedback would highlight the areas that a child performed well.
You are, in essence, giving a child positive reinforcement so that those
behaviors are more likely to occur in the future. You can also could give a
child corrective feedback. Corrective feedback consists of selecting a behavior a child needs to improve, giving additional instructions on how to
perform the behavior, and then modeling the behavior. Feedback can also
occur during role-playing.

I hope it has become apparent that teaching children social skills is no
different than teaching a child how to play tennis. In the latter, we instruct
a child on the rules of tennis and the various shots, show him various strokes,
have him practice or rehearse the strokes, and then we set up a role play. In
essence, the role play is having a child play tennis with whomever is providing
the instruction. The child is then given feedback before actually playing a
game with someone else.

Combating Negative Consequences

Not every child who is depressed and fails to obtain enough positive reinforcement from others lacks the social skills. Sometimes children who are
depressed simply stop engaging in behavior that is likely to be reinforced by
others. Usually these behaviors are not being produced because a child
believes that the consequences will be negative. Remember when Carla said

she no longer enjoyed the debate team. She believed that her teammates didn't think she was a very good debater. If Carla believed this, she would want to avoid the *perceived* negative interaction she would have with her teammates. By withdrawing from a situation, a child who is depressed can avoid what she *perceived* as negative interaction. Avoidance behavior then becomes reinforcing. That is, the more one avoids a situation, the less negative interaction one has with others in that situation. Obviously, since interaction is avoided altogether, the responses of others can't be negative. This makes perfect sense if you are depressed. Therefore, one of the easiest ways to help a child over this avoidance is to increase her activity level.

William Glasser, in his book *Positive Addiction*, described the importance of individuals developing positive habits. These habits can take the form of any activity—either performed individually, such as jogging, or performed with others, such as a weekly game of racquetball. However, Dr. Glasser put several stipulations on the activity: it must be performed on a regular basis, it must take effort, and it must be of perceived value to the individual. Dr. Glasser uses the word *addiction* in the sense that if an individual fails on occasion to perform the activity, he will feel bad, just as drug addicts feel bad when they miss a fix. Think of someone you know who is an avid jogger. Ask the jogger how she feels on days it rains and she is unable to jog. She will probably speak of feeling restless, empty or irritable. The reason for these feelings is that the jogger has developed a kind of addiction to jogging and when prevented from engaging in this activity experiences withdrawal, just as would a drug addict. However, unlike a drug addict, a positive addiction has value to the individual. As a result, engaging in the activity is very reinforcing. Therefore, it is quite helpful to get children who are depressed to develop some positive addiction—either developing a new one or engaging in a previously reinforcing activity. There are several considerations when selecting an activity for a child.

Possessing the skills

It is important that a child has the skills for participating in the selected activity. For example, it would not be a good idea to register a child to play water polo if she is a poor swimmer. Although this example is extreme and obvious, the point nevertheless should not be forgotten.

Absence of anxiety

It is important that a child's avoidance behavior is not a result of her experiencing high levels of anxiety related to the activity. Sometimes anxiety occurs simultaneously with depression. Forcing a child to participate in an activity, even one for which she possesses the skills, when she is experiencing anxiety will be counterproductive. Remember that a child who is depressed is avoiding activities because of the perceived negative consequences of participating. If a child is highly anxious when participating in an activity, that activity will remain negative and the child will continue to engage in avoidance behaviors, probably at an even higher rate than before being forced to participate. When a child experiences anxiety, another activity should be selected. If she is experiencing generalized anxiety—in other words, anxiety is present no matter what activity is tried—then professional help should be sought. A psychiatrist may want to treat extreme levels of anxiety with medication in order to stabilize the depression to a point where a child is less anxious about participating in activities. In any event, do not force a child to participate in an activity. Instead, try to select activities of short duration that initially take minimal effort. It is always easier to get a child to make a small initial change in behavior rather than requesting a large one.

Previously enjoyable activity

The identified activity should be one that a child previously found enjoyable. Parents can ask themselves if a child decreased participation in an activity about the time that he became depressed. An affirmative response indicates an activity with a likelihood of reducing a child's depression. For example, if a child previously enjoyed playing with neighborhood children, then you might want to take your child and a couple of children from the neighborhood to McDonald's or some other restaurant that also has some type of playground equipment. Most children enjoy going to Chuck E. Cheese's because of all the games they provide. This last suggestion may make parents cringe as some of them find children's entertainment restaurants quite trying; nevertheless, it can have a therapeutic effect on children who are depressed.

Determine activities

If you are unsure of activities that a child previously found reinforcing, then it is best to try several activities and see if any of them result in an improvement in a child's depressed mood. The suggested activities should be of short duration and should require little effort on the part of the child. These two considerations will increase the likelihood that the child will participate in the activities. For example, going to a zoo or amusement park may require a long drive to get there and lots of walking once you arrive. Children who are depressed are not likely to engage in these types of activities—they simply take too much effort.

An alternative to simply trying a variety of activities is to ask a child what type of activities he has enjoyed in the past. Parents would be surprised at the range of activities that children list. William Reynolds and Kevin Stark developed a form for determining children's pleasant activities. Briefly, their form uses three degrees of happy faces that a child marks, indicating whether an activity is "just OK," "really fun" or "in between OK and really fun." One of the drawbacks of this schedule is that a child must fill in the activities. However, some children who are depressed view thinking of pleasant activities too burdensome. An alternative approach is the use of inventories that present a variety of potentially reinforcing activities. In this way, children have only to check the degree to which they enjoy an activity rather than having to think up the activities. Joseph Cautela developed inventories that can be used to determine reinforcing events for children and adolescents. These inventories consist of a range of statements on various topics including family members and the home, friends, preferred age groups, school and school-related activities, free-time activities, appearance and eating. Children rate the degree to which they like each item using the following criteria: not at all, a little, a fair amount, much and very much. These inventories can help parents determine potentially reinforcing activities for their children.

A Cognitive Approach to Depression

A cognitive approach takes on specific importance in relation to depression. Aaron Beck developed a cognitive model of depression that states that individuals who are depressed often have a negative view of themselves, the world around them and the future, even when presented with positive information. The basis for these three negative views arises from the activation of negative schemas during periods of stress. According to Beck, individuals who are depressed engage in six basic irrational beliefs. They initially attach a correct but negative interpretation to an event, and through the concept of consistency, the interpretation is attached to less and less similar situations until the belief distorts reality in a negative way and, consequently, leads to depression. Figure 7.2 presents these six irrational beliefs that Beck and his colleagues describe in *Cognitive Therapy of Depression*. An example of each will help clarify how they contribute to depression.

Irrational beliefs associated with depression

An example of *arbitrary inference* would be the following: Jesse wants to make the school's soccer team. She has been through two days of trials. On the third day, the coach comes up to her and says, "Jesse, you're a good dribbler. Keep practicing! You're a natural as a center." Oh great, Jesse thinks to herself. He's just being friendly so I won't feel so bad when he cuts me from the team. In this example, Jesse arbitrarily concludes that her coach is

Irrational Belief	Description
1. Arbitrary inference	Drawing a specific conclusion in the absence of evidence to support the conclusion or when the evidence is contrary to the conclusion
2. Selective abstraction	Focusing on a detail taken out of context, ignoring other more important features of the situation and conceptualizing the whole experience on the basis of this fragment
3. Overgeneralization	Drawing a general rule or conclusion on the basis of one or more isolated incidents and applying the concept across the board to related and unrelated situations
4. Magnification and minimization	Errors in evaluating the significance or magnitude of an event that are so gross as to constitute a distortion
5. Personalization	The tendency to relate external events to yourself when there is no basis for making such a connection
6. Absolutistic, dichotomous thinking	The tendency to place all experiences in one of two opposite categories

Figure 7.2. Irrational beliefs that characterize depression.

reacting negatively to her without checking out whether this perception is factual or not.

Individuals who are depressed engage in the next irrational belief, *selective abstraction*, quite frequently. Take the case of Alberto, a tenth-grader who is a staff member of his school's newspaper. This year he desperately wants to be on the yearbook staff. Most of the staff is selected from students who have performed well on the school newspaper. Alas, Alberto sighs, and feeling quite inadequate, reconciles himself to the fact that he will not be selected because last year he had two grammatical mistakes in an article he wrote. Unfortunately, Alberto completely ignores that fact that he completed every article by or before the deadline, wrote an average of two more pieces than any other student, was complimented by both the newspaper sponsor and the school principal, and received a grade of "A" on every English assignment related to grammar and punctuation. Instead, Alberto focused on one detail, making two grammatical mistakes, and ignores this other more important information.

We all are guilty of engaging in *overgeneralization* on occasion. It is a natural tendency given our proclivity to apply the concept of consistency to interpret situations. However, when taken to an extreme, overgeneralization leads to feelings of helplessness, worthlessness and depression. Consider Charles, a 17 year old who believes that if he is not loved by anyone, he is worthless. Actually this is not that irrational a belief; although most people are loved by at least one person—their mother or father. However, in Charles' case, he is infatuated with Susan. He really wants her to love him. But alas, Susan tells him she does not love him and does not even want to date him. Charles is devastated and tells himself, If I don't have love, I'm worthless. Susan doesn't love me. Therefore, I'm worthless. Charles has just engaged in a major overgeneralization. As is the case with many teenagers, Charles is basing his entire self-worth on the love of one person, while ignoring the love of his parents, brothers and sisters, and grandparents. He is taking a major premise, "If I don't have love, I'm worthless," applying a special case, "Susan doesn't love me," and making a general conclusion, "I'm worthless."

Magnification occurs when a person thinks the worst is most likely to happen to her. *Minimization* occurs when a person inappropriately shrinks things until they appear tiny and insignificant—both her own desirable and undesirable qualities. To illustrate the former, Monica is getting ready to sing a solo in her church choir. She just knows that the organist will hit the wrong note, some small child will begin to cry, it will be so hot that the congregation will be fanning themselves with the offering envelopes rather than listening to her, she will begin to sweat and everyone will be able to see the sweat on her lip, and she will have to sneeze half way through. If any of these things happen, it will be the end of the world. *Magnification* is similar to the irrational belief of awfulization described in the previous chapter.

Individuals who are depressed often engage in *minimization*—especially in regard to their own ability. For example, Brian just received an "A" on his spelling test. He tells himself the following: I only did well this week because the words were easy. This belief immediately discounts his performance. Individuals who regularly minimize their accomplishments effectively trash their self-esteem, and often experience depression.

Jessica is waiting for her date to arrive and take her out for dinner. She met George several weeks ago and this would be their third date. The first two dates were pretty nerve-wracking for Jessica, who is a shy person. George was polite but didn't talk much, thus making for some awkward silences. Jessica was left asking her friends to ask George's friends whether he really liked her or not. Although she had received a positive reply, she just wasn't sure whether George really liked her. After all, she was shy and didn't say much. Sometimes she just wished she could be the life of the party like her friends Betty and Sally. Jessica glanced up at the clock and saw that George was 15 minutes late. Oh great, Jessica thought to herself. George is late and that must mean he doesn't want to have dinner with me because I don't have a good sense of humor. Jessica's last reflection suggests she is engaging in *personalization*. She is taking an event—George being late—and relating the reason to herself.

The last irrational belief, *absolutistic dichotomous thinking*, occurs when an individual views an event in extreme terms. This type of thinking can devastate one's self-esteem. Little children engage in this belief all the time: "Mommy, if you don't buy me the candy bar, that means you don't love me." If there is one speck of dirt on the floor, and you tell me the floor is filthy, you are engaging in *absolutistic dichotomous thinking*. This thinking style can result in feelings of hopelessness. After all, if one speck of dirt represents filthy, then what are the chances of ever having a clean floor!

Beck and his colleagues described techniques for combating these six irrational beliefs. I will describe them and provide an example for each.

Techniques for combating irrational beliefs

The first technique is to help children recognize the connection between thoughts, emotions and behavior. Remember the four parts of any experience—event, meaning/interpretation, feeling and behavioral response—and the story of Robert and Karen in Chapter 4 that illustrates these parts. I use this example to teach children the connection between their beliefs, emotions and behaviors. Most children readily understand this example and refer to it as "the flower story." You can use any example to help a child understand the connection between thoughts, emotions and behavior as long as it fits into the four parts of any experience. Here's another example.

Whitney waits impatiently for the bell to ring indicating the beginning of morning recess. After what seems like an eternity of watching the clock, the bell finally rings. Whitney jumps out of her seat and gets in line to go outside. As she enters the bright sunshine of the morning, she squints her eyes and looks for someone to play with. She sees a group of four girls standing next to the backstop watching a group of kids playing kickball. She recognizes the girls as being from the other fourth-grade class. Whitney doesn't really consider them her friends, but has talked to them occasionally. She looks around for other kids to play with. Her two best friends are playing kickball—a game at which Whitney is not very coordinated. Rather than standing alone at recess—a definite sign of a dork—she decides to approach the girls watching the kickball game. She strolls up to the four girls and says, "Hi, what are you..." But before Whitney can finish her sentence, two of the girls start laughing. Whitney thinks to herself, they must be laughing at me. I'm such a dork. Who would want to talk to me anyway? Whitney immediately feels sad and rejected, covers her eyes with her hands, and runs off toward the school door. One of the girls who was laughing at her friend's story, turns to another and says, "I wonder what's with her? She sure can act strange."

This interaction can be illustrated using the four parts of any experience described in Chapter 4, as follows:

1. *Event:* Whitney talks to a group of girls and two begin laughing.
2. *Meaning/Interpretation:* Whitney tells herself the girls are laughing at her because she's such a dork.
3. *Feeling:* Whitney feels sad and rejected.
4. *Behavioral Response:* Whitney puts her face in her hands and runs off.

The important point is to use examples that help children understand that it is their interpretation of an event, and not the event or the people involved, that influences how they feel and behave. Many children who are depressed fail to understand this point. Instead, they believe that the way others behave or the things that happen to them are responsible for how they feel. Of course, we cannot control events or the behavior of others. However, by maintaining the belief that "others do it to us," children are setting themselves up for experiencing feelings of helplessness—one of the benchmark indicators of depression.

The second technique Beck and his colleagues described is having children monitor their negative beliefs held in certain situations. Remember from Chapter 4 that as we activate a belief in certain situations often enough, it becomes unconscious and is activated automatically. Consequently, many children are not even aware of the belief they attach to a situation. But many children are aware of the negative feelings and behavior that the belief produces. Therefore, it is important to help children become more aware of the beliefs they activate in certain situations. This can be accomplished using the self-monitoring techniques described in the previous chapter. I have taken the same format for the Frustration Action Sheet and modified it for depression in Figure 7.3.

When children self-monitor their thoughts, they become more aware of them. Two things can happen as a result of this. First, a child's behavior may change simply by engaging in self-monitoring. I referred to this process as *reactivity.* Second, once a child is aware of his thoughts, he may independently notice how irrational the belief really is.

However, sometimes another strategy must be used to help children understand the irrationality of a belief. Therefore, the third strategy is

---

Daily Thought Log

1. Describe an event leading to an unpleasant emotion:

2. What emotion did you experience?

3. Rate the degree you experienced this emotion:

1	2	3	4	5
a little	some	average	a lot	very much

4. Describe your thoughts that came before the emotion:

5. Rate your belief in these thoughts:

1	2	3	4	5
a little	some	average	a lot	very much

6. What irrational thinking style did your thoughts represent?

7. Describe how you behaved during and after the situation:

8. Write a rational response to your thoughts:

9. Rate your belief in these thoughts:

1	2	3	4	5
a little	some	average	a lot	very much

Figure 7.3. Example of a daily thought log.

helping children examine evidence for and against the irrational belief. The story of Lori illustrates this technique.

Many years ago when I was a counselor at a psychiatric unit for adolescents with emotional and behavioral problems, I worked with Lori who was a depressed 15 year old. Other than being depressed, Lori was a fairly typical teenager: she had some friends, but wished she had more; she had boys interested in her, but didn't think she was very attractive; she argued with her parents, but thought they were basically okay; and she wanted more privileges. One of the main reasons for Lori's depression was the irrational beliefs she would attach to situations. I had her complete two self-monitoring sheets daily like the one in Figure 7.3. Yet she still engaged in irrational beliefs that contributed to the development and continuation of her depression. Lori would go to great lengths, even having privileges taken away, to avoid situations she *believed* would have a negative outcome for her. Therefore, I decided to design an intervention for her to collect evidence for and against her irrational beliefs. I was hoping that by conducting a "personal experiment," Lori would come to view her beliefs as irrational.

Everyday at 5:00 p.m. the patients were divided into two groups: one group went swimming and the other group played volleyball. Unlike many other girls who were self-conscious about boys seeing them in a swimsuit, Lori didn't mind one bit and enjoyed swimming. However, playing volleyball was another thing. Lori believed that she was not very good at volleyball. And I had to agree with her. She was one of those people who had a repertoire of three shots: missing the ball completely, hurting her fingers while hitting the ball, or hitting the ball backwards. However, she also held what I considered to be several irrational beliefs which were strongly applied on Fridays. Every Friday night the patients decorated the unit, got out the stereo, purchased chips and pop, and had a dance with patients from the other adolescent unit. It was particularly difficult to get Lori to play volleyball on Fridays. She would prefer receiving a variety of punishments instead of participating in volleyball. Here was her thinking:

"I think most of the kids on the unit like me. But I've seen them laugh and make fun of other kids when they make a lousy shot playing volleyball. Because I'm lousy at volleyball, if I were to play and make a bad shot, everyone would laugh at me and tell me I suck. Then they'd laugh and tease me when we got back on the unit. And tonight, no one would want to dance with me. The only decent thing about this place is the dances we have on Friday nights. So if the dance sucks, then my life pretty much sucks too."

It's easy to see the different irrational beliefs Lori is applying to this situation. First, she is making an *arbitrary inference* by jumping to the conclusion that because she is lousy at volleyball, her peers will no longer like her. Second, she is engaging in *selective abstraction* because she is focusing solely on one detail, her poor volleyball skills, dwelling on it and disqualifying the fact that she is well liked by her peers. Third, she is *overgeneralizing.* Her basic assumption is that if her friends don't like her, life sucks. The specific case is that she is lousy at volleyball. Therefore, she is making a general conclusion that if she is lousy at volleyball, her peers will no longer like her, and her life will suck. Fourth, Lori is engaging in *magnification* by catastrophizing that the worst will happen—if she is lousy at volleyball then her life ultimately will suck due to the fact that no one will like her anymore. Finally, she is engaging in *absolutistic dichotomous thinking* by viewing her poor volleyball skills as proof that her peers will make fun of her. She is not leaving room for any middle ground.

I viewed my task as to challenge the irrational beliefs Lori held about the consequences of playing volleyball. However, I am not using the word *challenge* in the traditional sense. It would be a mistake to try to convince Lori that her beliefs were irrational. That would only get her angry at me and, consequently, she would be less likely to follow any of my suggestions. Instead, I'm using the word *challenge* to mean setting up situations where Lori was confronted with the irrationality of her beliefs. It would not do any good for me to point out that her beliefs were irrational. Instead, she had to reach that conclusion herself by examining evidence for and against the beliefs. My job, therefore, was to set up a "personal experiment" for Lori. This is how I proceeded.

"Lori, I sure can understand where you're coming from. I know I wouldn't want my friends to begin making fun of me or blowing me off. If that happened to me my life would suck too." By making this response, I have validated Lori's concerns. Now she knows that I understand her problem. This is an important consideration when working with children—especially teenagers. You must initially let them know you understand where they're coming from, even if you disagree or think their beliefs are totally off the wall. We all like to feel we're understood by others. In Lori's case, I wanted her to know "I was with her" so that she'd be more receptive to my suggestions.

With these opening remarks, I had Lori's attention, so I continued. "Do you like to be punished when you don't go off the unit to play volleyball?"

"Hell, it's better than being made fun of," Lori exclaimed.

"Yeah, I can understand that, but if the other kids would not make fun of you, would you still prefer to be punished rather than playing volleyball?"

"Well, no, that would be stupid, but I know they will make fun of me."

"How do you know they would make fun of you?" I asked.

"Because they make fun of kids that are lousy at volleyball all the time."

"All the time?" I asked.

"You know what I mean."

Ignoring her last comment, I continued. "Are all the kids that play volleyball equally good?"

"Of course not," Lori responded. "Josh, Nancy, Steffie and Rob are probably the best players. Mark and Lewis aren't bad. I heard that Fred and Julie are really terrible."

"Do Fred and Julie have friends on the unit?" I inquired.

"Sure, most kids like Julie, because she's really friendly and not stuck up at all. I guess people like Fred, I always see him talking to someone."

"So even though Fred and Julie 'suck' at volleyball, they still have friends?"

"Well I guess so." Lori responded slowly, but quickly continued, "but I know they wouldn't like me because I'm so lousy at volleyball."

"Lori, would you be interested in finding out for sure whether the other kids would stop liking you if you did lousy at volleyball?" Before Lori could answer, I continued. "What I have in mind is really *easy* and *fun* to do and you will *not* have to play volleyball."

Lori responded to my last two questions cautiously. "Well, maybe if it's easy and fun. And you said I wouldn't have to play volleyball?"

"Nope. Not only that, but you won't lose any privileges if you decide not to play volleyball so there's really no risk involved. Would you be interested?"

"Yeah, sure, what do you want me to do?"

I had to proceed carefully. I tentatively had Lori's cooperation. But if the tasks were too difficult or if she perceived that they entailed too much of a personal risk to her, she would probably bail out. "Didn't I hear you tell someone that someday you wanted to be a newspaper reporter?"

"You bet," responded Lori enthusiastically. "I want to cover murder trials and expose people who try and con old people out of their money."

"Tell me how you think a reporter would go about covering a story."

"Well, I know they have to interview people that are involved in the story. I've seen them on TV asking lots of questions and taking lots of notes."

I responded to her last statement by asking, "Can reporters just write down anything they want to? I mean, can they write something bad about a person just because they may not like him?"

"Oh no," Lori responded passionately. "They must stick to the facts. Only people who write editorials can give their personal opinion." Lori appeared proud of her knowledge of the workings of reporters and newspapers.

"Well, here's what I'd like you to do," I began. "I want you to pretend you are a reporter for a newspaper that's been assigned to cover a story. To cover this story, you must be completely objective—that means just collecting the facts and not giving your opinion. Do you think you can do that?"

"Of course I can. But what story do you want me to cover?"

"The headline reads: *Will Poor Volleyball Performance Alienate Girl from Friends?* Your task is to interview the kids on the unit to determine whether this headline is true or false. The first thing any good reporter does is to come up with a list of questions to ask the people she is interviewing."

"You mean you want me to be a reporter for my own story?"

"You've got it," I exclaimed. "Do you still want to give it a try? Remember, you don't have to play volleyball and you won't be punished for not doing this. But most importantly, you'll find out what the other kids on the unit think of your volleyball skills and whether they will tease you or not."

"Well, it sounds kind of stupid," replied Lori, obviously disappointed that she would not be covering a more sensational story. "But I guess I can give it a try."

"Good," I said. "Now, as I mentioned, you first need to come up with a list of questions to ask all the kids on the unit."

"But I'm not sure what to ask them."

"Would you like me to help you?" I asked. With a nod of her head, Lori indicated to me that she'd like my help. I continued. "The first thing is to ask them how well each kid believes he or she plays volleyball. Then ask them if they have ever made a bad play. After that…"

"Slow down, I can only write so fast," exclaimed Lori.

"Sorry." After Lori indicated that she was ready, I proceeded. "Okay, then ask them if they would laugh at you if you made a bad play. Finally, ask them if they would still like you even if you were lousy at volleyball. Do you have all that?"

"Yeah, I think so. But what if they just give me nice answers so as to not hurt my feelings?"

"Lori, do you think that if they don't want to hurt your feelings that maybe that means they like you?"

"Well, I guess so. But they still could act differently during an actual game."

"That's true, but we'll cross that bridge when we get to it. Right now, I want you to begin interviewing everyone on the unit."

Lori began interviewing the other patients on the unit. Later that day, I met with her to go over the results of her interviews. She somewhat bashfully admitted that not everyone was good at volleyball, that no one would make fun of her if she were to play, and that they all would still be friends with her.

The interviewing served as a way for Lori to gather information for and against her beliefs. The information she obtained was contrary to her beliefs. I asked her what she made of this information.

"Well, maybe I overreacted a little. Some people even said I was stupid to think they wouldn't like me just because I wasn't very good at volleyball."

"What other information did you get?" I asked.

Lori had an expression as if she was a toddler whose parent had just caught her with her hand in the cookie jar when she said, "Josh, Nancy, Steffie and Rob—the best volleyball players—asked me if I was ever going to play volleyball. I couldn't believe they would actually want me to play."

Without commenting on her last statement I said, "Are you ready for the second part of your reporting job?"

"You said I don't have to play volleyball, right?"

"That's absolutely right," I replied. "Are you ready?"

"Sure," Lori said.

"Good," I began. "Now here's what I want you to do. Everyone goes down to play volleyball at 5:00 p.m. I want you to wait in your room until everyone is off the unit. Then after about five minutes have passed, come out and I'll be waiting for you over by the nurses' station. Bring your notebook and a pencil. Okay?"

"What are we going to do?" Lori inquired.

"You'll see, but I promise you won't have to play volleyball."

About five minutes after the other kids went to play volleyball, Lori came out of her room with pencil and notebook in hand. "Here's what we're going to do," I began. "I'm going to take you down to where the kids are playing volleyball. However, you're just going to watch from the doorway. You shouldn't feel too stupid doing this because a lot of kids from other units stop to watch. And if anyone asks, you can just tell them I'm making you take notes as one of your program assignments. Then I want you to write down the names of the kids playing volleyball. Next to their names, I want you to make a tally mark every time someone makes a bad play. Then put the initials of anyone who makes fun of the kid who just made a bad play next to the tally mark. This way, you'll have a record of who made a bad play and whether anyone made fun of them."

Lori somewhat hesitatingly agreed as long as if anyone asked, she could blame me for her having to do this. I agreed that would be fine. To Lori's surprise, everyone made bad shots. Even more surprising to Lori, no one made fun of anyone who made a bad shot. In fact, many of the kids offered encouragement after someone missed a shot. Rob and Steffie twice asked Lori if she wanted to play. Although Lori wasn't in a hurry to drop her notebook and pencil and rush out on to the court, she eventually joined the game for the last five minutes.

Through this "personal experiment," Lori demonstrated to herself that her beliefs were irrational—that is, they were not grounded in fact. The final step in cognitive therapy is to substitute more reality-oriented interpretations for irrational beliefs. One approach for accomplishing this goal is to use the techniques presented in the second half of Chapter 4. Another approach is to use the five-step self-instruction training technique described earlier in this chapter. Even though a child may have gathered evidence indicating her beliefs about a situation are irrational, because of the concept of consistency, that evidence may only have a short-term effect and the irrational beliefs may return. Therefore, we want to make sure a child replaces the irrational beliefs with more rational ones. In Lori's case, we together worked out a simple self-instruction she began repeating to herself right before she was going to play volleyball. The self-instruction was as follows: "Chill out, no one is going to make fun of me. And if I make a lousy shot, how bad is it anyway?"

To summarize: The purpose of a cognitive approach to depression is first to make a child aware of her negative self-talk. Because self-talk is habitual and activated automatically, self-monitoring techniques are helpful for increasing a child's awareness of her self-talk. After a child is aware of the self-talk, we want to set up "personal experiments" so that she can obtain evidence either for or against that belief. Finally, we want to replace the irrational belief with one that is more rational and factual and will eventually become habitual and activated automatically.

Self-Control Approach

The final approach for understanding depression and developing therapeutic activities is based on the feedback model of self-control described in the previous chapter. To review briefly, self-control is conceptualized as a three-phase feedback loop involving self-monitoring, self-evaluation and self-administered consequences. A self-control approach to depression was developed by Lynn Rehm. He characterized self-control problems in one or more of the three processes in the following ways for individuals who are depressed.

Problems in self-control

First, children who are depressed may selectively monitor or attend to negative events to the exclusion of positive events. For example, a child may focus all his attention on the fact that he was scolded by his father for leaving toys in the living room. This child may ignore the fact that his father just spent an hour playing basketball with him, that he praised him for receiving a "B" on a math quiz, and that he thanked him for taking his little sister to the park that morning to play on the swings. When children selectively ignore positive interactions and activities, depression is often a natural reaction.

Second, children who are depressed may selectively monitor immediate as opposed to delayed consequences of their behavior. The concept of immediate versus delayed consequences was described at the beginning of Chapter 4. This concept can be applied to depression. For example, a child who has to cut the lawn on Saturday morning may focus on how terrible this is. She may ignore the fact that she is being paid $8.00 and that after lunch she can use that money, along with $15.00 she has saved, to buy a new baseball mitt. Or a child may get upset because her teacher requires her to write the three spelling words she missed on the pretest 10 times each. She completely ignores the fact that now she will most likely be better prepared for the spelling bee at the end of the week with its prizes for the winner and runner up.

Third, children who are depressed often set overly harsh self-evaluative criteria. Remember from Chapter 4 that if a child reaches or exceeds his self-evaluative criteria, he is likely to engage in positive self-statements. The opposite is true if the child fails to meet his self-evaluative criteria. Therefore, when promoting self-control, it is important that children set realistic criteria for their performance. Unfortunately, many children who are depressed are too perfectionistic and, consequently, are harsh on themselves. Sometimes this surfaces in absolutistic dichotomous thinking. For example, a child may set a goal of getting 25 out of 25 division problems correct and anything less than a perfect score, even missing just one, indicates he performed terribly. Setting overly stringent criteria is very apparent when watching children play a sport, such as little league baseball. If a child strikes out once, or grounds out, or fails to get a hit every time at bat, he evaluates his performance as completely lousy. How many parents have placed their arms around a child's shoulders trying to console him. Some children are devastated by not reaching perfection.

Fourth, overly stringent evaluative criteria lead to negative self-statements regarding one's performance. These negative self-statements become habitual and are activated automatically and in situations less and less similar to the original one. Because most children are not aware of the negative self-statements they tell themselves, they are left with only the feelings of depression.

Fifth, many children who are depressed infrequently engage in self-reinforcement. This could be expected since they tend to self-monitor negative events and set overly stringent evaluative criteria.

Sixth, they frequently administer excessive self-punishment. This often takes the form of negative self-talk—put-downs, discounting performance or believing success is due to external factors. In some instances, children will engage in self-injurious behaviors as a form of self-punishment, such as burning themselves with a cigarette or making cuts on their skin with a knife or needle.

Activities for combating self-control problems

Activities for combating self-control difficulties are the same as those described in the preceding chapter. First, we want children to self-monitor positive activities and interactions that they have throughout the day. By becoming more aware of these positive things, children's perceptions begin to change. As their perceptions about events change, so do their emotions and behaviors. Second, we want to train children to look at long-term versus short-term consequences. One of the easiest ways to accomplish this is to have children set their own goals. I like to have children set daily morning and afternoon goals as well as a weekly goal. Goal-setting helps children stay focused on the long term rather than reacting to short-term events. Third, we want to help children set more realistic evaluative criteria for their performance. Sometimes it is helpful to have children determine what the "average" same-aged peer's performance would be and use that as a starting point. Finally, children are taught to engage in more positive self-statements. All the techniques presented in the previous chapter apply here.

8

Dealing with Resistant Children

It just wasn't fair, thought Jerry Orchard as he walked home from school. He was in a bad mood and didn't care about spring or anything else. He had been excited about going to the zoo with his class on Friday. Then it happened during music. Something always happens during music, Jerry thought to himself. It's because of that stupid kid Lance and that even stupider music teacher, Mrs. Schmidt. On this particular day, Lance had brought a tennis ball into the music room. When he thought Mrs. Schmidt wasn't looking, he threw it at the clock on the wall next to the blackboard. The ball ricocheted off the wall, bounced in between chairs, and eventually came to a stop by Mrs. Schmidt's feet.

Jerry couldn't resist laughing. And that was his downfall. Mrs. Schmidt glared at Jerry. Jerry knew that look. He had seen it a hundred times before. Therefore, he quickly pointed at Lance and said, "He's the one who threw the ball, not me." Lance began to protest but quickly saw that wouldn't get him anywhere.

Mrs. Schmidt had made up her mind: "Lance, get down to the principal's office this instant." Jerry couldn't help smiling and was trying to muffle a chuckle when Mrs. Schmidt added, "You too, Jerry, get yourself to the principal's office."

"But why?" whined Jerry. "I didn't throw the ball. It's not fair that I should have to go to the principal's office. I heard other kids laughing too. Why don't you send them to the principal's office?" From the expression on Mrs. Schmidt's face, Jerry knew he shouldn't have made this last comment. He quickly sulked out of the class to make the trip down the hall to the principal's office.

As the boys explained what happened to the principal, Mr. Rodriguez, they had the feeling he had already made up his mind they were guilty. Mr.

Rodriguez reached for a calendar of school events on the credenza behind him as the boys finished their side of the story. He laid it on his desk, sighed and said, "It appears that your class is going on a field trip to the zoo this Friday. It that correct, boys?" Each boy nodded numbly. Jerry began to understand where Mr. Rodriguez was heading with this line of questioning and quickly said, "It's not fair that I can't go on the field trip, I didn't throw the ball and besides, a bunch of other kids were laughing."

"That's beside the point, "Mr. Rodriguez said sternly. "I think a fitting punishment would be for you boys to stay at the school while your class is at the zoo, so you can help Mrs. Schmidt. She is going to spend much of the day Friday cleaning and rearranging the music room. I think she would appreciate some help." Mr. Rodriguez picked up the calendar and returned it to the credenza, indicating the conversation was over.

As Jerry was walking home, he couldn't help replaying the situation in his mind. It was so unfair, he thought. He was sick and tired of being told what to do by adults who didn't bother to understand his point of view. By the time Jerry turned into the driveway of his house, he had worked himself into a highly agitated state. Just let my mom try and tell me what to do when I walk in the door and I'll show her, Jerry thought to himself.

"Hello, dear," Mrs. Orchard said sweetly to her son. "How was your day?"

"Fine," Jerry responded, not wanting his answer to give his mother the satisfaction of knowing what really happened at school.

"Your sister convinced me to make some rice crispy treats. You can have some after you put your books away."

There weren't too many things Jerry liked better than rice crispy treats. He amazed himself and his parents at how many he could eat in one sitting. But even rice crispy treats weren't going to get him into a good mood. Instead, he thought how his mother offered them to him as a way for yet another adult to control him. And Jerry was fed up with adults telling him what he could and couldn't do. He turned back toward his mother, who was still smiling at him while she was cutting up vegetables for a dinner salad. He then dropped his books on the kitchen floor and glared at her challengingly.

Mrs. Orchard's smile faded but she nevertheless responded in a calm voice that just irritated Jerry more. "Jerry, please pick your books up and place them on the desk in your bedroom."

"No! I won't pick up my books. And I'm not going to put them on my desk either. You can't make me—nobody can make me!"

At this point Jerry could be considered "oppositional," and his mother had to deal with his resistance. As his mother, the adult in authority, she couldn't back down to his challenge. She needed to let Jerry know he can't do whatever he wants to. Like any parent whose authority has been threatened by a child, Mrs. Orchard believed she needed to teach Jerry respect.

Still maintaining her patience and self-control, Mrs. Orchard responded to Jerry's challenge, but without any of the sweetness evidenced earlier. "Jerry, if you want any rice crispy treats, you had better pick those books up and put them on your desk right now." Jerry just stood there, his bottom lip stuck out like the perch on a bird house, his silence communicating his answer. "Fine, young man, you can either put those books on your desk or spend the rest of the afternoon in your bedroom and then your father can deal with you when he gets home from work," Mrs. Orchard responded with none of the calmness previously exhibited.

"I hate you," Jerry yelled as he stomped into his room, purposely kicking his books into the foyer on his way. He had decided that as long as he was stuck in his room for the afternoon, he wasn't going to give his mother the satisfaction of picking up his books.

Mrs. Orchard shook her head in puzzlement and disgust as she bent over and picked up his books. Kids can be so strange. I wonder what set him off, she thought as she dropped the books on her son's desk without saying a word to him.

The situation that occurred between Jerry and his mother is a fairly common one that is repeated in many households across this country. Jerry is not a problem child, nor did his mother overreact to his seemingly strange behavior. In fact, she kept her cool amazingly well. Yet her goal, to get Jerry to pick up his books and place them on his desk was not achieved. Most of us would view Jerry as the source of the problem. Two terms come to mind to describe Jerry: oppositional and resistant. But I would like to pose the following question based on this situation: Who was really being resistant—Jerry or his mother? In order to answer this question, we must understand the concept of *resistance.*

Understanding Resistance

Resistance was originally described by Sigmund Freud in the context of psychoanalysis. Although many aspects of Freud's theory either have not withstood the test of empirical study or have few practical implications for parents, his conceptualization of resistance is quite illuminating. Freud used this term to describe why many of his patients failed to participate in therapy despite their request for help. Why would a person be motivated enough to seek out therapy for a troubling problem but then resist the therapist's help? Freud speculated that resistance served an adaptive function: it maintained internal equilibrium and avoided emotional conflict. In other words, if an individual was to comply with the therapist, he would be exposing himself to the anxiety associated with the problem that initially prompted the need for help. But by being resistant to therapy, he could keep the anxiety at an unconscious level which, in the short run, would be less emotionally painful than confronting it directly.

Family therapists hold a similar view of resistance. From their perspective, individuals cling to the way things are rather than exposing themselves to the uncertainty and threat that changing their behavior implies. This need to change but remain the same is at first quite puzzling. For example, why are some children who complain of not having enough friends, needing more money, or being bored so resistant to suggestions to join a club, apply for a job, or develop a hobby? I believe the answer to this question has to do with risk—all the suggestions expose the child to the potential of being rejected or failing. Therefore, the pain implied in the risk of changing may be more severe than remaining the same, even when remaining the same is also painful. Consequently, we all repeatedly engage in certain behaviors that are ineffective. In essence, we all try to maintain *homeostasis*—a term family therapists use to describe our desire for consistency in our life. Consistency breeds predictability which, in turn, reduces anxiety by engendering feelings of comfort and a sense of self-assurance. However, it is this perceived sense of comfort that often keeps us behaving in ineffective ways. Students repeatedly engage in the same inappropriate behavior and we, in turn, respond in predictable and often ineffective ways.

From our discussion thus far, we could easily conceptualize resistance as avoidance of anxiety or fear of taking a risk. These factors certainly contribute to resistance and often result in children being labeled oppositional, stubborn and inflexible. However, I would like to offer a more basic definition of resistance: any behavior that interferes with or reduces the likelihood of a successful outcome. Although this definition may seem vague, it is meant to point out that resistance can originate from a variety of factors. Traditionally, we view resistance as behavior a child engages in to avoid complying with a request. And sometimes this may be true—children certainly do engage in oppositional behavior with the sole purpose of trying to frustrate us. However, it is more difficult to become frustrated if we expand our repertoire of responses to children's behavior. Therefore, although I describe three different factors accounting for resistance, the recommendations are mostly based on how you can alter your responses to manage resistance.

Resistance Due to Child Factors

We are quick to point to a child as a source of resistance. This response reflects the medical-disease model often used in psychiatry that was described in Chapter 5. Remember that this model considers behavior problems to be manifestations of clinical entities much like physical diseases. Although there is insufficient evidence to warrant a generalized medical model of all behavior problems or to imply that such problems exist within persons as do physical diseases, we nevertheless rely on labels generated from this model to explain why a child is being resistant. In fact, there is a

psychiatric label for highly resistant children—oppositional defiant disorder—which is characterized by a recurrent pattern of negativistic, defiant,
disobedient and hostile behavior toward authority figures. These labels are
supposed to inform us about the nature of a child's problem and to guide
treatment. However, they also have the unintended effect of minimizing the
influence our behavior has on a child's functioning. I will be describing a
different conceptualization of child-specific factors—one that focuses on
whether or not a child possesses the requisite skills in her repertoire to
comply with a request.

The model of behavior shown in Figure 8.1, developed by Ken Howell
and his associates at Western Washington University, can be used to understand the dynamics of resistance due to child factors. In this model, a child's
resistant behavior can be examined in relation to two general categories:
can't versus can.

If a child can't perform a behavior, it is because of one of two possible
reasons. First, a child may actually lack the skill necessary to comply with a
request. For example, a parent may tell a child to stop irritating her brother.
However, the child may not know what "irritate" means. Consequently, she
is unable to comply with the request and instead appears resistant or
oppositional. Second, some aspect of the environment may be reinforcing
the child for continuing to irritate her brother. She may receive a lot of
attention, albeit negative, from her brother. Consequently, she is being

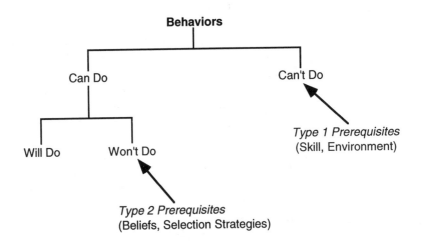

Figure 8.1. Model for understanding resistance due to child factors.

reinforced for engaging in the undesirable behavior despite her parents' directions to desist.

If a child can perform the requested behavior, he either will or won't perform it. If a child performs the behavior, he is not going to be considered resistant but, instead, compliant. However, it is possible that a child can perform the desired behavior but nevertheless won't. There are a variety of reasons for this. A child's perceptions about a situation may interfere with performing the desired behavior. Sometimes when a child gets into a neighborhood fight he is required to apologize to the other child. However, he may be quite resistant to making an apology—not because he lacks the skills for apologizing, but because he believes his peers will think he is a sissy for apologizing.

Another reason why children won't perform a behavior they possess is that they may select an inappropriate strategy to guide behavior. Strategies are used to help us analyze a given situation, select a behavior to perform based on our analysis, and evaluate the possible consequences to ourselves and others of performing the behavior. For example, a child may respond to teasing from a peer by hitting him. As a result, the child is grounded for two days. This behavior can occur repeatedly with the same outcome because a child fails to evaluate the consequences of hitting a peer, or may have been successful using this behavior, without consequences, to get his sibling to stop teasing him.

I want to stress that when a child *won't* perform the appropriate behavior, it means he has selected, from among a variety of behaviors in his repertoire, the wrong behavior—one that makes him appear resistant or oppositional. I am not suggesting that he consciously, and with intent to irritate, selected to do so. When a child purposely performs a behavior to irritate you he is reacting to you as much as you are reacting to him. In this instance, I believe resistance is not due to child factors but rather to adult factors—a point I will elaborate upon shortly. However, more often *selecting* an inappropriate behavior is not the same as *deciding* to behave inappropriately. We select behaviors automatically. Automatic responses are those that have become habitual through repeated use and thus are activated unconsciously. In this instance a child automatically selects an inappropriate behavior without giving conscious thought to the consequences. Given this brief overview, I will now describe in more detail resistance due to specific child factors and ways to manage them.

Children Who Lack the Necessary Skills

Some children fall under the *can't* category in Figure 8.1, because they lack the necessary skills to comply, or due to environmental factors which I will discuss in the next section. A child may experience a variety of skill deficiencies. For example, a child may seem resistant because she simply does not understand what to do or how to go about performing a behavior or task. In some instances a child is too preoccupied to understand an adult's instructions or feels inept at carrying them out. Other children may not understand an adult's instructions or the rationale for engaging in a particular behavior or task. Resistance due to these difficulties can be managed with the following techniques.

Provide detailed instructions

Providing children with detailed instructions is an important component to increase compliance. Instructions refer to rules that indicate that specific behaviors will pay off in particular situations. Sometimes rules clearly identify reinforcers or punishers associated with following the rules. An example would be telling a child "if you finish your vegetables in 10 minutes you can have an ice cream sundae for dessert, but if you don't finish your vegetables in 10 minutes you will not get any dessert." In other cases, consequences are implied. When a parent says to a child in an excited voice, "Wow, would you look at that!" looking in the implied direction will likely enable the child to see something interesting. On the other hand, if an adult sternly says to a child, "Sit down right now!" the instruction carries the implication that the child's refusal to sit down is likely to lead to punishment. There are several simple guidelines for giving instructions:

1. Instruction should be within the understanding of the child.
2. Instruction should specify the behavior in which the child is to engage.
3. Instruction should specify contingencies involved in complying (or not complying), and these contingencies should be applied consistently.
4. Complex instruction should be broken down into easy-to-follow steps.
5. Instruction should be sequenced so that it proceeds gradually from very easy to more difficult behavior for the child.
6. Instruction should be delivered in a pleasant, courteous manner.

To ensure that a child understands an instruction, ask her to repeat it to you. Sometimes she will refuse to repeat an instruction, especially if she is angry at the prospect of engaging in some unpleasant activity. In this situation, as when managing *any* resistance, it is important to be flexible and exude a "matter-of-fact attitude." For example, you could tell her that if she prefers, instead of saying it out loud, she can write down the instruction or say it into a tape recorder. If you are still engendering resistance, you can say, in a matter-of-fact voice, that she can choose to stay in her room as long as it takes for her to paraphrase the instruction. You want to convey to the child that you really don't care whether she paraphrases the instruction now or sits in her room. If you really don't care that a child stays in her room until she is ready to paraphrase an instruction, and if you are pleased that she has the opportunity to spend time thinking about it, then she most likely will not involve herself in a power struggle by refusing to paraphrase it. After all, if she does, she will not anger you, but only invite some time thinking about the instruction. And if she senses that you really do not care, she will figure that she may as well repeat the instruction now and be done with it.

Provide skill training

Children who lack the necessary skills to perform a task or behavior will not comply simply because a teacher asks them to do so. Therefore, resistance is reduced when children are taught the specific skills necessary to comply and are provided with practice in the skills. Specifically, you should break the skill to be taught into small, manageable steps of increasing difficulty, model the skill for the child, provide him with opportunities to rehearse the skill, set up a role-play to provide additional real-life practice, and provide reinforcement and feedback. However, even after a skill is learned, a child sometimes fails to perform it for one reason or another. When this happens, additional practice is warranted. One such type of practice that is particularly well suited for managing resistance is called *overcorrection*.

Provide opportunities for practice

Overcorrection is a procedure that was initially developed to reduce inappropriate behaviors exhibited by children with autism and mental retardation. There are two types of overcorrection: *restitutional overcorrection* and *positive practice overcorrection*.

Restitutional overcorrection requires that a child corrects the consequences of his inappropriate behavior by altering the situation to a condition greatly improved from that which existed before the misbehavior. For example, a child who throws food in the school lunch room would be required not only to clean up his food, but also any other food or garbage in the entire cafeteria.

Positive practice overcorrection provides a child with opportunities to engage in appropriate behavior. In this case, a child who casually tosses her clothes on the floor would be required to repeatedly place her clothes in the hamper. It is this latter type of overcorrection that can be quite helpful for managing resistance. Positive practice is based on the belief that in order to help resistant children learn responsibility, they must spend time and effort engaging in the appropriate behavior. In this way they experience the inconvenience suffered by other people who must otherwise correct the disturbance. To understand how to implement positive practice for managing resistance, I will elaborate on the example of the girl who threw her clothes on the floor instead of putting them in the hamper.

When a child throws her clothes on the floor rather than putting them in the hamper, your goal is to have her assume responsibility for her behavior without imposing on others. In a matter-of-fact way, you explain to the child that you have noticed she has difficulty putting her clothes in the hamper. Therefore, she will devote one hour this morning to *practice* putting her clothes in the hamper. You further clarify that different people require different amounts of practice time to learn skills in different areas. You are confident that she will be able to master the skill, but are uncertain if one hour will be adequate time for her to practice and really learn to do it well. Tell the child that you are more than willing to let her practice again if necessary. Appear genuinely enthusiastic about this process. Let the child know you are confident that she will catch on and that she can take her time.

The key component in getting children to comply with practicing is to appear as if you really do not care; then a power struggle is diffused. If you really do not care that a child is spending one hour learning how to put his clothes in the hamper and, in fact, are pleased that he has the opportunity to practice and master the skill, he will probably not be resistant by tossing his clothes on the floor, but instead will put them in the hamper and be done with it. And if he does toss the clothes on the floor, he will not anger you, thereby controlling the situation and receiving negative attention, but instead will invite practice time. Remember, always give a child a choice: either pick up the clothes when asked the first time, or receive practice. In this way, a child always has the *choice* to avoid practice. And if a child chooses to practice, never feel sorry for him. After all, practicing putting clothes in the hamper for one hour has never caused illness, death or permanent disability.

Children Who Have Pessimistic Expectations

There are two types of expectations: efficacy expectations and outcome expectations. *Efficacy expectations* refer to a person's belief that she can perform the specific behaviors required for a desired consequence. *Outcome expectations* refer to a person's belief that a specific behavior will, in fact, lead to a certain outcome, such as reinforcement. A child might believe that asking a friend for assistance would result in the friend's providing help, but have little confidence that she could nevertheless perform the behaviors successfully. Or the child might think she could successfully ask for help but believe those behaviors would not result in assistance from the friend or, worse, that the friend might criticize her for asking for help. In either case, the child may not perform the requested behavior and, therefore, will appear resistant.

Sometimes children's beliefs are not grounded in reality. In the previous example, the child may believe the friend will criticize her for asking for help, without having any proof that the friend will engage in such behavior. However, once a belief is formed, it attains factual status. Therefore, it is important to acknowledge children's pessimism as real. This suggestion may at first sound a little strange, or even uncaring. Our typical response to children who express pessimistic ideas or expectations is to counter such beliefs with expressions of optimism. If a child is feeling some type of hurt, whether it be physical or emotional, we naturally want to comfort him. However, in many instances, our attempts to counter with optimism have the opposite effect—they elevate rather than reduce resistance. Regardless of the good intentions behind our statements, they often run counter to a child's position of pessimism. Take a situation where a child believes he will flunk his math test, even though you know he possesses the skills for passing. When a child states this pessimistic expectation, it's common to counter with a statement such as, "Oh, that's ridiculous, you'll have no problem passing the test." Although this comment is meant to cheer a child up, it runs counter to his belief. Therefore, he is likely to say to himself, My mother doesn't understand me, she's no help at all. Instead of countering with optimism, it is better initially to acknowledge a child's pessimism. You could tell the child, "I can understand your point and it's probably better to be uncertain or doubtful at this time." This statement sounds strange because we are so conditioned to try to ease a child's emotional or physical pain. But by doing so, we often create resistance because we are saying things that run counter to a child's current beliefs.

By initially matching your comments to those of a child, you are implying that you recognize his discouragement and validate it as being real. This reduces resistance so that you can move the child in a more desirable direction. In the previous example, after acknowledging the boy's pessimism about not doing well on his math test, you could ask, "Have there been any other math tests which you didn't flunk?" The idea behind this statement is to get the child to put his pessimistic beliefs into perspective by comparing them to past experiences. A child is more likely to reflect logically and respond honestly to this statement once you have acknowledged his pessimism. If, on the other hand, you first try to counter with optimism, the child will think you do not understand his position. Therefore, your next statement is likely to fall on deaf ears—he will either not answer truthfully or will make up some reason why your question is irrelevant.

Milton Erickson, once considered an unorthodox and controversial psychiatrist, utilized this technique with both his patients and his children. Erickson's approach, known as *strategic therapy*, has increased in popularity and is studied and taught widely. Since his death in 1980, Erickson has assumed the stature of a cult figure with thousands of admirers attending large conferences addressing aspects of his unique approach. It is not easy to describe this approach because of the curious way Erickson stood on the line between healer and poet, scientist and bard. But in a nutshell, strategic therapy is a name given to a variety of techniques in which the therapist takes responsibility for directly influencing people. The strategic therapist identifies solvable problems, sets goals, designs approaches for each problem, and examines the client's responses to make corrections in order to achieve the goals. Because it is difficult to categorize Erickson's techniques, I have instead interwoven various examples of his work throughout the remainder of this chapter.

Erickson once described how he handled an incident involving his son Robert who, when he was almost four years old, fell down the back stairs of his house, split his lip and knocked his upper tooth back into the maxilla. The boy was bleeding and screaming with pain and fright. Erickson and his wife rushed to him and realized it was an emergency. But instead of picking their son up and comforting him, Erickson said, "That hurts awful, Robert. That hurts terrible. And it will keep right on hurting." Erickson did not try to console his son with some optimistic response such as "Oh, Robert, it will be okay, it will stop hurting soon." Although such a comment is meant to provide comfort to a child, it usually has the opposite effect. The child knows it hurts, and by failing to acknowledge this fact you create resistance to any further efforts to move the child beyond the pain. As an adult, Robert reflected back on this situation: "When my father agreed with me, I realized that he clearly understood the pain I was experiencing, so I was ready to listen. My father had established credibility with me."

Children Who Have Negative or Anxious Thoughts

Some children exhibit resistance because they have negative or anxious thoughts at the prospect of changing their behavior. Such children may view the short-term negative consequences of looking foolish, not knowing what to do, or experiencing "put downs" from others as more significant than the potentially reinforcing long-term consequences of changing their behavior. Several techniques can be used in such situations.

Explore children's expectations and fears

It is important to encourage children to share with you their fears and anticipated reactions to changing their behavior. Contrary to what some would expect, expressing anxious thoughts actually helps children gain control over them. Sometimes we are reluctant to have children discuss their fears, believing that talking about them will make them come true. However, children's anxieties are usually reduced when discussed in the presence of a warm, nonjudgmental parent. Having children share their fears about changing their behavior also enables you to identify and correct any irrational beliefs about the situation using the RET techniques described in Chapter 4. These techniques diffuse unrealistic and catastrophic expectations that prevent children from performing new behaviors.

Set up a small alteration in behavior

Children who hold negative beliefs are more likely to comply with a request to make a small rather than a large change in their behavior. This suggestion is congruent with one of the principles of reinforcement presented in Chapter 3: *Reinforce approximations*. Remember that I discussed how behavior is not performed in one swoop and that it needs to be shaped using a step-by-step process. I illustrated this point by describing a student who was resistant to completing multiplication worksheets. My solution was to give the student a piece of paper with only one multiplication problem on it. It was difficult for the student to be resistant since the requested change in behavior was so minor. Although my end goal was to have the student complete more math problems, I had to set up a situation where resistance was initially reduced. Behavior change is like a kaleidoscope. Although it is possible to turn the tube only a fraction of an inch, the entire pattern nevertheless changes. And so it is with changing behavior: A small change seems inconsequential to children and doesn't require a radical departure from the status quo, yet it has the effect of setting in motion larger changes in behavior, thereby reducing resistance. Again, the techniques of Milton Erickson illustrate this point.

Sidney Rosen, in his book *My Voice Will Go with You*, describes how Dr. Erickson worked with a woman who was claustrophobic—she couldn't tolerate being confined in a small room. She agreed to sit in his office if the door was left wide open. Dr. Erickson responded by saying, "Suppose instead of having the door wide open it lacked one millimeter of being wide open?" She agreed. Dr. Erickson then worked up to two millimeters, three millimeters, a centimeter, half an inch, an inch and so on. Dr. Erickson was telling us to deal with difficult problems a little bit at a time.

Use a force-field analysis

Although the name of this technique sounds like something from a science fiction movie, it was developed by Kurt Lewin to help individuals who were resistant to change. Using this technique, the parent assists a child in listing all possible ways to avoid complying with a request, called *resisting forces*. Although a parent could easily list all the avoidance behaviors in which a child engages, it is more effective to have a child do it since it takes advantage of their resistant point of view. Having a child give all the possible reasons for and ways to be noncompliant with the required behavior or activity serves two purposes.

First, by listing ways to avoid the task, a child is actually being cooperative. That is, she is following your direction and, by so doing, is being compliant. Once a child is compliant in one area, it is easier to get compliance in others. This technique is considered paradoxical since in order for a child to resist, she must comply. In a force-field analysis, a child can resist engaging in a task by listing all the ways of resisting. But by listing those ways, the child is complying with the request to list them.

Second, by having a child list ways to avoid the task or activity, the context surrounding the resistant behavior is changed. Changing the context also changes the meaning of the behavior and, consequently, the purpose for engaging in it. Remember from Chapter 2 that all behavior is purposeful and engaged in to achieve a specific outcome. For example, a child may refuse to follow a parent's direction to come in the house because he believes his resistance will impress his peers. The resistant behavior is purposeful since it is engaged in to achieve the outcome of impressing peers. Achieving the desired outcome is dependent upon the context of resistance being unacceptable to the parent. However, when a parent requests that the child list all the ways of avoiding the request, the context surrounding resistant behavior is changed—it no longer serves the purpose of impressing peers.

After listing all possible avoidance behaviors, the parent and child list all possible approach behaviors, called *driving forces*. Driving forces refer to behaviors a child can engage in to approach rather than avoid a task or activity. Children are more likely to list approach behaviors after first listing avoidance behaviors because the latter are more congruent with a child's resistant frame of reference.

The final step requires that the parent and child plan ways to reduce the number and impact of the avoidance behaviors while increasing the number and impact of the approach behaviors. For example, a child may identify reading a comic book as an avoidance behavior rather than cleaning his room. An appropriate approach behavior may be allowing the child to read a comic book after cleaning his room. This suggestion also makes use of the Premack principle, described in Chapter 3, in which access to a desired behavior or activity is contingent upon the performance of a less desirable behavior or activity.

Use rehearsal to practice new behaviors

Children frequently are reluctant to try new behaviors, either because they feel unable to perform them or are unsure of the outcome. Resistance due to these two common concerns can be reduced by arranging for a child to practice the desired behaviors before actually using them in real life. Practice provides a child with confidence that she can, in fact, adequately perform the behaviors while also giving her feedback about the possible reactions she will receive from others. The techniques of instruction, modeling, rehearsal, role-playing and feedback described previously can be used here.

I once worked with a 10-year-old girl who was deadly afraid to order her own meal when she was at a restaurant with her parents. This problem had been ongoing since she was old enough to talk sufficiently well for others to understand her. Any attempts by her parents to get her to give a waiter or waitress her order were met with severe resistance—she would either cry or run to the car. Both the girl and her parents reported that she was afraid of messing up the order and the subsequent reactions of the waitress or waiter and the other patrons who, she believed, would laugh at her. A simple and straightforward method for reducing her resistance to placing her own order was to have her rehearse these behaviors under various situations. I set up a table with dishes, silverware and glasses. We then role-played ordering and observing the reactions of others.

Providing a child with repeated practice increases his confidence level and allows him to anticipate and prepare for any negative reactions he may receive from others. Initially set up role-play scenarios that guarantee a positive outcome. One of the key points I have made throughout this book is to set up children for success—start small and reinforce as soon as possible. After a child becomes proficient at performing certain behaviors during a role play that guarantee a positive outcome, the scenarios can gradually be modified to include more real-life responses from others. We want to teach children that no matter how socially appropriate their behavior is, they will not always get a positive response from others. But by slowly interjecting more real-life responses from others, you are building up a child's ability to handle negative reactions.

Resistance Due to Environmental Factors

We are all familiar with the term *environment*. It refers to the conglomerate of circumstances and events, involving both animate and inanimate objects, in which we interact on an instance-to-instance basis. And most of us would agree that it exerts a powerful influence on our behavior. We rely on environmental cues to help us select and perform appropriate behaviors for a given situation. Remember the example of the differences in behavior required when attending church versus a baseball game I provided in Chapter 1 when discussing the limitations of punishment. There are certain behaviors we display in church that we would not display at a baseball game, and vice versa. These two environments serve as cues to help us select appropriate behaviors. However, the environment has no personal agenda—

it is not a sentient being. Therefore, it can exert either a positive or a negative influence on our behavior. And sometimes the negative influence it can exert results in children exhibiting resistant behaviors.

There are a variety of environmental factors that can interfere with the achievement of a successful outcome. These factors, however, can be classified under two general, and somewhat similar, categories: environmental variables incompatible with change and environmental variables maintaining problem behavior. The techniques used to manage resistance due to these variables are based on the principles described in the first four chapters of this book.

Environmental Variables Incompatible with Change

When aspects of the environment are at odds with a desired behavior, resistance often occurs. In these instances, the environment may be failing to provide sufficient cues to activate appropriate behavior. In a little league baseball game, it is customary for the next batter to wait in an "on deck" circle where he can warm up by stretching or practice his timing by swinging along with the pitches thrown to the batter at the plate. However, if it has rained and the lines designating the "on deck" circle have been washed out, some little leaguers may forget to engage in this behavior.

In other instances, certain aspects of the environment may be competing with a child displaying an appropriate behavior. Many college students may find it hard to study if the norms of their sorority sisters are "to party." These norms compete with or distract the student from completing the desired responses of studying. Other competing stimuli for studying may include such activities as sports, band and work.

A final environmental variable incompatible with change may simply be the negative habits children have developed. Students may find it difficult to study because good study habits have never been incorporated into their daily routine. Simply having a student continue the same pattern with the addition of inserting a time and a place for studying is not likely to work because the new behavior does not fit with or is not supported by the old pattern.

There are a variety of techniques that can be used for each of these three situations where the environment is incompatible with change.

Arrange cues that make the desired behavior more likely to occur

Cues involve anything that prompts the occasion for a desired behavior to occur. We are confronted with a variety of cues every day—traffic lights and a ringing phone are two examples. As we approach a traffic light and the color turns from yellow to red, that cue prompts us to stop. When we hear a phone ring, the ring is a cue to pick up the phone. It is tempting, although inaccurate, to say that these antecedent cues *control* our behavior. Instead, it is the *consequences*—reinforcement or punishment—that actually control our behavior.

Let's examine this assertion by applying it to a traffic light turning from yellow to red and the ring of a phone. In the first situation, we stop when the light turns red because of the perceived consequences of not doing so. If we fail to stop, we could get a traffic ticket, get into an accident with another car, or worse, injure or kill someone. The threat of these negative consequences prevents us from running a red light—most of the time. There are some occasions when the consequences of running a red light are not that great. In these instances, a red traffic light has no effect on our behavior. I can remember driving up to a red traffic light late at night. It was one of those pressure-activated lights. Because traffic is usually so light coming in one direction, the light will only turn green when the weight of a car activates the traffic light to change. However, if there are not a lot of cars waiting behind this type of traffic light, it sometimes won't turn green. This was the case as I stopped at a red light around midnight. I waited for about five minutes. The light wouldn't change. During these five minutes, not one car passed going in the opposite direction. Therefore, I ran the light. The point is that when the perceived consequences (in this case negative) are too weak, the red light was insufficient to *control* my behavior.

The same principle is in effect when we answer a telephone. The ring only serves as a cue there will be a positive consequence if we answer the phone—someone will be on the other end. However, if every time we answered the phone when it rang, no one was on the other end, we quickly would stop answering the phone. It was not the ring that *controlled* our behavior but the perceived positive consequences of someone being on the other end.

You see, the red light or the ring of a phone only serves as a cue to access a behavior we believe will either lead to a positive consequence or avoid a negative one. As described in Chapter 4, our unconscious activates our beliefs which include evaluating possible outcomes for performing different behaviors before we select a behavioral response. Because we have gone through this process for many years, we do not have to allocate any conscious awareness to it. In some instances we have been so well conditioned that we perform certain behaviors after being exposed to a stimulus even when the consequences are absent. We have been strongly conditioned to stop when a railroad crossing gate is down and its lights are flashing. People are extremely hesitant to go around the gates, even when a train is not approaching in either direction. In essence, we behave as if the consequence were present when, in fact, it is not.

However, in some situations, the stimulus is not strong enough to set the occasion for a behavior to occur. A child may not pick up on the stern look she receives from a parent, when house guests are present, to stop whining. In other cases, a child may require additional learning to make the connection between a stimulus and the appropriate response. It is common for a toddler who just learned to say "Daddy" in the presence of her father to say "Daddy" in the presence of a variety of other men—the mailman, a clerk in a store or a neighbor. Although this general stimulus phenomenon has been the brunt of many jokes, it is quite common and a child usually learns to make the distinction between her father and other men with a little additional instruction from a parent.

In Chapter 4, I described several ways to arrange the environment to help promote children's self-control. The first technique was to provide extra cues for appropriate behavior. This technique also can be used in the context of managing resistance due to environmental factors. For example, you may place a Polaroid picture of a child brushing his teeth in a place where it would serve as a cue for engaging in this behavior.

Reduce competing sources of reinforcement

Children frequently resist changing their behavior because of the reinforcement—attention from others—they receive for continuing to engage in the inappropriate behavior. In Chapter 1, I described how punishment does not eliminate the attention a child receives for engaging in a behavior. I gave two examples: the class clown who makes animal noises and a child who places a string bean up her nose at the dinner table. Both children engaged in these behaviors because of the attention they received from their peers and siblings, respectively. It is a difficult task to reduce a child's level of resistance to engaging in inappropriate behavior when he is receiving a pay-off. Therefore, your efforts to manage resistance need to shift temporarily away from the child to the people in the environment providing attention to the inappropriate behavior.

There are several techniques for managing the attention others give a child for engaging in inappropriate behavior. One technique is simply to provide reinforcement to children who ignore the inappropriate behavior. The children in the class with the boy who made animal noises could receive a sticker for every five minutes that they did not look at or talk to him when he made animal noises. However, any children who looked at or talked to the boy when he made animal noises would lose one sticker. At the end of the class period, children could exchange their stickers for desirable free-time activities. A similar approach can be used with the siblings of the girl who stuck a bean up her nose at the dinner table. Her parents could instruct them that every time they ignored their sister when she stuck a bean up her nose, a poker chip would be placed on the corner of the table. Conversely, if they looked at or talked to her, one chip would be removed. If a total of 15 chips were accumulated on the table, the sister's siblings could earn a special dessert. In each of these examples, the child engaging in the misbehavior also could receive stickers or chips for not engaging in the inappropriate behavior during specified time intervals.

There are two other techniques that can be used to reduce competing sources of reinforcement for inappropriate behavior. Both techniques are *group-oriented* since the presentation of a reinforcer to the entire group is contingent upon the behavior of either one member of the group or the entire group.

The first technique is a *dependent group-oriented contingency*. In this arrangement, reinforcement is delivered to everyone in the group *only* if an identified child performs the desired behavior. The advantage of this technique is that it can motivate other children to "root for" the identified child to perform the desired behavior so that everyone can enjoy the reward. Consequently, this technique is often referred to as the "hero procedure" since one child, by performing the desired behavior, can become the "hero" by earning the entire group a reward. Here's how it could be employed with our two examples. The teacher of the boy who made animal noises could tell the class that for every five minutes that passed in which the boy did not make the noises, the entire class would earn a point, and if 20 points were earned by the end of the day, everyone would be able to participate in a popcorn party. Similarly, the girl who stuck the bean up her noise could be informed by her parents that for every two minutes that passed in which she did not perform the bean trick, she would earn a chip which would be placed on the corner of the table. If she accumulated 10 chips by the end of dinner, then all the children would get a special dessert of their choosing. In both examples, points or chips could be taken away for engaging in the misbehavior.

Although dependent group-oriented contingencies can be extremely effective, you must assess two factors that could severely limit its success. First, determine the level to which the other children will threaten, criticize or harass the child whose behavior is linked to their getting the reward. Some children derive pleasure from seeing the identified child fail. When this type of scapegoating occurs, you can simply tally the number of scapegoating-type comments of the other children. If this number exceeds the number of intervals in which the identified child refrained from engaging in the inappropriate behavior, then those children making excessive use of scapegoating are excluded from receiving the reward. Second, assess the extent to which the identified child finds it reinforcing to prevent others from getting a reward by purposely engaging in the inappropriate behavior. I have previously stressed that reinforcement is *individual.* Therefore, it is possible that the identified child finds it more reinforcing to prevent the group from receiving the reward than to receive the reward himself. In these situations, you can either find an appropriate reward that is more reinforcing to the identified child than the thrill of preventing others from receiving the reward or abandon the use of this technique until an appropriate reinforcer has been found.

The second technique is an *interdependent group-oriented contingency*. In this approach, the group can only earn the reward if all members perform the desired behavior. If successful, this approach will have the children working together to earn a reward in which they all share equally. Returning to our examples, the teacher could say that *everyone* must refrain from making animal noises in order for *anyone* to earn the popcorn party. Or the parents could require all their children to refrain from playing with their food at the dinner table in order for any of the children to earn a special dessert. As with the dependent group-oriented approach, you must watch out for individual children who derive pleasure from spoiling the reward for everyone by misbehaving. You can combat this problem by removing points from the children doing the scapegoating as described above, or you can individualize the behavioral requirements for certain children. Therefore, in the class with the boy who made animal noises, some children may also have to refrain from making such noises while others may have to refrain from teasing. At the dinner table, a sibling may derive pleasure from trying to get his sister to stick a bean up her nose by making funny faces. In this case, that sibling's behavior would be to refrain from making funny faces. As with any group-oriented approach, if scapegoating or sabotaging persists despite efforts to stop it, the technique should be abandoned in favor of the other approaches described in the previous chapters.

Change a child's pattern and routine

Children, like adults, develop patterns or routines specific to certain contexts or situations. Some children sit in the back of class in order to daydream or write notes. As long as they continue to sit in there, efforts at getting them to be attentive will be difficult. In essence, we pair certain behaviors with specific contexts or situations so that the context or situation serves as an antecedent cue to perform the behavior. Through this repeated pairing, the behavior is activated automatically with little conscious awareness of how it is prompted by the environment. Therefore, resistance often can be managed by changing a child's pattern or routine. This recommendation is based on the notion that behavior is meaningful in some but not all contexts. And when the context changes, the meaning of the behavior also changes. Consequently, it is no longer necessary to perform the behavior.

In his book *My Voice Will Go With You*, Sidney Rosen described a unique approach that Milton Erickson used to break the pattern and routine of a woman who sought his help in losing weight. The woman weighed 180 pounds, but wanted to weigh 130 pounds. In the past, when the woman would reach 130 pounds, she would rush to the kitchen to celebrate her success—promptly gaining back the 50 pounds. Dr. Erickson told her he could help, but that she would not like the solution. At this point in her life, she was so desperate to lose the weight permanently that she agreed to do anything. Dr. Erickson then told her to gain 20 pounds, and when she weighed an even 200 pounds she could start reducing. For every pound the woman gained she implored Dr. Erickson to let her start reducing. Dr. Erickson insisted that she gain an even 20 pounds if his intervention was to be effective. When the woman reached 200 pounds she was thrilled to finally begin reducing. And when she reached 130 pounds she was certain that she would never gain again.

Sidney Rosen provides some insightful commentary on this case. The woman's pattern and routine had been to reduce and gain. Dr. Erickson reversed that pattern and made her gain and reduce. Once the woman had broken the pattern, she could no longer go through the same sequence repeatedly, as she had done all her life. She apparently had learned to tolerate gaining weight only up to 180 pounds. Many people with weight problems seem to have a tolerance level corresponding to a certain weight, at which point they urgently feel the need to reduce. Dr. Erickson succeeded in making the woman's tolerance level intolerable because he made her go beyond it.

When Inappropriate Behavior is Maintained by the Environment

I previously described a child who made animal noises because of the attention he received from peers and adults even though such attention was primarily negative. This begs the question, How can any child *like* receiving a verbal reprimand from a teacher or vicious comments from peers? For some children, the consequences of their behavior—the negative attention from others—only serve to reinforce their belief that they can control others. And the perception of being able to *control* others represents a powerful reinforcer to many individuals.

In other situations, a child may resist changing his behavior because of the negative comments he believes his peers will make. In this situation, the consequences would be considered punishing rather than reinforcing. And since most people work to avoid punishment, a child would not want to place himself in a position to be teased for changing a behavior. In Chapter 2, under the "So what" test, I described how many therapists try to teach their clients to be assertive. But teaching young people to be assertive will probably result in their peers ridiculing them for engaging in behavior outside of the norm. This ridicule is a form of punishment which, by definition, has the effect of reducing or eliminating the behavior. Consequently, you may see children appearing to be resistant to try new behaviors because they are afraid their peers will make fun of them. How many times have parents told children who are being teased by peers in school to simply tell the teacher. Children typically respond to this suggestion like this: "Oh right, Mom. That'll be a big help. Then I'll get teased even more for tattling on them."

There are several recommendations you can use when environmental consequences are either reinforcing inappropriate behavior or punishing appropriate behavior. Each of these recommendations shares common elements with much of the information presented in the previous chapters. Therefore, I will present these recommendations briefly and refer the reader back to sections of the book where they were discussed.

Find effective reinforcers for the new behavior

Using the principles of reinforcement discussed at the beginning of Chapter 3, it should make sense that compliance is enhanced when the desired behavior is followed by reinforcement. Reinforcement *always* works! If a behavior does not increase after administering something, then by definition that something was not a reinforcer. Remember from our discussion that the most difficult aspect of reinforcement is finding something that will be reinforcing to a child. Reinforcement is individual and what one child will find reinforcing another child may not. Of course, for the reinforcer to be effective, a child must only have access to it *after* performing the desired behavior.

To use reinforcement most effectively to manage resistance, start with changes that are likely to make a child feel better in a short time or are likely to result in dramatic or at least visible improvement. When children notice the benefits achieved from engaging in a behavior, they will be more likely to engage in subsequent behaviors that make greater demands on them and take longer to get a desired result. This recommendation follows the principle of *shaping* or *successive approximations* that was discussed in Chapter 2. Briefly, it is easier to get compliance when asking a child to engage in a small and easy-to-perform behavior. Then, with the use of effective and immediate reinforcement, a child will become less resistant to changing his behavior.

Find alternative sources of reinforcement

When peers or siblings either reinforce a child for engaging in inappropriate behavior or punish her for engaging in appropriate behavior, the focus of your efforts to reduce resistance need to shift from the child to her peers or siblings. And unless you shift your focus, the child will most likely be resistant to give up the inappropriate behavior. The shift I am referring to is getting a child's peers or siblings to ignore the inappropriate behavior and provide positive comments when he engages in the appropriate behavior. This approach is known in the literature as promoting *entrapment*. If you looked up the word entrapment in the dictionary, you would most likely find the following definition: "to catch in a trap; to lure into danger or difficulty." We think of entrapment as something undercover detectives or vice cops do to catch a criminal. However, in the present context, it refers to restructuring the existing reinforcement contingencies in peer interaction groups so that these new contingencies will reinforce the appropriate behavior to be performed. In essence, you are teaching peers or siblings positive responses to give the child when he exhibits the desired behavior and reinforcing the peer group for making these positive comments.

As an undergraduate student I had a practicum experience in a fourth-grade classroom for children with behavioral problems. One child was particularly withdrawn. To complicate matters, his peers would tease him mercilessly on the playground at recess. Consequently, his social withdrawal was negatively reinforced in that the more he withdrew, the fewer negative comments he would receive. A very simple two-step program was developed to increase his socialization at recess. First, the boy was taught (using modeling, rehearsal and role-playing) how to interact appropriately with peers during a game of four-square. The second step of the program shifted to the peer group. Specifically, a number of fourth-graders from several classes who played four-square at recess were recruited to participate in the program. They were told that an adult observer would make a tally mark next to their names every time one of them asked the boy to join in the game and subsequently made a positive statement to him. The number of tally marks each child received could then be used to purchase free time. This technique was highly effective in getting the target boy to become more socially active with his peers. However, the most common criticism I receive after telling this story is that the program was "artificial." I readily acknowledge this criticism as valid. However, I just as quickly point out that managing resistance requires initially making small changes in the desired direction. Once a desired pattern was established, more natural consequences could be initiated.

Teach adaptive means of attaining reinforcement

Recall that all behavior is purposeful—children engage in behavior to achieve some outcome. This assertion carries two implications for managing resistance. First, the outcome a child desires is most likely socially acceptable and appropriate. Second, if we can determine the desired outcome, then we can teach a child a replacement behavior—one that represents an appropriate way of achieving the same outcome.

It is common in a family of three or more children for two of the siblings to join forces to tease another. As most parents realize, these alliances are fragile at best and frequently switch. A common outcome of teasing is that it brings the other two siblings together in a common interest. As a result, the two children who formed the alliance may play harmoniously with each other for a period of time as a result of sharing the common experience of teasing their sibling. Their desired outcome—sharing a common experience—is an appropriate one desired by most adults. We all feel a social connectedness when we are introduced to individuals with whom we share some common experience—either from our past or current life situation. Therefore, by identifying the desired outcome, as described in Chapter 2, it is possible to teach a child an appropriate behavior to reach that outcome. Therefore, if two of your children are teasing a third, you may want the two to simply find another activity in which they share a common interest. In this way, their behavior can be changed while still having it reach the same desired outcome.

I cannot overstate the point that almost all child behavior, no matter how bizarre it may seem at first, can result in some appropriate outcome. In Chapter 5, I discussed the social implications of labels. I showed how society uses labels to create an alien niche for people who disturb the mainstream of society. We may view the behavior of such people as extremely aberrant. Yet when you examine the outcomes those behaviors served, they may be normal and desirable. When a child is engaging in resistant behavior, try to determine the desired outcome by using the techniques described in Chapter 2. This approach has two advantages. First, it requires you to engage in problem-solving in order to unearth the possible desired outcome. Second, you are less likely to personalize a child's resistance since you are actively involved in determining the potential outcome of the behavior. Any time you can avoid personalizing resistance, you are more likely to have access to a wider variety of options for dealing with the problem. On the other hand, when you personalize a child's behavior, you are more likely to respond in a typical manner that may not be effective. And this is the crux of the problem when resistance is due to adult factors.

Resistance Due to Adult Factors

In many respects we are a stubborn and inflexible species. When a solution is not working, most of us respond by trying it more frequently. We continue to respond to children in a similar fashion even when what we are doing is not working, for a couple of reasons. First, if we personalize a child's behavior, we are more likely to overreact emotionally and engage in resistance-engendering behavior. In this respect, the information presented on controlling emotions and behavior presented in Chapter 4 should be applied here. Whenever children "push our buttons" we tend to respond in ways we have in the past—it's an automatic, habitual reaction that is difficult to break. Second, responding to children's resistance differently than we have in the past is risky—both for a child and for us. We may be concerned about the potential outcome if we do something *really different* with children. After all, any risk is threatening because it upsets the stability of our daily routine. And stability is comforting, even when the habitual behavior does not result in a desired outcome.

This homeostasis results in what are called *linear interventions,* or *more of the same.* For example, if a teenager comes home after his curfew, his parents may ground him for a week. The problem is presumed to have been addressed by this punishment. But what if the boy stays out past his curfew again? The linear solution would be to ground him for two weeks. This is why I call these types of solutions *more of the same,* and they rarely work. Like any intervention, if they worked, you would be using them less often rather than more often. In essence we limit our options for responding to children's oppositional behavior. Consequently, ordinary difficulties become more severe because the initial problem was mishandled and remains unresolved. And here is where the crux of the matter lies. We need to abandon our preconceived notions about what we *should* do or say to a child and expand our perspective to consider alternative options.

Adopting New Patterns of Behavior

We generally have more knowledge of how to deal effectively with children than we realize. It is amazing what we could do if we recognized all our available options. Unfortunately, we often follow a very careful routine without seeing that we are restricting our behavior. We tend to place limits on so many things, and in turn are limited in our patterns of behavior. Every magician will tell you not to let children too near or they will see through the trick. This is not the case with adults. Adults have closed minds. We think we are watching everything—but we have a routine way of looking. Therefore, in order to effectively manage resistance, it is important to be comprehensive and unrestrictive in our behavior and not do what we have done in the past. This recommendation is difficult to follow because we learn parenting skills from several very predictable sources.

For the most part, we parent our children based on how we were parented. We either apply the same techniques or go to the opposite extreme because of our distaste for the methods used by our parents. I can remember my father not liking to spank me because his mother routinely spanked him. My grandparents were first-generation Americans who emigrated from Switzerland. My grandmother was particularly strict. My father once told me that when he was seven years old he worked as a caddie at a local golf course. He naturally had to give the money he earned to his mother as his contribution to the family finances. Once he lost his money on the way home from the golf course. His mother proceeded to cut a willow branch from the tree in their front yard and gave my father a "meaningful" spanking. Although my father loved and respected his mother very much, he went to the opposite extreme with me because of his experience with spanking as a child.

We also learn to parent from our interactions with friends who have children—again applying what we agree with and avoiding techniques we dislike. Parenting skills also can be acquired by watching television programs. Unfortunately, television's depiction of parents handling children's difficult behavior is not very instructive. The TV solution is simply to reason with children—as if they are amenable to larger doses of reason from their parents. Finally, parenting skills can be acquired through books presenting a variety of approaches.

My point is that the sources we draw upon to parent our children are very predictable. And our patterns of behavior in dealing with resistance are predictable and habitual. It has been my experience that both parents and teachers are on a perpetual quest for "the technique." We want techniques that are practical, easy to use, and produce quick results—as if we can produce change in children's resistant behavior as easily as getting the carburetor adjusted on our car. But in fact we already possess a variety of potential techniques for responding to children's resistant behavior. These techniques are based on the multitude of experiences we have had throughout our lives. These experiences may include how you dealt with being lost on a vacation, putting up with Uncle Elmer's pontifications at the Thanksgiving dinner table, dealing with a slow checker at a department store, or telling a friend she has an irritating habit without hurting her feelings. Unfortunately, the difficulty is in getting ourselves to perceive different options for responding.

When speaking to a group of people on the topic of resistance, I often illustrate the difficulty of perceiving different options by having every other person make a fist. Then on the count of three I tell the persons next to them to get that fist open as quickly as possible. Invariably, people try to force the other person's fist open. I then inquire how many people simply *asked* the persons to open their fist. After the laughter and sighs of mild embarrassment subside, I point out that *asking* is well within our repertoires, yet we often do not perceive this simple option.

Milton Erickson was asked to provide a psychiatric consultation concerning a catatonic schizophrenic who was not responding to conventional psychiatric interventions. Schizophrenia is a disorder characterized by a severe disruption of thought processes that results in a sharp break with reality and a withdrawal from social interaction. Delusions and hallucinations are common. In catatonic schizophrenia, the individual suddenly loses all animation and remains motionless for hours or even days. Dr. Erickson walked into the room where the patient was sitting in a catatonic state. Several psychiatrists were standing over the patient discussing various conventional treatment approaches such as the use of psychotropic medication, electroconvulsive shock therapy and psychoanalysis. These psychiatrists asked Dr. Erickson for his recommendation. Without hesitation, Dr. Erickson walked up to the patient and stomped on his feet several times. The patient came right out of his catatonic state. Now I am not suggesting that parents stomp on their resistant children's feet, but rather that many potentially effective ways of responding to children are available if we would only expand our perceptions to encompass other areas of our experiences. Foot-stomping was well within the skill repertoire of the other psychiatrists, but they were too narrowly focused on "psychiatric techniques" to access this approach. In contrast, Dr. Erickson was unrestricted and comprehensive.

Join a Child: Accept or Encourage Resistance

Too often, intentionally or unintentionally, we attempt to inculcate our children with a way of looking at and dealing with the world that has worked well for us and others but which may be clumsy and inappropriate with respect to a child's view of the world. We expect children to accept our authority. Trying to lecture or otherwise force a child to comply with our version of the world often results in resistance. If we are to deal effectively with resistance, we must learn to join a child in his frame of reference. No two people are alike, no two people understand the same sentence the same way, and in dealing with children we must not try to make them fit exactly into our concept of what they should be. We should try to discover what their concept of themselves happens to be.

I began this chapter with the story of Jerry, the young boy who came home in an oppositional frame of mind. His mother asked him to place his books in his room. Upon hearing this request, he promptly dropped them on the floor. This behavior was perfectly rational. Jerry was feeling oppositional. Therefore, in order to keep in this oppositional frame of mind, he naturally had to resist his mother's request to put his books away. His mother dealt with the situation using a very traditional method. Here is another approach that *uses* Jerry's oppositional frame of mind. After Jerry responded to his mother's request to pick up his books by saying "No, I won't, and you can't make me—nobody can make me," his mother could counter by saying, "You're right, I can't make you pick up those books. I can't even make you move those books one inch. And I know you *can't* move those books one foot ... you certainly can't move those books into your bedroom. *And* I know there's no way you can put those books on your desk!"

This response acknowledges Jerry's oppositional frame of reference and uses it to get him to comply with his mother's request. In order for Jerry to continue to be oppositional, he had to comply. By telling Jerry he can't move the books, he may move them to continue being resistant, in which case you have achieved the desired outcome. If he refuses to move the books, then he is no longer being oppositional since he is agreeing with you. Although in the latter case the books still remain on the floor, Jerry's oppositional frame of reference has been disrupted, which makes it easier to direct him toward the desired outcome. I described this approach earlier as being paradoxical because by encouraging or accepting resistance, you are putting a child in a position where his attempts to resist are defined as cooperative behavior. A child finds himself following your directives no matter what he does, because what he does is defined as cooperation. Once a child is cooperating—that is, once his resistant frame of reference has been broken—it is easier to divert him into the desired behavior.

Milton Erickson was an expert at using this technique. In his book *Uncommon Therapy*, Jay Haley describes Dr. Erickson's skill at joining a 10-year-old boy's resistance. This boy had been brought, against his will, to see Dr. Erickson because he wet his bed every night. The boy's parents brought him yelling into Dr. Erickson's office. When the boy paused to catch his breath, Dr. Erickson told him to go ahead and yell again. After the boy yelled and paused to take a breath, Dr. Erickson yelled. The boy turned to look at Dr. Erickson and was told it was now his turn to yell. The boy and Dr. Erickson took turns yelling. After several turns, Dr. Erickson told him they could continue taking turns yelling but that would get awfully tiresome. Dr. Erickson then told the boy he would rather take his turn sitting down in his chair, which he did. He pointed to a vacant chair and the boy took his turn sitting in the other chair.

In this example, Dr. Erickson joined the boy's resistance by yelling himself. By so doing, he broke the boy's resistance by establishing the expectation that they were taking turns yelling. Once the boy's resistant frame of reference was changed, Dr. Erickson led the boy in another direction by changing the game to taking turns sitting down. He had established rapport, the opposite of resistance, and was able to address the problem of the boy's bedwetting. Dr. Erickson has described this approach as being analogous to trying to change the course of a river. If you oppose the river by trying to block it, the river will merely go over and around. But if you accept the force of the river and divert it in a new direction, the force of the river will cut a new channel.

Provide a Worse Alternative

One of the common themes I have stressed throughout this book is the influence context has on behavior. Context is what gives behavior meaning. Lifeguards have more meaning in the context of a swimming pool than on a ski slope. Cutting open a person's skin with a knife has a positive meaning in the context of a surgeon performing a life-saving operation and a negative meaning for a mugger attempting to steal someone's wallet. Many of the recommendations and stories I have presented throughout this book have focused on changing the context surrounding a behavior: the couple required to argue in the garage and the girl and her screaming chair are two examples. There are two other ways to change the context of a behavior, thereby changing the meaning and reducing resistance: providing a worse alternative and stressing the positive aspects of the behavior.

A way to provide a worse alternative is to have a child engage in what is called *negative practice*. In this technique, a child is required to repeatedly engage in the inappropriate behavior as a way to change its context and meaning. Many parents and teachers frequently use this technique. One teacher dealt with a child who spit on a peer by having the offending child repeatedly spit into a can for 30 minutes. Other teachers deal with children who throw wadded-up paper across the room into a trash can by having them repeatedly throw the paper into the can for a specified period of time. One of my graduate students told me how he used this technique as a substitute teacher in a class for children with emotional and behavioral problems. After assigning the students a page of math problems to complete, one boy was instead writing the name of his school followed by the word "sucks" all over his paper. The substitute teacher went up to the boy and told him that he had a very distinctive handwriting, but that he was sure he could be even more creative. He suggested trying to write the two words in a variety of print styles and colors. The boy quickly lost interest in the task and began to do his math assignment.

The substitute teacher had suggested a worse alternative and by so doing, changed the context and meaning the behavior had for the boy. The substitute teacher employed a paradoxical technique because by asking the boy to do what he was already doing, the boy was caught in the position described previously where oppositional behavior is defined as cooperation. If the boy resisted the teacher's request to write on his assignment, then the desired goal would be achieved. And if the boy did as the teacher requested, he was no longer being resistant because he was complying with the direction. At the same time, the context and meaning were changed and, consequently, the desire to engage in the behavior vanished.

Milton Erickson used this approach with his daughter who came home from grade school one day and said, "Daddy, all the girls in school bite their nails and I want to be in style too." He replied, "You certainly ought to be in style and you have a lot of catching up to do. Now the best way to catch up is to bite your nails for 15 minutes three times a day, every day." His daughter began enthusiastically at first. Then she began quitting early and one day she said, "Daddy, I'm going to start a new style at school—long nails." By joining his daughter in her desire to be in style, Dr. Erickson proceeded to make the "stylish behavior" into an ordeal. It became more of a bother to keep the behavior than to give it up.

Stress the Positive Aspect of a Behavior

Stressing the positive aspect of a behavior comes out of the belief that every behavior is appropriate given some context or frame of reference. The name for changing the context and, consequently, the meaning of a behavior is called *reframing*. Reframing is an approach that modifies a person's perceptions or views of a behavior. Parents use reframing whenever they ask children to see an issue from a different perspective. Reframing can focus on the meaning of a behavior or the context wherein behavior occurs.

Meaning reframe

When you reframe meaning, you are challenging the meaning that a child has assigned to a given problem behavior. Usually the longer a child attaches a particular meaning to a behavior, the more necessary the behavior itself becomes in maintaining consistency and predictability. In other words, the longer a particular meaning is attached to a behavior, the more a child is likely to see things in only one way or from one perspective. Reframing helps children by providing alternative ways to view a problem behavior without directly challenging the behavior itself and by loosening a child's frame of reference.

Once the meaning of a behavior changes, the person's response to the situation usually also changes, provided the reframe is valid and acceptable to the person. The essence of a meaning reframe is to give a situation or a behavior a new label or a new name that has a different meaning. This new meaning always has a different connotation, and usually it is a positive one. A child's "stubbornness" might be reframed as "independence," or "greediness" might be reframed as "ambitious." Here is an example of context reframing described by Richard Bandler and John Grinder in their book *Reframing.*

A therapist was working with a woman who had a compulsive behavior—she was a clean-freak. She was a person who dusted plant leaves and venetian blinds. Her husband and three kids could handle almost all her efforts to keep the house clean except for her attempts to care for the carpet. She spent a lot of her time trying to get people not to walk on it, because they left footprints—not mud and dirt—in the pile of the rug. When this woman looked down at the carpet and saw a footprint, she experienced an intense negative reaction in her stomach, as if someone rung it out like a washcloth. She would rush off to get the vacuum cleaner and vacuum the carpet immediately. She vacuumed the carpet several times a day and spent a lot of time trying to get people to come in the back door, nagging them if they didn't, or getting them to take their shoes off and walk delicately.

The family seemed to get along fine if they were not at home. If they went out to dinner or a movie, they had no problems. But at home, everybody referred to the mother as being a nag mainly because of her carpet behavior. After hearing this story, the therapist turned to the mother and said, "I want you to close your eyes and see your carpet, and see that there is not a single footprint on it anywhere. It's clean and fluffy—not a mark anywhere." The mother closed her eyes and began smiling contentedly. The therapist continued, "And realize fully that that means you are totally alone, and that the people you care for and love are nowhere around." The mother's expression shifted radically and she began to frown. The therapist ended by saying, "Now, put a few footprints there and look at those footprints and know that the people you care about in the world are nearby."

This example of a meaning reframe was effective because the new meaning was acceptable to the woman. Although she valued a clean carpet, she valued her husband and children even more. Therefore, when the meaning of having a clean carpet was reframed to mean her loved ones were gone, the desire to keep the carpet clean vanished. Here is another example of a meaning reframe I used with a 10-year-old boy.

I used a meaning reframe with Benjamin, a boy I had been seeing in my private practice. At one of our sessions, Benjamin began really tearing into his mother about always having to go on errands with her. I immediately motioned for his mother to leave the room for a few minutes. I then let Benjamin relate every rotten aspect of going on errands with his mother. Here is an excerpt of what he said: "This isn't fair. I always have to go on errands with my mom. I just know she's trying to make me suffer because she knows how much I hate going with her. She'll even drop off my little sister at my aunt's house to play with our cousins. Now that really sucks. She gets to stay and play with our cousins while I'm forced to go with my mom to all these stupid stores. That really tells me my mom likes my sister better than me. She never lets me stay at my aunt's house to play—I always have to go with her."

After Benjamin tired of repeating these same charges against his mother, I turned to him and said, "Let me ask you a couple questions, Benjamin. Your sister is three years younger than you. How much fun is it when she goes on an errand with you and your mom?"

"It really sucks," Benjamin replied. "She's really a pain—nagging all the time. It's terrible. And then my mom gets angry at her and starts yelling."

"Does that happen when just you and your mom go to the store?" I asked.

"Well, no. We usually talk about something."

"I see. You know, Benjamin, you're getting to be a pretty big boy. In fact, you'll be a teenager before you know it. It seems to me that your mother wants you to go on errands with her because she really enjoys your company. You're like the man of the family when you're running errands with your mom. She probably depends on you. And she obviously likes talking to you more than to your sister with whom she fights. That's probably why she drops your sister off at your cousin's house, so that she can spend some good quality time alone with you. That must mean she really values your friendship and likes to treat you as an equal when you are running errands with her."

Benjamin sat there with a frozen look. Then his facial expression changed dramatically and a little smile began to crease the corners of his mouth. At this point, I knew he had accepted the meaning reframe. The previous meaning Benjamin attached to going on errands was that his mother was trying to punish him. The new meaning was that his mother valued his company and treated him, on these occasions, like an equal. Benjamin bought into this new meaning because it was congruent with what most boys want from their mothers—to believe they are needed and thought of as an equal.

Context reframe

Besides reframing the meaning of a behavior, you can also reframe the context in which a problem behavior occurs. Reframing the context helps a child explore and decide *when, where,* and *with whom* a given problem behavior is useful or appropriate. In essence, context reframing helps children answer the question, "In what place in your life is a particular behavior useful and appropriate?" Context reframing is based on the assumption that every behavior is useful in some but not all contexts or situations. Thus, when a child says, "I won't clean my room," a context reframe would be "In what situations, or with what people, is it useful or even helpful to be oppositional?" Two situations immediately come to mind: if a child is being solicited by another child to experiment with drugs or if an adult is trying to convince a child to get into his car, oppositional behavior is quite desirable.

It is easy to confuse context and meaning reframing. In meaning reframing we are directly trying to change the meaning of a behavior. In context reframing we are trying to find another context where the inappropriate behavior becomes appropriate. I believe the confusion arises because when you change the context, you automatically change the meaning of a behavior. In fact that's the goal when using a context reframe: by changing the context to point out appropriate situations where the inappropriate behavior is appropriate, the meaning attached to the behavior in the problem situation changes and, consequently, the desire to engage in the behavior vanishes. Therefore, both meaning and context reframing try to change the meaning of a behavior. In the former the meaning is directly challenged, and in the latter the context is changed to elicit a change in meaning. Here is an example of a context reframe used by the noted family therapist Virginia Satir, as described by Bandler and Grinder in their book *Reframing*.

The father in the family Virginia Satir was treating was a banker—professionally stuffy, yet very well intentioned. He was a good provider for his family and was concerned enough to seek therapy. His wife was an "extreme placater" in Satir's terminology. A placater is a person who will agree with anything and apologize for everything. When you say, "What a lovely sunset," the placater says, "Yes, I'm sorry." The daughter was an interesting combination of the parents. She thought her father was the bad person and her mother was the good person, so she always sided with her mother. However, she acted like her father. The father's chief complaint was that his wife hadn't done a very good job raising their daughter because the daughter was so stubborn. At one point when he made this complaint, Satir looked at the father and said, "You're a man who has gotten ahead in your life. Is this true?"

"Yes," replied the father.

"Was all that you have just given to you? Did your father own the bank and just say, 'Here, you're president of the bank'?"

"No, no. I worked my way up."

"So you have some tenacity, don't you?"

"Yes," said the father.

Satir then got to the crux of the context reframe. "Well, there is a part of you that has allowed you to be able to get where you are, and to be a good banker. And sometimes you have to refuse people things that you would like to be able to give them because you know if you did, something bad would happen later on."

"Yes."

"Well, there's a part of you that's been stubborn enough to really protect yourself in very important ways," Satir noted.

"Well, yes. But, you know, you can't let this kind of thing get out of control," the father protested.

Ignoring the father's last statement, Satir went on. "Now, I want you to turn and look at your daughter, and to realize beyond a doubt that you've taught her how to be stubborn and how to stand up for herself, and that that is something priceless. This gift that you've given to her is something that can't be bought, and it's something that may save her life. Imagine how valuable that will be when your daughter goes out on a date with a man who has bad intentions."

In this example, Virginia Satir changed the context of being stubborn which was initially viewed by the father as a bad trait in the context of the family. However, it becomes good in the context of banking and in the context of a bad date. Satir changed the context that the father used to evaluate his daughter's behavior. Her behavior of being stubborn with him no longer will be seen as her fighting with him. Instead, it most likely will be viewed as a personal achievement—he taught her to protect herself from men with bad intentions.

The underlying realization is that with children, every experience and every behavior can be appropriate, given the right context or frame of reference. In much of the behavior children exhibit that we tend to label as resistant, the context turns out to be internal and based on past experiences. When a father says to his son, "You really did a great job mowing the lawn," and the son responds with "Fine, but I don't really care and I didn't do that good a job, so I wish you wouldn't lie to me," that's a pretty good indication that the boy is operating out of a unique internal frame of reference. Upon further exploration, it may become apparent that from past experience, the boy takes a compliment to mean that he'll just have to do more work in the future. A lot of our ability to deal with resistance rests on appreciating that what may seem bizarre and inappropriate could simply be a statement about the failure to appreciate the context from which that behavior proceeds.

Manipulate Children

I realize that the word *manipulate* probably has negative connotations for most people. In fact, one of the situations that adults find particularly troublesome is when children try to manipulate them. The classic example is when a child asks her father if she can go to a party, receives the answer "no," and then asks her mother the same thing. Parents feel set up and often get angry at each other and the child. We dislike manipulation just as much when it originates from other adults. Scam games and rip-off contests that are commonly exposed on TV programs like *60 Minutes* really get us angry. However, the use of manipulation is not as devious as it may first appear. The very process of rearing children is manipulative. We manipulate the very techniques we use to teach children. For example, we may try to scare a child into not smoking by telling him horror stories about people who got cancer. Or we may let a child smoke a cigarette in front of us while inhaling deeply. In fact, every interaction with others can be considered a manipulation since the goal is usually to elicit a response. Therefore, we might as well manipulate effectively, relevantly and constructively. By manipulating appropriately we can reduce resistant behavior.

One of the easiest ways to manipulate children is through the use of surprise or shock. This technique helps break up rigid mental sets that we all possess. The unexpected always helps in dealing with resistant children— avoid doing what is expected. As a counselor at a psychiatric hospital for adolescents, I was working with a particularly oppositional boy named Allen. He hated to talk to his mother on the phone. When his mother called, he would become extremely resistant—throwing a tantrum that often escalated to the point of having to place him in a time-out room. Of course, being placed in the time-out room was just what Allen wanted because he could avoid talking to his mother. As part of his treatment plan, he had to talk to his mother when she called during free time so that they could begin discussing some of the issues that resulted in his hospitalization. If he refused to talk to her, he was placed in a time-out area and lost all his daily points.

One day during free time when the phone rang and I told Allen that the call was for him, he immediately became resistant and said, "No way, I'm not going to talk to her," as he started walking to the time-out area. I put the phone to my ear and loudly said, "Yes, Mr. Simmons, Allen is right here." Mr. Simmons was Allen's school principal. Allen looked at me with a terrified expression on his face—after all, it is not everyday that a child gets a call from his principal. Allen slowly approached the phone and tentatively said "Hello." Well, Mr. Simmons was not on the other end—his mother was. Allen was so surprised and relieved not to have to talk to his principal that he said, "Oh Mom, am I ever glad it's you on the phone!" It's when you do the unexpected that you cause a lot of rearrangement in a child's thinking.

A second way to manipulate children is to encourage an appropriate response by initially frustrating it. In this approach you direct a child to behave in a certain way, and as she begins to do so, cut off the response and shift to another area. When you return to that directive, the child will be more responsive because she has developed a readiness to respond but was then frustrated.

I was working with a family consisting of a mother, her three children (two boys and a girl) and a stepfather. One of the complaints the mother had was that her youngest child, the daughter, never participated in family discussions. The other family members agreed that she hardly ever spoke at the dinner table or on family outings. I observed that the family spent a lot of time complaining about how the young girl would not voice her opinion while simultaneously talking for her. And the more the family tried to encourage her to talk, the less she responded. From spending some time alone with the girl, I found out that one of her favorite hobbies was collecting stuffed animals—dogs in particular. And she could talk about dogs for hours. This topic really excited her. During one of the family sessions, the issue of going on a vacation was raised. The two boys were in favor, the girl was silent and the parents were hesitant, primarily because they didn't know who could watch their dog for a week. I saw an opening in this conversation to get the daughter involved. Therefore, I started talking about the needs of dogs and purposely made several glaring factual errors in the process. Out of the corner of my eye, I could see that the daughter was becoming upset with my lack of knowledge about dogs and their needs. Consequently, she tentatively opened her mouth and, in a very soft voice, began stating how much exercise a dog should get. But before she got more than two words out, I told her we were having a serious conversation about taking care of the dog and could she just wait her turn. I then proceeded to provide more incorrect information. This process was repeated two more times—each with the same result: I would make errors, the girl would begin to correct me, and I would frustrate her response by continuing to talk. However, on the fourth occasion, the girl stood up and in a loud voice that no one in her family had heard before, she said, "I want you all to shut up and listen to me. This is what we need to do...." By preventing her from talking, it was possible to increase her desire to talk.

Conclusion

There is a simple axiom you should follow: if what you're doing isn't working, try something else—*anything else*. If we think of intervening as the introduction of variety and richness into children's lives, then our goal is to become creative and unrestrictive in our interactions with them.

In a wonderful article entitled "Insanity in the Classroom," Ann Hassenpflug describes her approach for managing her disruptive students. She demonstrates an amazing ability to be flexible and creative:

> On that day when all the classroom management systems I had diligently absorbed in years of inservices completely collapsed, I tried insanity. As I approached the classroom, students were not doing what they were supposed to be doing, and the noise level reached an ear-piercing volume. I refused to start screaming or shouting commands and threats. I simply walked into the room, looked down at the floor as if addressing a small dog, and said, "Toto, I don't think we're in Kansas anymore." As students began to turn toward me to see what was going on, I asked one of the worst offenders if he would like to take Toto out into the hall to play for a while. More heads turned and more mouths shut.
>
> The noise and activity were still out of control, though, so I called for the ward nurse and inquired about the name of the asylum for the inmates of the room. While waiting for her arrival, I talked to an imaginary elf (but a stuffed animal or small statue would have done as well) about the unbelievable behavior of these students. When I ran out of conversation, I started watching an imaginary wasp flying around the room. Almost everyone's eyes were on the teacher now.
>
> One particularly nasty individual, however, was still putting on a show of his own. I took my clipboard and stood by him and silently noted down everything he did as if I were an entomologist studying a new species.
>
> Shortly, this student was so fed up that he sat down without my ever having to say a word. I sauntered over to another offender and began speaking politely in a mixture of French and German. The student turned red and sat down.
>
> Class was ready to begin now, and the preliminary claiming procedures had taken only five minutes in comparison to the usual ten to fifteen of yelling.

Hassenpflug demonstrates a marvelous ability to be flexible, creative, and have a sense of humor about herself and her students. The ability to modify what we do by not restricting ourselves to set patterns of behaving allows us to tap and make available those resources we have in order to help deal with resistance. Hassenpflug also described one of her students who regularly stood by her desk and whined about not wanting to work and instead demanded to know why she could not be sent to the gym instead. One day, Hassenpflug jumped up, slammed down her book, and walked out of the room for two minutes. When she returned the student was doing her assignment. She also described how she diverted the class's attention from ongoing incidents of misbehavior by pointing out the window and describing all the imaginary beings, events and objects she saw out there.

I believe the lesson to be learned from Hassenpflug's accounts is that we must go beyond the perceived approaches of dealing with resistance and try something new. One thing that all children teach you is that there are different ways of looking at situations. Dealing with resistance should not be a massive job. We usually know what to do—but don't always know that we know.

On a final note, I was in the middle of a family therapy session focusing on developing a behavioral contract when the mother stood up and said, "It sure would help the situation out if my husband didn't leave his clothes around the house all the time." Although I was taken quite by surprise at this unexpected digression, I asked the woman how long her husband had left his clothes around the house. She replied that he had been doing it for the entire 10 years of their marriage. I then asked her what she did when her husband left his clothes around the house. She responded that she yelled at him. I looked at her squarely in the eyes and said, "Congratulations, you're very persistent. You really gave yelling a chance to work—10 years is a long time to try one thing. Now are you ready to try something different?"

Epilogue

Throughout this book I have tried to provide information and techniques for proactively managing children's difficult behavior. So often we view discipline in terms of punishment that is administered after children misbehave. This approach is reactive rather than proactive. And any reactive approach gives children an incredible amount of power—they can, in essence, "push our buttons" which is very reinforcing to them. But when we assume a proactive stance—one in which we anticipate situations where inappropriate behavior may occur and rearrange our behavior and the environment accordingly—children are unable to obtain the satisfaction from controlling our behavior. In addition, children begin to develop self-control since they are placed in a position to make choices on how to behave and evaluate the potential positive and negative consequences of those choices.

There are also several themes that I purposely repeated throughout this book. First, I tried to stress the importance of targeting appropriate behaviors on which to focus. Appropriate behaviors are those that can be operationally defined so that both parents and children know exactly what is expected of each other. The behaviors should be ones that increase, rather than decrease, a child's repertoire. Focusing solely on decreasing behavior results in a punishment mentality which has numerous drawbacks. However, I also realize that there are times when parents must punish their child. But remember, the desired effect of punishment is to decrease an inappropriate behavior. Therefore, if you are going to decrease an inappropriate behavior through punishment, it is important to identify a positive behavior to reinforce that can take its place. The principle of targeting appropriate behaviors applies to various interventions including externally administered techniques such as a token economy or behavioral contract; self-management techniques such as self-monitoring, self-evaluation and self-reinforcement; and strategies for dealing with resistance.

A second point I have reiterated is that people engage in behaviors to achieve some outcome. The behaviors are intentional and purposeful. That is not to say that children always know why they are engaging in a behavior. So asking children *why* they behaved in a certain way is counterproductive. You already know why: because they wanted to achieve some outcome. Your task is to determine what outcome a child was trying to achieve through the inappropriate behavior displayed. And although this is not an easy task, it does help you maintain a problem-solving focus rather than taking the inappropriate behavior personally. Any time you take children's behavior personally, you give them an incredible amount of power and control over you.

One way to avoid taking things personally is to apply the techniques described in the second half of Chapter 4. Specifically, it is important simply to accept that a child has directed some type of unwanted behavior toward you. You don't have to approve of the behavior, but by accepting that a reality occurred, you are less likely to engage in demandingness. Remember that demandingness is characterized by the use of *should* or *shouldn't*. When we say to ourselves, "My child shouldn't have said 'shut up' to me," we are engaging in demandingness since, in essence, we are trying to change reality. The child should have said "shut up" because he did. By applying these techniques, you will increase your repertoire of ways to respond to children because you won't be hampered by overreacting emotionally to the situation.

A third theme stressed throughout this book is the role context plays in behavior. All behaviors—both those deemed appropriate and inappropriate—obtain their meaning from the context in which they are exhibited. When we change the context of a behavior we also change the meaning or significance that behavior has for a child and, consequently, the desire to engage in the behavior. I provided several examples of changing context, including the boy who swore in school, the husband and wife who were told to argue in the garage, and the girl who got her own "screaming chair." By focusing on context, we are less likely to view a child's behavior as the *source* of the problem.

There is a tendency to take a particular behavior and use it to label a child. Thus a child who exhibits aggressive behavior becomes known as an "aggressive child." Although this at first may appear to be an inconsequential semantic difference, it has a profound impact upon how we view children and respond to them. When we take a behavior and use it to label a child, we intentionally or perhaps unintentionally create mental disorders analogous to physical disorders. That is, we view the onus of the problem to reside within the child and if the problem is severe enough, it is the child, rather than his behavior, the environment, or our responses, that needs to be modified.

This tendency to label a child rather than addressing his behavior at face value is a byproduct of our mental health system which is based on a medical-disease model of deviance. This model is the one under which most physicians operate. In medical school, great emphasis is placed on a proper diagnosis. The diagnosis is everything because it leads to appropriate treatment. For example, if I see a physician about a stomach ache, the doctor will want to determine the cause of the problem. Determining the cause leads to an accurate diagnosis which, in turn, dictates the type of treatment I am to receive. If, upon being questioned, the physician ascertains that I was out late the previous night, ate too much pizza with anchovies and onions, and drank several dark beers, the diagnosis may be heart burn. This diagnosis leads to an appropriate treatment—taking an antacid. On the other hand, if I complain of a stomach ache specifically on my right side—one that doesn't hurt when I press my stomach in with my hand, but hurts terribly when I release my hand—the doctor may diagnose my condition as appendicitis. This diagnosis leads to an appropriate treatment: appendectomy.

Personally, I am very pleased that physicians operate out of this model. And there are some severely disabling biological conditions for which this model also works quite well. For example, phenylketonuria (PKU) is a genetic disorder in which an enzyme is missing for metabolizing phenylalanine (a substance found in many foods including some that are artificially sweetened). The accumulation of phenylalanine prevents the brain from developing normally and, consequently, results in mental retardation and secondary behavior problems such as hyperactivity and temper tantrums. The implication of accurately diagnosing PKU is straightforward: avoid feeding a child foods that contain phenylalanine.

But I believe it becomes problematic to apply this model of diagnosis leading to treatment for common behaviors that all children exhibit to some degree. For example, the "symptoms" of attention deficit disorders are displayed by all children at some time during their development. In Chapter 6, I illustrated this point using a "normal curve." It is not specific behaviors that separate "normal" from "deviant," but rather the frequency, duration and intensity of the behaviors and the context in which they are displayed. Therefore, it should come as no surprise that when we examine childhood "conditions" such as attention deficits or depression, the only treatment implication specific to these labels is medication. And while I believe medication plays a critical role in the treatment of these two conditions, it only represents one aspect of an overall treatment approach. When one examines the nonmedical treatment options available for these so-called disorders, there are none specific to any condition of childhood. In my opinion, these labels only serve to obscure the real issue: analyzing and targeting specific behaviors for intervention and applying one or more of the techniques described in this book. I have seen too many parents waste their money on "experts" who presume to have "the treatment" for a number of conditions—

as if a label has any more implications than what we already know: a child is exhibiting inappropriate behaviors and a robust intervention is required.

Another recurring theme throughout this book has been the concept of consistency. This little concept is incredibly powerful and serves a multitude of purposes—both positive and negative. On the positive side, it helps us accurately interpret new situations. You see, we obtain meaning from a new situation by matching it to past situations that we believe to be similar in some way to the new experience. Therefore, if someone had never eaten at Wendy's, but had previously eaten at McDonald's or Burger King, she would most likely know how to behave since all three share the common characteristic of being fast food restaurants. The concept of consistency is how children learn to extract meaning from books when learning how to read. Once words are recognized we automatically access past experiences to assign meaning to the written words.

The concept of consistency is an extremely powerful one that helps us maintain stability and predictability in our everyday interactions. Stability and predictability result in feelings of comfort, which enables us to avoid the anxiety that accompanies the unknown. However, there is a down side to the concept of consistency as well. We have a tendency to apply a specific interpretation to events that are not logically connected to each other. Therefore, even when something is not working for us or a certain way of behaving results in bad feelings, we nevertheless continue the same pattern. We usually view the emotional pain of behaving in a predictable but ineffective way as better than the emotional pain of changing what we are doing and entering the realm of the unknown. I think that whoever said the definition of insanity is doing the same thing in the same way but expecting different results had in mind the negative impact the concept of consistency has on human functioning. In addition, the concept of consistency can act as blinders that filter information to fit our preconceived notions of how things should be. I began Chapter 2 with a discussion of paradigms and in Chapter 4, I talked about an irrational thinking style called tunnel vision. Both of these concepts affect us by allowing us to only see what we want to. Consequently we have strongly held beliefs that serve as obstacles to the expansion of our own repertoire for managing children's difficult behavior.

One of the most powerful obstacles for adults is that we often think only in terms of targeting a child's behavior for intervention while ignoring our own behavior. In the second part of Chapter 4 and Chapter 8, the focus was largely on changing our behavior. If we are able to apply to ourselves the principles of rational emotive therapy discussed in Chapter 4, we are less likely to get overly upset and, consequently, be in a better position to select ways to respond to children that achieve our goal. The important points of RET are not to take things personally, to accept that a reality occurred, to interpret the situation using a factual and literal approach, and to select an appropriate emotion and behavior for that interpretation. Once you do this, it will become quite easy to alter your behavior in the ways I described in Chapter 8 for dealing with resistance. The essence of managing children's resistance is to alter *our* patterns of responding verbally and nonverbally to children. A general rule is never to fight with children. Don't try to convince them to see your point of view—that will only lead to more resistance. I'm not suggesting that you give in to children or behave the way they do. Instead, try to figure out where the child is coming from, and use this frame of reference to affect a small change in the child's behavior.

I believe there is no secret to managing children's difficult behavior. And it is not an easy task. If it was easy, certain behaviors children exhibit wouldn't be considered *difficult*. A book about managing children's easy behavior probably wouldn't be necessary, although the title might be catchy enough to get some people to buy it. It takes hard work, perseverance, a thick skin and resilience to manage children's difficult behavior. On the other hand, managing the techniques is straightforward and can be applied by most people. I also believe there is no such thing as a true "expert" at managing children's behavior. We all have certain techniques that have worked for us. And we should continue using what works. However, if we continue to use a technique even when it doesn't result in a desired outcome, then we are stuck and probably at the mercy of the negative aspects of the concept of consistency.

Children do not learn the troublesome behaviors that they exhibit overnight. Therefore, don't expect these behaviors to change overnight. Changing children's difficult behavior is not like taking a car in for repairs. You can't *fix* kids. However, you can apply the basic principles of management discussed in this book. Yet, all the techniques I have provided here won't work if you don't change your mindset and agree to try new things. No matter what you choose to try with children, don't have a closed mind. Don't let the negative effects of the concept of consistency control your life—you do have a choice to view things differently. So I would like to end with a tale containing a problem. If you can solve it, you will be on your way to freeing yourself from set patterns of thinking and behaving.

There is an old story of a father who leaves his earthly belongings, consisting of 17 camels, to his three sons with the instruction that the eldest son is to receive one-half, the second one-third and the youngest one-ninth. No matter how they try to divide the camels, they find it impossible—see if you can divide 17 into these fractions. Eventually a mullah comes along on his camel, and they ask him for his help. "There is nothing to it," he says. "Here, I add my camel to yours, which makes 18. Now you, the eldest, receive one-half, which is nine. You, the middle son, are entitled to one-third, which is six. And you, the youngest, get one-ninth, that is, two camels. This leaves one camel, namely, my own." And having said this, he mounts it and rides off.

References

Chapter 1

Azrin, N.H. and Holz, W.C. (1966). Punishment. In W.K. Honig (ed.), *Operant behavior: Areas of research and application.* New York: Appleton-Century Crofts.

Howell, K.W., Fox, S.L. and Horehead, M.K. (1993). *Curriculum-based evaluation: Teaching and decision making*, 2nd Ed. Pacific Grove, CA: Brooks/Cole.

Maag, J.W. (1990). Social skills training in schools. *Special Services in the Schools* 6:1-19.

Nelson, C.M. and Rutherford, R.B., Jr. (1983). Timeout revisited: Guidelines for its use in special education. *Exceptional Education Quarterly* 3(4):56-67.

Newsom, C., Favell, J.E., and Rincover, A. (1983). The side effects of punishment. In S. Axelrod and J. Apsche (eds.), *The effects of punishment on human behavior.* New York: Academic Press.

Rutherford, R.B., Jr., and Neel, R.S. (1978). The role of punishment with behaviorally disordered children. In R.B. Rutherford, Jr., and A.G. Prieto (eds.), *Severe behavioral disorders of children and youth*, Vol. 1. Reston, VA: Council for Children with Behavioral Disorders.

Rutherford, R.B., Jr. and Nelson, C.M. (1982). Analysis of the response contingent time-out literature with behaviorally disordered students in classroom settings. In R.B. Rutherford, Jr. (ed.), *Severe behavioral disorders of children and youth*, Vol. 5. Reston, VA: Council for Children with Behavioral Disorders.

Skinner, B.F. (1990). *Beyond freedom and dignity*, Rev. Ed. New York: Bantam Books.

Walker, H.M., and Rankin, R. (1983). Assessing the behavioral expectations and demand of less restrictive settings. *School Psychology Review* 12:274-284.

Chapter 2

Bandler, R., and Grinder, J. (1982). *Reframing: Neuro-linguistic programming and the transformation of meaning.* Moab, UT: Real People Press.

Barker, J., and Christensen, R.J. (1989). *Discovering the future: The business of paradigms,* 2nd Ed. Burnsville, MN: Charthouse International Learning Corporation.

Cessna, K.K. (ed.). (1993). *Instructionally differentiated programming: A needs-based approach for students with behavior disorders.* Denver: Colorado Department of Education.

Kaplan, J.S. (1991). *Beyond behavior modification: A cognitive-behavioral approach to behavior management in the school,* 2nd Ed. Austin, TX: Pro-Ed.

Kuhn, T.S. (1970). *The structure of scientific revolutions,* 2nd Ed. Chicago: University of Chicago Press.

Laing, R.D. (1969). *The divided self.* New York: Pantheon Books

Neel, R.S., and Cessna, K.K. (1993). Behavioral intent: Instructional content for students with behavior disorders. In K.K. Cessna (ed.), *Instructionally differentiated programming: A needs-based approach for students with behavior disorders.* Denver: Colorado Department of Education.

Chapter 3

Cooper, J.O., Heron, T.E., and Heward, W.L. (1987). *Applied behavior analysis.* Columbus, OH: Charles E. Merrill.

Dardig, J.C., and Heward, W.L. (1981). *Sign here: A contracting book for children and their parents,* 2nd Ed. Bridgewater, NJ: Fournies Press.

Fisher, R., and Ury, W. (1981). *Getting to yes: Negotiating agreement without giving in.* New York: Penguin Books.

Levitt, L.K., and Rutherford, R.B., Jr. (1978). *Strategies for handling the disruptive student.* Tempe, AZ: College of Education, Arizona State University.

Skinner, B.F. (1969). *Contingencies of reinforcement: A theoretical analysis.* New York: Appleton-Century-Crofts.

Walker, J.E., and Shea, T.M. (1991). *Behavior management: A practical approach for educators.* New York: Macmillan.

Chapter 4

Cooper, J.O., Heron, T.E., and Heward, W.L. (1987). *Applied behavior analysis.* Columbus, OH: Charles E. Merrill.

Ellis, A. (1962). *Reason and emotion in psychotherapy.* New York: Lyle Stuart.

Ellis, A. (1976). The biological basis of human irrationality. Journal of Individual Psychology 32:145-168.

Glasser, W. (1992). *The quality school,* 2nd Ed. New York: Harper Perennial.

Haley, J. (1973). *Uncommon therapy: The psychiatric techniques of Milton H. Erickson, M.D.* New York: Norton.

Kanfer, F.H., and Gaelick-Buys, L. (1991). Self-management methods. In A.P. Goldstein and L. Kranfer (eds.), *Helping people change*, 4th Ed. Tarrytown, NY: Pergamon Press.

Martin, G., and Pear, J. (1992). *Behavior modification: What it is and how to do it*, 4th Ed. Englewood Cliffs, NJ: Prentice Hall.

Miller, T. (1986). *The unfair advantage.* Manlius, NY: The Unfair Advantage Corporation.

Miller, T. (1993). *Self-discipline and emotional control* (cassette recording no. C134 293). Boulder, CO: CareerTrack.

Perry, D.C., and Bussey, K. (1984). *Social development.* Englewood Cliffs, NJ: Prentice Hall.

Wallace, I. (1977). Self-control techniques of famous novelists. *Journal of Applied Behavior Analysis* 10:515-525.

Chapter 5

American Psychiatric Association (1987). *Diagnostic and statistical manual of mental disorders*, 3rd Ed. Rev. Washington, DC: APA.

Noblit, G.W., Paul, J.L., and Schlechty, P. (1991). The social and cultural construction of emotional disturbance. In J.L. Paul and B.C. Epanchin (eds.), *Educating emotionally disturbed children and youth: Theories and practices for teachers*, 2nd Ed. Columbus, OH: Charles E. Merrill.

Sleeter, C.E. (1986). Learning disabilities: The social construction of a special education category. *Exceptional Children* 53:46-54.

Szasz, T. (1961). *The myth of mental illness.* New York: Hoeber-Harper.

Chapter 6

American Psychiatric Association (1968). *Diagnostic and statistical manual of mental disorders*, 2nd Ed. Washington, DC: APA.

American Psychiatric Association (1980). *Diagnostic and statistical manual of mental disorders*, 3rd Ed. Washington, DC: APA.

American Psychiatric Association (1987). *Diagnostic and statistical manual of mental disorders*, 3rd Ed. Rev. Washington, DC: APA.

Barkley, R.A. (1990). *Attention deficit hyperactivity disorder: A handbook for diagnosis and treatment.* New York: Guilford.

Dodge, K.A. (1989). Problems in social relationships. In E.J. Mash and R.A. Barkley (eds.), *Treatment of childhood disorders.* New York: Guilford.

Feingold, B.F. (1975). *Why your child is hyperactive.* New York: Random House.

Lerner, J.W., and Lener, S.R. (1991). Attention deficit disorder: Issues and questions. *Focus on Exceptional Children* 24(3):1-17.

Martin, G., and Pear, J. (1992). *Behavior modification: What it is and how to do it*, 4th Ed. Englewood Cliffs, NJ: Prentice Hall.

Reid, R., Maag, J.W., and Vasa, S.F. (1994). Attention deficit hyperactivity disorder as a disability category: A critique. *Exceptional Children* 60:198-214.

Reid, R., Maag, J.W., Vasa, S.F., and Wright, G. (1994). Who are the children with attention deficit-hyperactivity disorder? A school-based survey. *Journal of Special Education* 28:117-137.

Still, G.E. (1902). The Coulstonian Lectures on some abnormal physical conditions in children. *Lancet* 1:1007,1018,1163.

Strauss, A.A., and Lehtinen, L.E. (1947). *Psychopathology and education of the brain-injured child.* New York: Grune & Stratton.

Swanson, J.M., McBurnett, K., Wigal, T., et al. (1993). Effect of stimulant medication on children with attention deficit disorder: A "review of reviews." *Exceptional Children* 60:154-163.

Whalen, C.K. (1989). Attention deficit and hyperactivity disorders. In T.H. Ollendick and M. Hersen (eds.), *Handbook of child psychopathology,* 2nd Ed. New York: Plenum.

Zametkin, A.J., Nordahl, T.E., Gross, M., et al. (1990). Cerebral glucose metabolism in adults with hyperactivity of childhood onset. *New England Journal of Medicine* 323:1361-1366.

Chapter 7

American Psychiatric Association. (1987). *Diagnostic and statistical manual of mental disorders,* 3rd Ed. Washington, DC: APA.

Beck, A.T., Rush, A.J., Shaw, B.F., and Emery, G. (1979). *Cognitive therapy of depression.* New York: Guilford.

Cautela, J.R. (1981). *Behavior analysis forms for clinical intervention, Vol. 2.* Champaign, IL: Research Press.

Cormier, W.H., and Cormier, L.S. (1985). *Interviewing strategies for helpers: Fundamental skills and cognitive behavioral interventions,* 2nd Ed. Monterey, CA: Brooks/Cole.

Glasser, W. (1976). *Positive addiction.* New York: Harper & Row.

Kaslow, N.J., and Rehm, L.P. (1991). Childhood depression. In T.R. Kratochwill and R.J. Morris (eds.), *The practice of child therapy,* 2nd Ed. Tarrytown, NY: Pergamon Press.

Lewin, K. (1951). *Field theory in social science.* New York: Harper & Row.

Maag, J.W., and Forness, S.R. (1991). Depression in children and adolescents: Identification, assessment, and treatment. *Focus on Exceptional Children* 24(1):1-19.

Rehm, L.P. (1977). A self-control model of depression. *Behavior Therapy* 8:787-804.

Weisskopf-Joelson, E. (1955). Some comments on a Viennese school of psychiatry. *Journal of Abnormal and Social Psychology* 51:701-703.

Chapter 8

Bandler, R., and Grinder, J. (1982). *Reframing: Neuro-linguistic programming and the transformation of meaning.* Moab, UT: Real People Press.

Cormier, W.H., and Cormier, L.S. (1985). *Interviewing strategies for helpers: Fundamental skills and cognitive behavioral interventions*, 2nd Ed. Monterey, CA: Brooks/Cole.

Erickson, M.H. (1980). Pediatric hypnotherapy. In E.L. Rossi (ed.), *The Collected Papers of Milton H. Erickson on Hypnosis*, Vol. 4. New York: Irvington.

Haley, J. (1973). *Uncommon therapy: The psychiatric techniques of Milton H. Erickson, M.D.* New York: Norton.

Hassenpflug, A. (1983). Insanity in the classroom. *English Journal* 72(8):4-6.

Howell, K.W., Fox, S.L., and Horehead, M.K. (1993). *Curriculum-based evaluation: Teaching and decision making*, 2nd Ed. Pacific Grove, CA: Brooks/Cole.

Meichenbaum, D. (1985). *Stress inoculation training.* Tarrytown, NY: Pergamon Press.

Index